T0341650

Politics
& Social Justice

AFRICAN LITERATURE TODAY **32**

Editor:	Ernest N. Emenyonu
Assistant Editor:	Patricia T. Emenyonu
Associate Editors:	Jane Bryce
	Maureen N. Eke
	Stephanie Newell
	Charles E. Nnolim
	Chimalum Nwankwo
	Ato Quayson
	Kwawisi Tekpetey
	Iniobong I. Uko
Reviews Editor:	James Gibbs

HEBN Publishers PLC

JAMES CURREY

GUIDELINES FOR SUBMISSION OF ARTICLES

The Editor invites submission of articles on the announced themes of forthcoming issues. Submissions will be acknowledged promptly and decisions communicated within six months of the receipt of the paper. This is the estimated minimum time it takes to receive reports from peer reviewers. Your name and institutional affiliation (with full mailing address and email) should appear on a separate sheet, plus a brief biographical profile of not more than six lines. The editor cannot undertake to return materials submitted, and contributors are advised to keep a copy of each material sent. Please note that all articles outside the announced themes cannot be considered or acknowledged. Articles should be submitted in the English Language.

Length and format: Articles should not exceed 5,000 words. Articles should be double-spaced, and should use the same type face and size throughout. Italics are preferred to underlines for titles of books. For the purpose of peer review, please do not insert your name, institutional affiliation and contact information on the article itself.

Style: UK or US spellings are acceptable, but be consistent. Direct quotations should retain the spellings used in the original source. Check the accuracy of citations and always give the author's surname and page number in the text, and a full reference in the Works Cited list at the end of the article. Italicize titles of books or plays. Use single inverted commas throughout except for quotes within quotes which are double. Avoid subtitles or subsection headings within the text. Do not use footnotes or endnotes.

Citations: Limit your sources to the most recent, or the most important books and journals, in English, avoiding general reference books. Cite works in foreign languages only when no English-language books are available. If citing from the internet/websites give full references as for printed sources.

For in-text citations, use (Surname: page number). No year of publication unless needed for clarity. All details should be presented in the Works Cited list at the end of the article in alphabetical order by author. Consistency is essential. Eg:

Cazenave, Odile. *Rebellious Women: The New Generation of Female African Novelists.* Boulder, CO: Lynne Rienner Publishers, 2000.

Duerden, Dennis. 'The "Discovery" of the African Mask.' *Research in African Literatures.* Vol. 31, No. 4 (Winter 2000): 29-47.

Ukala, Sam. 'Tradition, Rotimi, and His Audience.' *Goatskin Bags and Wisdom: New Critical Perspectives on African Literature.* Ed. Ernest N. Emenyonu. New Jersey: Africa World Press, 2000: 91-104.

Copyright: It is the responsibility of contributors to clear permissions.

All articles should be sent online as Word attachment to the Editor. There is no need to send a hard copy by mail:
Ernest N. Emenyonu, African Literature Today
Email: eernest@umflint.edu   Fax: 001-810-766-6719

Reviewers should provide full bibliographic details, including the extent, ISBN and price, and submit to the Reviews Editor:
Obi Nwakanma
English Department, Colburn Hall
University of Central Florida
12790 Aquarius Agora Drive
Orlando, FL 32816, USA
Email: obi.nwakanma@ucf.edu

AFRICAN LITERATURE TODAY

Volumes 1-14 were published from London by Heinemann Educational Books
and from New York by Africana Publishing Company

Editor: Eldred Durosimi Jones
  1, 2, 3, and 4 Omnibus Edition
  5 The Novel in Africa
  6 Poetry in Africa
  7 Focus on Criticism
  8 Drama in Africa
  9 Africa, America & the Caribbean
  10 Retrospect & Prospect
  11 Myth & History

Editor: Eldred Durosimi Jones
Associate Editor: Eustace Palmer
Assistant Editor: Marjorie Jones
  12 New Writing, New Approaches
  13 Recent Trends in the Novel
  14 Insiders & Outsiders

Backlist titles available in the US and Canada from Africa World Press
and in the rest of the world from James Currey, an imprint of Boydell & Brewer
ALT 15 Women in African Literature Today
ALT 16 Oral & Written Poetry in African Literature Today
ALT 17 The Question of Language in African Literature Today
ALT 18 Orature in African Literature Today
ALT 19 Critical Theory & African Literature Today
ALT 20 New Trends & Generations in African Literature
ALT 21 Childhood in African Literature
ALT 22 Exile & African Literature
ALT 23 South & Southern African Literature
ALT 24 New Women's Writing in African Literature
ALT 25 New Directions in African Literature

Note from the publisher on new and forthcoming titles
James Currey Publishers joined Boydell & Brewer Ltd in 2008.
African Literature Today continues to be published as an annual volume under the
James Currey imprint
North and South American distribution:
Boydell & Brewer Inc., 68 Mount Hope Avenue, Rochester, NY 14620-2731, US
UK and International distribution:
Boydell & Brewer Ltd., PO Box 9, Woodbridge IP12 3DF, GB.
Nigeria edition: HEBN Publishers Plc
ALT 26 War in African Literature Today
ALT 27 New Novels in African Literature Today
ALT 28 Film in African Literature Today
ALT 29 Teaching African Literature Today
ALT 30 Reflections & Retrospectives in African Literature Today
ALT 31 Writing Africa in the Short Story
ALT 32 Politics & Social Justice
Call for papers
ALT 33 Children, History & the Tales Told

Politics
& Social Justice

AFRICAN LITERATURE TODAY **32**

James Currey is an imprint of
Boydell & Brewer Ltd
PO Box 9, Woodbridge,
Suffolk, IP12 3DF (GB)
and of
Boydell & Brewer Inc.
668 Mt Hope Avenue,
Rochester, NY 14620-2731 (US)
www.boydellandbrewer.com
www.jamescurrey.com

HEBN Publishers Plc
1 Ighodaro Road, Jericho,
PMB 5205, Ibadan, Nigeria
Phone: +234 2 8726701
info@hebnpublishers.com
hebnpublishers@yahoo.com
http://www.hebnpublishers.com
www.facebook.com/pages/HEBN-PublishersPlcs
www.twitter.com/HEBNPublishers

British Library Cataloguing in Publication Data
A catalogue record for this book is available on request from the British Library

ISBN 978-1-84701-097-1 (James Currey paper)
ISBN 978-978-081-462-5 (HEBN paper)

The publisher has no responsibility for the continued existence or accuracy of URLs
for external or third-party internet websites referred to in this book, and does not
guarantee that any content on such websites is, or will remain,
accurate or appropriate.

This publication is printed on acid-free paper

Designed and set in 10.5/12 pt Berkeley Book by
Kate Kirkwood Publishing Services, Cumbria, UK

Dedication

James Gibbs

Since 1997, James Gibbs has served as the Book Reviews Editor of *African Literature Today*. In this capacity, he helped in no small way not only to shape, mentor and nurture the journal to great heights, but also made other contributions that ensured sustainability for the journal. With this issue, he steps down as the Book Reviews Editor. We will dearly miss his wisdom, astuteness and pragmatism. This issue on 'Politics and Social Justice' is appropriately and deservedly dedicated to James Gibbs, our colleague and friend.

Ernest N. Emenyonu, Editor
for, and on behalf of, the Editorial Board

With effect from *ALT 33*, Dr Obi Nwakanma, inspiring poet, erudite scholar and teacher, assumes the position of Book Reviews Editor. We welcome him to the Editorial Board and look forward to his building on the solid foundations laid by James Gibbs – Ed

***

STOP PRESS/ TRIBUTE TO NADINE GORDIMER
1923–2014

Nobel Laureate NADINE GORDIMER (1923–2014) acclaimed 'one of the most powerful voices against apartheid', died while we were going to press with this issue. We will carry a Tribute to her legacy in the next issue, *ALT 33*.

Contents

Notes on Contributors

Prince Kwame Adika is a Lecturer in the Department of English, University of Ghana, Legon. He received his PhD from Illinois State University in 2009 and has published on the intersections between transnationalism and global African literatures. He is a member of the Adjudicating Panel of the Burt Award for African Literature.

Mawuli Adjei (PhD) is a Senior Lecturer in the Department of English, University of Ghana, Legon. He is the author of two novels *The Jewel of Kabibi* (2011), *Taboo* (2012) and a collection of poetry *Testament of the Seasons* (2013).

Kofi Anyidoho is Professor of Literature, Director of the CODESRIA African Humanities Institute Programme and former head of the English Department, University of Ghana and is well known for his poetry in English and Ewe. He is a Fellow of the Ghana Academy of Arts and Sciences and was the first occupant of the Kwame Nkrumah Chair in African Studies, University of Ghana.

Emilia V. Ilieva is a Professor of Literature at Egerton University, Kenya. Most recently, she has contributed an essay to *Teaching the Novels of Ngugi wa Thiong'o* (2012). She has also translated Ngũgĩ's novel *Petals of Blood* into Bulgarian.

Ikenna Kamalu holds a PhD in English from the University of Ibadan and currently teaches in the Department of English Studies, University of Port Harcourt. He is the editor of *Working Papers: Journal of English Studies*, University of Port Harcourt.

Nicholas Kamau-Goro is a Senior Lecturer in Literature at Laikipia University, Kenya. He has published articles on Ngũgĩ in *Egerton Journal of Humanities, Social Sciences and Education*; *Studies in World Christianity*; and an essay in *Christianity and Public Culture in Africa* (2011).

Deborah L. Klein taught in Plateau State then Akwa Ibom State, Nigeria, for five years followed by eight years at the University of Jos where she was active in the Association of Nigerian Authors (ANA). She teaches English in Montgomery, Alabama.

Rachel Knighton is a PhD student at Cambridge University, where she is researching African prison writing. The article included in this journal forms a chapter of her MA dissertation on recent Kenyan writing.

Ghirmai Negash is a Professor of English and African Literature in Ohio University, and a general editor of the *Modern African Writing Series* of Ohio University Press. He taught at the University of Asmara from 2001 to 2005 and is the author of several books and essays on Eritrean literature and poetry, and articles on South African and Horn of Africa literatures.

H. Oby Okolocha is a Senior Lecturer in the Department of English and Literature, University of Benin, Benin City, Nigeria. She teaches several courses in drama and prose fiction. Her research interests are in gender studies, feminist literature and criticism and literature dealing with war, conflict and trauma; areas in which she has published articles inside and outside Africa.

Richard K. Priebe, PhD, is Emeritus Professor of English and African Literatures at Virginia Commonwealth University. He is now retired in Richmond, Virginia.

Edward Sackey, PhD, is a Senior Lecturer in the Department of English, University of Ghana, Legon. His area of research interest is the African Novel and Ayi Kwei Armah's contribution to its formation.

Laura Wright is Associate Professor and Department Head of English at Western Carolina University. She is author of *Writing Out of All the Camps: J. M. Coetzee's Narratives of Displacement* (2006 and 2009) and lead editor, with Jane Poyner and Elleke Boehmer of *Approaches to Teaching Coetzee's* Disgrace *and Other Works* (2014).

Eric Nsuh Zuhmboshi is a Lecturer in the Department of African Literature and Civilisations of the University of Yaounde 1, Cameroon. He is also a PhD candidate (awaiting defence) in the same department. His areas of research interest include postcolonial studies, orature, critical theory, political economy and ideology, and the interconnections between literature and the social sciences.

Editorial

Fiction & Socio-Political Realities in Africa: What Else Can Literature Do?

ERNEST N. EMENYONU

Chinua Achebe once said something to the effect that no country has ever handed its government to writers. It was not so much a statement about the administrative capabilities or lack thereof, of writers in government, as of the true significance of creative imagination in the shaping of human destiny at a point in time. 'The pen' they say, 'is mightier than the sword'. But whereas soldiers and armed forces overthrow civilian governments and impose dictatorships and totalitarian regimes across the globe, no association of writers by whatever name, has ever carried out a coup d'état to topple a country's government, constitution and its political institutions with a stroke of the pen.

Defining the role of a writer in a new nation particularly in Africa, Achebe declared that a writer with a proper sense of history can 'explore in depth the human condition' and show the populace in clear terms 'how the rain began to beat them' – the causes and effects, actions and reactions, events and consequences in the life of a people. He revealed his own mission, commitment and vision as an African writer in near-crusading terms:

> I should be satisfied if my novels especially the ones I set in the past did no more than teach my readers that their past, with all its imperfections, was not one long night of savagery from which the early Europeans, acting on God's behalf delivered them.

That assertion included a still reverberating sentiment generally shared by the first generation of African writers that it is possible to reclaim that distorted past creatively in order to show and understand where and when the rain started beating them and how best to dry their bodies. It has remained an exciting, long and arduous journey from the past to the present with all genres and forms of literary and cultural production recalling and

1

recording, charting and constructing, assessing and critiquing, blaming or exculpating, reconfiguring that past and projecting a new confident African future steeped in all the fundamental values of self-determination. The spectrum of that complex engagement could be rightly said to encompass critical issues in politics and social justice in all their ramifications, which form the focus of this issue of *African Literature Today*.

Achebe opted to tell 'the African story' for Africans and the rest of the world alike; to tell the outside world in general and Europe in particular that 'Africans did not hear of culture for the first time from Europeans'. And to Africans, that huge responsibilities and transparent accountabilities come with political independence and self-determination. Elsewhere, he specifically identified a vital goal/ purpose of the African writer who tells the story of his/her people, the travails and tremors of nation-building namely: to dramatize complex human experiences so that people and generations caught in similar circumstances, can make the right choices and decisions. Ezekiel Es'kia Mphahlele precisely called such a writer, 'the conscience of his/her society'.

As 'the consciences' of their societies, African writers have in varying degrees, painstakingly at the risk of lives, exposed without fear or favour, injustices, corruption, abuse of human rights, gender inequities, degradation of womanhood, obnoxious patriarchy, religious intolerance, domestic violence, child abuse and trafficking, and other forms of crimes against humanity at the hands of rulers or the ruled. Some of these have not gone down well with the majority of African rulers especially the self-seeking, opportunistic ones who perceive their primary role at the helm of affairs in their countries as that of looting their national treasury, and regarding their countries' resources as their personal franchise to dispense at will. To secure their grips on their 'empires' they take steps on assumption of office to entrench themselves as perpetual rulers and are quick to change the constitutions of their countries to enable them rule for life, and at death, ensure that their offspring succeed them to the end of time if possible. Any opposing individuals or groups are crushed with reckless abandon.

Since the modern era (post-independence), African writers have battled such rulers who stole the fruit of independence and dashed the hopes of the citizenry for sustainable progress and development in their new nation. Nobel Laureate Wole Soyinka went to jail in Nigeria and during the era of one particular military dictator, was declared 'wanted dead or alive'. Ngũgĩ wa Thiong'o went to prison in Kenya, and during the rule of a particular intolerant head of state, was singled out for assassination and hounded into exile. Ken Saro-Wiwa of Nigeria was persecuted, hounded down, tortured and executed with immeasurable indignity – it took the hang-man seven sordid tries to sniff out Ken Saro-Wiwa's life! Dennis Brutus and many of his anti-apartheid compatriots spent years in maximum security prisons in South Africa; some died in anguish while there, and others were hounded into exile with diminished dignities. Nawal El Saadawi was imprisoned in Egypt, and under one particular autocratic president a death sentence was passed on her mainly for her indefatigable crusade for women's rights amidst obnoxious patriarchal fundamentalism. And these are just some of the most glaring cases that caught international attention.

If the above scenario looks like the targetting of hot-headed and maverick pioneer African writers, it should be pointed out that it has not been paradise for some of the younger generation contemporary African writers under rulers in some particular countries. In 2003, Human Rights Watch (HRW) documented the sordid tales of African writers who had been relentlessly persecuted, imprisoned or ruthlessly tortured for exposing corrosive corruption and other heinous crimes in high places. Included were Njanu Phillip and Niji Renatus (Cameroon), Khaled Abdul and Aaron Berhane (Eritrea), Lubaba Said (Ethiopia) and Tom Kamara (Liberia). However, one case from Nigeria reported by HRW, seems to top it all in its horrific absurdity, and deserves to be quoted in full:

> Chris Abani, a Nigerian poet and novelist was arrested in 1985 and again in 1987 when plots of his novels were said to be plans for attempts to overthrow the government (Chris, born on December 27, 1966 was a teenager in 1985). Abani spent six months in prison in 1985 and in 1987, he was held in Kiri-Kiri Maximum Security Prison (Lagos) for a year and tortured. On his release, Abani entered Imo State University (for his undergraduate studies in English). Inspired by Wole Soyinka's use of theatre as protest, Abani formed a theatre group that wrote and performed anti-government sketches. In 1990 he wrote a play, *Song of the Broken Flute*, for the University's Commencement exercises which the military head of state and military governor were scheduled to attend. The play, a series of monologues that decried government corruption and its effects on the people, landed him back in prison on treason charges. Released after 18 months, he graduated from Imo State University and joined national service (National Youth Service – a mandatory one-year national service required of

Nigerian graduates). Several attempts on his life while in boot camp prompted him to flee to England. Abani lived there quietly until the publication of his prison memoir (*Kalakuta Republic*) in 1997 when he began speaking out. As a result, the Nigerian government applied to have him extradited to stand trial for treason again. In December 1999, following the doorstep murder of his next-door neighbor, the only other Nigerian in the building, Abani left England for the US. (*Panapress*, Dakar, Senegal, 28 July 2003)

What Achebe said in 1983 about Nigeria – 'the trouble with Nigeria is leadership' – is true today of the entire continent of Africa. Africa is never in short supply of leaders, what is lacking is leadership with vision and integrity; leadership that has the interest and welfare of the people at the centre of all its policies and actions. Africa does not lack eloquent and articulate leaders, what is greatly missing among African political leaders are those who are not hypocrites, who do not take their people for granted by saying one thing to get into office and doing the very opposite once there; Africa is not lacking in educated politicians and leaders, what is in short supply is a crop of incorruptible statesmen and stateswomen who will not sell their country and its citizens to amass wealth and property in leading capital cities of the world at the expense of much needed developments at home. It seems to be only in Africa that presidents and governors have immunity from prosecution in crimes against their people and humanity while in office. It seems only in contemporary Africa that politicians who could hardly afford money to fuel their beat-up cars (if they owned any at all), become owners of private jets so soon after getting into office. It seems only in Africa that leaders of countries use security votes to make themselves billionaires while their countries number among the world's most poverty-stricken, and their citizenry are at the mercy of armed robbers and daring terrorists.

African writers have depicted these vices and crimes against humanity with flawless accuracy in their imaginative works and performing arts. Novelists, poets, dramatists, short story writers, musicians and spoken-word artists have made them subjects of their creativity to no avail. The criminals are not swayed. It becomes the norm that politics is where you go not to serve your country and people but the place to go to steal and loot without being caught, and if caught, you have limitless resources to escape justice. African writers have depicted these in all forms and techniques – direct language, imagery, symbolism, sarcasm, satire, lampoonery, jests and derisions, realistic fiction and non-fictional memoirs. Do African politicians and leaders listen to what the creative and performing artists say about them? Do African leaders and politicians hear the outcries of their people relayed in multiple art forms? Do African politicians and leaders read the portraits of them in the literatures of their times? If they do and care not, what else can literature do?

This issue of *African Literature Today* on 'Politics and Social Justice' has tried to shed light on how writers from various parts of the continent have, in multiple languages and techniques 'told the African story' in their particular regions, countries, communities and other social environments. The writers discussed in the accompanying chapters cut across generations and cultures. Nicholas Kamua-Goro and Emilia V. Ilieva discuss 'The Novel as an Oral Narrative Performance' using Ngũgĩ wa Thiong'o's *Matigari ma Njirũũngi* as the platform for a discourse on postcolonial Kenya. Readers will find it a refreshingly different approach to the analysis of this Ngũgĩ's unique novel. With their mastery of the Gikuyu language, the authors capture the meanings of major words, concepts and names in the novel. Eric Nsuh Zuhmboshi further reinforces Ngũgĩ's portrayals of Kenya with sound arguments in his 'The Rhetoric and Caricature of Social Justice in Post-1960 Africa'. Ikenna Kamalu's 'Abiku in Ben Okri's Imagination of Nationhood' builds his discussion and analysis on a sound theoretical foundation that is easy to read and supported by relevant references to Okri's novels particularly *The Famished Road*. In 'Refracting the Political: Binyavanga Wainaina's *One Day I Will Write About This Place*', Rachel Knighton sets out to use Ato Quayson's theory of 'liberatory politics in writing' to interrogate Binyavanga Wainaina's perspectives on Kenya in the novel, thereby providing for the reader a detailed textual analysis. Readers will find Edward Sackey's article on '*The Resolutionaries*: Exoteric Fiction, the Common People and Social Change in Post-Colonial Africa', a well-argued and valuable intro-duction to Armah's most recent work, after '*Osiris Rising* and *KMT: In the House of Life*. In her article 'In Quest of Social Justice: Politics and Women's Participation in Irene Isoken Salami's *More Than Dancing*', H. Oby Okolocha uses the play to discuss the playwright's proposals for social change in relation to gender equality, and to test Mola ra Ogundipe-Leslie's controversial diagnosis that one of the biggest obstacles to African women's progression is 'the mountain of self'. Readers will find the arguments intriguingly entertaining. Laura Wright's 'Breaking the Laws in J.M. Coetzee's Oeuvre: *The*

Childhood of Jesus – Philosophy and the Notion of Justice', is a vital discourse which provides useful insight into the Nobel Laureate's fiction – an admixture of narrative dexterity and philosophical profundity. In her article '"Manhood" in Isidore Okpewho's *The Last Duty*: Authenticity or Accountability?', Deborah Klein investigates perceptions of manhood with a focus on a novel which explores war, a fit setting for unravelling such perceptions. Klein uses the methodology of character analyses and reveals the extent to which the author of the novel has based his entire construction on the thorny issue of what manhood means in a time of war. Readers will find Klein's analysis not only vibrant but interesting and revealing.

As we were going to press in 2013 with ALT 31: Writing Africa in the Short Story, we heard the terrible news that Ghanaian poet Kofi Awoonor, one of Africa's pioneer and most versatile writers of the twentieth century, was among those killed during the shootings in the Westgate Mall in Nairobi, Kenya, on 21 September 2013. We promised that we would carry a full tribute on his life and work in ALT 32: Politics and Social Justice. Kofi Awoonor had fought for, and been uncompromising in the advocacy of social justice in both his real life and his writings. The last section of this issue titled 'Remembering Kofi Awoonor' is our promised tribute. Kofi Awoonor will ever be remembered as one of Africa's greatest writers of all time. We thank Kofi Anyidoho for his immeasurable assistance and wonderful support to bring this tribute to our readers worldwide.

The Novel
as an Oral Narrative Performance
The Delegitimization of the Postcolonial Nation
in Ngũgĩ wa Thiong'o's *Matigari Ma Njirũũngi*

NICHOLAS KAMAU-GORO & EMILIA V. ILIEVA

Matigari Ma Njirũũngi (1986) (*Matigari*, 1989), Ngũgĩ wa Thiong'o's second novel in Gĩkũyũ, is the most disparaged of his works. Critics like Nkosi (1995: 197-206) and Gurnah (1991: 169-72) have raised questions about the identity of the novel, its place in the changing canon of African literature and its aesthetic strategy. Ogude accuses Ngũgĩ of abandoning the depiction of 'moral complexity' of his earlier novels in favour of what the scholar dismisses as 'simple minded ... allegorising' (1991: 13-14) . How can we account for this critical hostility towards the novel?

In this article, we argue that with *Matigari Ma Njirũũngi*, Ngũgĩ reaches the apogee of his intellectual crusade for the democratization of African literature, an endeavour which, in the possibility of its fullest realization, is forbidding for an elitist literary establishment. This democratization, in Ngũgĩ's view, calls for the use of indigenous African languages as vehicles for 'thought, feeling and will' (2009: 95). It presupposes a notion of audience that includes the vast majority of the African people who are mostly the oppressed and the marginalized in the post-colonial dispensation. It manifests itself in the literature's rootedness in the folklore of the people, which Ngũgĩ understands in the Herderian sense of it being the expression of the character and soul of a people. German philosopher, poet and literary critic (1744-1803) Johann Gottfried von Herder insisted that each people should develop on its own cultural foundation. Embracing an alien cultural foundation would result in 'breaking the continuity of past development and disrupting the nation's organic unity', in the 'stultification of native cultural forms and ultimately the death of the nation itself' (Wilson, 1978: 823). In Ngũgĩ's view, a democratic literature is also one that reflects the historical accomplishments of the African people, their life experience, philosophy, mindset, their moral and creative potential, their patriotism. It is a literature that rejects despotism, tyranny, oppression, spiritual and physical slavery, that condemns depravity and immorality. The main purpose of such a literature is to find the way towards bringing about a cardinal change in the destiny of the people. *Matigari Ma Njiruungi* becomes a veritable model for such democratic African literature.

Ngũgĩ models himself on the traditional artist in Gĩkũyũ society who was 'the spokesman of the little people, the underprivileged' (Kabira, 1983: 35). Orature not only authorizes the agency of the 'little' people but also reifies Ngũgĩ 's determination to intervene in the contested historical, political and cultural discourses in Kenya on behalf of the oppressed. Aesthetically, the poetics of oral storytelling help the author to retool the novel as an oral narrative in performance. The novel opens with formulaic 'ĩĩtha!' which, in Gĩkũyũ storytelling, is the response of the recipient(s) of the story. It implies that the listeners have taken the cue and are ready to be transported to the world of imagination and make-believe. This is followed by the author's/storyteller's own voice that, mimicking the oral narrator, goes on to tell us the nature of his story. These formulae imply that Ngũgĩ deliberately created the novel for oral reception. We are told that the story is fictive ('rũgano rwa gwĩtungĩra') and it has no specific setting. The story then commences with the formulaic, 'Tene, tene mũno ...' (Once upon a time). The oral world of Ngũgĩ's novel resembles a village, an organic face-to-face community that forms around the storyteller.

As a form that easily lends itself to didactic instruction, orature helps the author in what he sees as the urgent task of creating 'an alternative to the bourgeois public sphere inherited from colonialism and perpetuated in postcoloniality' (Gikandi, 2000: 226). *Matigari Ma Njiruungi* challenges the collocation of textuality with the development of individual consciousness characteristic of the Western realist novel. The novel does not merely represent but actually crosses the class boundary between the discursive communities defined by literacy and orality. As a written text, however, the novel assumes a literate – if only in Gĩkũyũ – reading audience while at the same time creating within itself a textual community of oral storytellers and listeners. Ngũgĩ's desire is to empower his audience and 'to make the act of reading one in which the audience participates and one that awakens the people to direct, revolutionary political action' (Lovesey, 1994: 153).

Oral storytelling involves a variety of forms including the folktale, songs, allegory, fable, myth, ancestor veneration, legend, proverbs and jokes. The qualities of fluidity, instability and liminality that mark the internal imaginative world of these oral forms are concentrated in the fantastic in art. The fantastic can be a powerful tool for a political literature of subversion in that it 'traces the unsaid and the unseen of culture: that which has been silenced, made invisible, covered over and made "absent"' (Jackson, 1981:4). It makes us aware of the real world not as a world within which we do and must operate, but as one that can and must be changed (Julien, 1992:159).

The choice of an allegorical setting for his novel is a strategy of evasion which Ngũgĩ uses to indulge his radical politics in defamiliarizing ways. The author transports his readers to a fantastical level of experience, which is not only different but larger than that of the realistic novel.

What distinguishes *Matigari Ma Njirũũngi* is the readability of its allegorical tropes. Ngũgĩ' s novel tells the story of Matigari Ma Njirũũngi, a former Mau Mau freedom fighter who returns from the forest years after the armed struggle for land and freedom is over and independence has been attained. Turning away from his military past, Matigari begins a search for his family with the aim of rebuilding his home and starting a new life of dignity. The novel is structured by the journey motif based on a Gĩkũyũ folktale about a man who, suffering some mysterious illness, undertakes a search for a cure.

As the embodiment of the nation, Matigari's illness is a public rather than an individual's affliction. His is a quest for a cure for a communal malady. Although the novel ostensibly eschews referentiality, Matigari's story reasserts the unnamed country as post-colonial Kenya. The radio broadcasts recall events in Kenya's recent post-colonial history. President Ole Mũgathe is a composite figure of the first two Kenyan presidents – Jomo Kenyatta and Daniel arap Moi. 'Mũgathe', a translation of 'his Excellency' into Gĩkũyũ, was the term used in all references to President Kenyatta. The soubriquet 'Ole' (meaning 'son of' in the Maa languages) is a reference to President Moi ('arap' meaning 'son of' in the Kalenjin languages). Other parallels recall a mutiny by elements of the Kenya army in 1967 which was suppressed with assistance from Britain and the outlawing of opposition under President Moi who declared Kenya a de jure one-party state in 1982. The novel insists that the truths of the nation are not contained in the propaganda purveyed by the state but in its actual realities as experienced by the people. By documenting these realities, the nation is combatted and its legitimacy put to question for its failure to deliver on the aspirations of the freedom struggle.

Matigari Ma Njirũũngi is divided into three parts. Part one entitled, 'Ngarũro wa Kĩrĩro' (Wiping Your Tears Away), focuses on Matigari's return to the neo-colony after years of absence and his search of his family. In part two, 'Macaria Ma na Kĩhooto' (Seeker of Truth and Justice), Matigari traverses the neo-colonial state and comes to terms with the painful fact that the ideals he, and others, sacrificed for in the struggle for independence have been betrayed. His anguished quest reveals the absence of truth and justice, and the pervasive oppression and exploitation of the poor (*MMN*, 59-114). In the final part, 'Gũthera na Mũriũki' (The Pure and the Resurrected), the novel imagines new post-colonial futures emerging from the success of a second liberation struggle that is, significantly, to be spearheaded by the oppressed – symbolized by Gũthera, a former prostitute, Mũriũki, a former street boy, and Ngarũro wa Kĩrĩro, a worker (*MMN*, 115-56). The structure of the novel is episodic with the centre of focus shifting cinematically over carefully foregrounded incidents. These 'snapshots' illuminate the deplorable state of the nation.

The theme of the novel revolves around the failure by the neo-colonial state to initiate a decisive break with its colonial past. Matigari Ma Njirũũngi, whose name translates as the 'remnants who survived the bullets', is a figure from history and popular culture. In popular Gĩkũyũ discourses, the phrase 'matigari ma Njirũũngi' was at first proudly used as a badge of honour by those who had participated in the liberation struggle as they mobilized themselves in the task of nation building. As it became clear that the ruling elite were not intent on delivering on the hopes and aspirations that had energized the struggle for independence, the term became a lament of exclusion. Often truncated to 'Matigari' (thus eliding reference to bullets), the term became a coded expression of the hope that one day, the Mau Mau survivors or their children will return to the forest to complete the aborted task of national liberation.

As used in the novel, 'matigari ma Njirũũngi' is a symbolic term. It recuperates the suppressed history of the struggle for independence and celebrates the agency of a group of people who have been marginalized in the Kenyan public sphere. The retrieval of past heroes in the novel is a clever way of raising issues of dissent and silence about Kenya's past.

This recovery, however, is not only historical. It is also cultural and linguistic. Mediated through indigenous storytelling codes, it allows Ngũgĩ access to an arcane language of representation that firmly places the novel within Gĩkũyũ indigenous cosmological and epistemological worldviews. Ngũgĩ turns to Gĩkũyũ sacred notions of reincarnation to imagine the 'return' of the Mau Mau to the post-colony and the birth of a new nation free from all forms of oppression. Significantly, when he returns, among his first acts is the rehabilitation of the orphaned children of former Mau Mau partisans – Mũriũki, the street boy, and Gũthera, the prostitute. We see the fusion of Biblical, African and Marxist codes as he declares: 'Let the will of the people be done! Our Kingdom come as once decreed by the *Iregi* revolutionaries' (*MMN*, 55). This is temporal, unlike the heavenly Kingdom promised in Christian eschatology. There are numerous such allegorical transformations of the Biblical discourse in the novel. Allegory, however, is not meant to be an escape from reality. It is a form of 'defamiliarisation necessary for concretisation' (Lovesey 1996: 184). This defamiliarization comes to acquire temporality in the fictional world of the novel because the victims of oppression finally come to see themselves as Matigari's children.

Matigari Ma Njirũũngi's return to the post-colonial world is presaged by an elaborate performance in which he buries his weapons under the mũgumo tree and girds himself with a belt of peace (*MMN*, 3-4). Orature provides the lexicon for Matigari's celebratory performance. Traditionally, the 'mararanja' songs he remembers were performed on the eve of circumcision. In the songs, the initiates expressed their longing for dawn to show that they did not fear facing the circumciser. In the text, the song is recast as a celebration of the end of colonialism. With the dawn of a new post-colonial era (*MMN*, 4), Matigari hopes to gather his 'family' that was displaced during the struggle and lead them home to begin a new life.

As Matigari begins his quest, his celebratory performance soon becomes melancholy as he comes face to face with the realities of the post-colonial state. Years after independence, the unnamed country to which he returns is ruled by corruption, fear and misery. It is a land of contrasts, of extremes of wealth and poverty. Matigari's home has been appropriated by the sons of Settler Williams and John Boy and his family scattered. The light of 'dawn' degenerates into a source of angst for Matigari as an uncharacteristically hot sun scorches the country. In this context, Matigari's quest is described in the familiar Ngũgĩan idiom of patriotism and national restoration. Matigari undertakes to 'rise up now and go to all the public places, blowing the horn of patriotic service and the trumpet of patriotic victory' (*MMN*, 6).

The most intriguing question in the novel regards Matigari's identity. This question is frequently evoked in a song (*MMN*, 111, 112, 114). But it is Ngũgĩ's use of language that creates the greatest suspense. The author uses verbs in the ungendered third person singular for Matigari's actions, e.g. 'aagwete' (held), 'aakĩĩra' (mused) (*MMN*, 3). Not until the incident where Matigari is stoned by the street boys at the dumpsite is he referred to by the gendered noun 'm thuri' (old man) (*MMN*, 16). Later in the novel, Ngũgĩ uses the term as a pun turning it into an adjective to refer to somebody who 'chooses' (from the verb 'thuura' to choose) to refer to choosing sides in the struggle against neo-colonialism.

Apart from taking advantage of the capacity of the Gĩkũyũ language to create ambiguities about gender, Ngũgĩ also uses the hero's name to depict Matigari as a symbolic character. The 'remnants who survived the bullets' can be anybody – men, women and even children – who survived Kenya's freedom struggle. This fact is evoked in Matigari's recollection of the Mau Mau song that extols the unity of the Mau Mau partisans, women ('atumia') and children ('ciana'), during the struggle (*MMN*, 5). It is also implied by Matigari's mission in the first part of the novel to search for 'ciana ciakwa' (my children) and his 'mũciĩ' (home) (MMN, 14). Matigari's notion of home is quite telling. One question that he asks himself as he begins his quest is: 'Mũciĩ wa mũndũ nĩ kĩĩ?' (What is a person's home?). He answers himself thus: 'Nĩ andũ aake: arũme, atumia, na ciana' (It is his people: men, women, and children) (*MMN*, 5). Matigari's idea of home is shaped by the egalitarian and communal ethos of Gĩkũyũ culture where a 'home' is not merely a dwelling but the family that lives therein. His 'people' turn out to be all the oppressed. Matigari is thus depicted as an androgynous hero who embodies the yearning of all the oppressed for a place in which they can feel at home. In other words, home is an allegory for the nation.

The ambiguity about Matigari's gender and the transformations in his persona enhance his qualities as a legendary hero who has been there from the beginning of time – from long before the time of the Arabs and the Portuguese (*MMN*, 40). This longevity makes Matigari privy to the Gĩkũyũ myths and prophecies of national origins, persecution and eventual deliverance purveyed by the likes of Mũgo wa Kĩbiro in *The River Between* (Ngũgĩ, 1995). This is apparent from his evocation of the *Iregi* (refusers) – a mythical pre-colonial generation of revolutionaries who, according to Gĩkũyũ mythology, were the first to rise up against oppression (*MMN*, 55). This depiction of Matigari interleaves with Ngũgĩ's historical consciousness. The author interprets Kenyan history as a continuum of domination and resistance that reached its peak during the Mau Mau struggle in the 1950s.

Thus, Matigari returns to the post-colonial public sphere as a national hero who symbolizes the nation in its ideal form. He speaks a polyglot language that represents the nation in all its diversity. His language is laden with the idioms of the indigenous gnosis, popular culture, myth, historical struggles and contemporary post-colonial politics.

In a sense, Matigari can also be read as a Christ figure. In his journeys, he meets and consoles representatives of the oppressed whom he inducts into the history and ethos of resistance. The first of these is Mũriũki, an orphaned street boy whose father died in the struggle for freedom. The war started a long time ago (tene) when Matigari – and Mũriũki's father – were fighting 'Kabuuũ' Williams (Settler Williams) in the forest (*MMN*, 14). Linguistically, the use of the term 'kabuurũ' – a derivative from the Kiswahili term 'kaburu' (Boer) – in the place of 'nyakeerũ' (whites) – the term Gĩkũyũ speakers would ordinarily use is a strategy of thematic expansion through language. The Kiswahili term draws parallels between the struggle against neo-colonialism and that against the racist apartheid regime in South Africa. Indeed, Ngũgĩ depicts the Kenyan struggle as an allegory, not just of the African, but also of the struggles of all the oppressed in the world for freedom and human dignity. In Matigari's reappropriation of Christian language, these struggles are depicted in Bunyanesque idiom as a 'holy war'. Hence, as Matigari explains to Mũriũki, the death of his father was 'blessed' because it was a sacrifice for the higher ideal of freedom (*MMN*, 14).

Another representative of the oppressed that Matigari meets is the worker, Ngarũro wa Kĩrĩro. The character's name means 'one who wipes away tears'. In his organic mindset, Matigari uses the language of Gĩkũyũ kinship nomenclature when he refers to Ngarũro as 'mbarĩ ya Kĩrĩro' (Kĩrĩro's clan, i.e. extended family) (*MMN*, 18). This reference implies that Ngarũro who is an activist and leader of a workers' strike symbolizes the workers' 'family'. In the nuanced sense in which the language is used, this means that the workers are also part of the family Matigari is looking for to lead home. In fact, later on when Matigari wonders whether Ngarũro might have seen his people in the factory, the latter responds rhetorically: 'Matigari's family? And whose family do you think we all are?' (*MMN*, 21).

A major figure of the oppressed is Gũthera who Matigari meets in a derelict roadside bar and restaurant. Gũthera is hiding from a policeman who has been pestering her for an affair. After Matigari rescues her from her harasser, Gũthera tells Matigari the story of her life. The story takes the form of an oral narrative within the novel and recalls Kareendi's story in *Caitaani Mũtharaba-inĩ* (1980). Gũthera uses the formulaic 'ĩtha' and an allegorical fictive persona 'mũirĩĩtu gathiraange' (a virgin girl) as a distancing strategy from her emotive story. The story also has a lively listening audience – Mũriũki, Matigari, who keeps interjecting, and others in the bar who might be listening in. The story contrasts the role of the indigenous and nationalistic African Independent Church and the missionary PCEA Church in the liberation struggle. A pious Christian in her youth, Gũthera's mother died in childbirth. Later her father, an elder of the African Independent Church was hanged by the colonialists for smuggling bullets hidden in his Bible to the Mau Mau fighters. Gũthera refused to yield to the sexual demands of a senior police officer who could have saved her father's life. Abandoned by her colonial PCEA Church because it would not be seen to associate with the daughter of a Mau Mau terrorist, Gũthera was ironically forced into prostitution in order to take care of her siblings. But to the Biblical Ten Commandments, she added an eleventh – that even as a prostitute she would never be involved with a policeman (*MMN*, 30-35).

Gũthera frequently refers to Matigari's action of rescuing her as 'kũhonokia' (save) – the term the Gĩkũyũ Bible uses for the Christian notion of salvation. Gũthera's salvation is not only moral. Like Mũriũki, Gũthera is literally a 'remnant' because her father was killed for being a Mau Mau supporter. A symbolic name is again important in divulging the role she plays in the novel. She is linked to Matigari's celebratory performance after his emergence from the forest. In his song, Matigari uses the verb 'gũthererũka' (to dawn completely/ shine bright), a pun on 'gũthera' (dawn/lighten up/also, pure) (*MMN*, 4). Transposed into a proper noun, the name 'Gũthera' plays on the ideas of 'dawn/'light'/'purity' to represent the birth of a new order. As she learns the causes and possible remedies to the problem of oppression in the land, Gũthera gradually transforms from a political novice to an agent of revolutionary change. In the end, she embodies the nation's yearning for a new dawn and restoration as the symbolic mother of the envisaged new dispensation.

Together with Matigari, Mũriũki and Gũthera form a pseudo-family of resisters similar to that of Abdulla, the Mau Mau veteran, Wanja and their unborn child in *Petals of Blood* (Ngũgĩ, 1977) or that of the Mau Mau woman in *The Trial of Dedan Kimathi* (Ngũgĩ and Mũgo, 1996) who similarly rehabilitates Boy and Girl and imbues them with the Kimathi spirit of resistance against neo-colonial oppression.

Before Matigari can lead his children home, he first must reclaim his house from John Boy Junior. As an allegory of the nation, the history of Matigari's house is a narrative of betrayal. During the colonial period, the house was appropriated by Settler Howard Williams. This character reminds us of Settler Howard in *Weep Not, Child* (Ngũgĩ, 1964) who had similarly taken over what used to be Ngotho's ancestral land. It is this appropriation of African properties that led to the Mau Mau struggle. But – and this is the major point the novel makes – even after independence, the house did not revert to its owners. Instead it was bought by John Boy Junior, the son of John Boy who had been the settler's cook. The continuation of oppression gives impetus to Matigari's quest that unfolds as a preparation for a new struggle, this time against neo-colonial oppression.

Nevertheless, Matigari's quest is not only about recuperating the nation (house). It is a quest for the truth about the nation. In other words, it is an epistemological struggle which, ultimately, 'is a struggle over the state' (Kortenaar, 2000: 243). Matigari is posed against a powerful ideological and epistemological system that ails the nation. This system finds expression in language, iconography, history and Christianity.

Ngũgĩ reinterprets and rewrites Biblical discourse to express the yearning for freedom and to satirize the colonial-missionary appropriation of the Bible to rationalize the imperial mission. Abraham's two sons in the Bible are used symbolically to represent the relationship between the white colonial elite and their local lackeys. Described as twins out of the womb of the same ogre, the story of Robert Williams and John Boy Junior captures the Manichaeism of the colonial world and its projection into the post-colonial public sphere. The story of the two 'brothers' maps the evolution of the exploiter class through history. Derived from Gĩkũyũ folktales, the image of the ogre depicts colonialism and neo-colonialism as a monster that has given birth to two sons. One is white (Robert Williams) and the other is black (John Boy Junior). The two are united by the fact that like the ogre, they devour the oppressed. The two 'brothers' are responsible for the 'darkness' that Matigari encounters as he re-enters the post-colonial state.

In his challenging quest, Matigari finds solace in indigenous proverbial wisdom when he notes that 'gũtirĩ ũtuku ũtakia' (there is no night that does not pass). In other words, Matigari, despite his initial melancholy, is optimistic that the oppressed will undo the 'twinning' of the colonial and the neo-colonial exploiter classes. These classes must be dislodged if the oppressed are to reclaim their nation.

Although Matigari is a hybrid figure from Christianity and Kenyan history, his most abiding features are derived from the indigenous gnosis. Traditional songs such as the 'mararanja' initiation songs herald the passing of his mantle of resistance to a new generation of resisters. Indeed, the novel stages this transition through the relationship between Matigari and Mũriũki. When they first meet at the dumpsite, Matigari refers to Mũriũki as 'kahĩĩ (young uncircumcised boy). But towards the end of the novel, Mũriũki's 'initiation' – to use the language of the 'mararanja' song – to manhood is completed when he inherits Matigari's weapons. This completes Ngũgĩ's fictional transposition of Kenya's history of resistance against oppression – from the mythical heroes (Iregi, Matigari), through historical heroes (Kĩmathi, Mathenge), to the present heroes (Mũriũki, Gũthera). Like Matigari, Mũriũki, whose name means 'born again' or the 'resurrected', is the reincarnation of all the past heroes.

Matigari emerges as an epic hero sui generis. His origins cannot be traced to one particular established oral tradition. Rather, he is a composite hero, whom Ngũgĩ conceives of in the manner of a traditional epic poet and whom he refashions as a character in a novel which is itself cast as an oral narrative performance. Ngũgĩ's novel thus corroborates Kotlyar's view that:

> the triumph of African literature as national literatures may well come as a result of the inclusion in literary works of epic traditions, whose value lies above all in the fact that it was in epos, more than in any other genre of folklore, that we find expression of the national consciousness of people. (Kotlyar, 2010: 26)

What happens to Matigari at the end? Significantly, the novel is inconclusive. The lack of clarity regarding Matigari's fate is appropriate because he, above all, symbolizes the spirit of resistance. He fades from the scene but also, as a spirit, remains central as an inspiration to the new generation in their ongoing struggles against oppression. Indeed, reading the oral codes in the novel not just as aesthetic codes but as 'strategies of remembering and recuperating viable values from the past in order to forge new relations between people in the present' (Vambe, 2004: 7) we would suggest that Matigari's character turns on indigenous Gĩkũyũ notions of elder veneration and 'spirit' worship. The obvious pun between his name and 'mũtiga irĩ' suggests as much. 'Mũtiga irĩ' is a revered elder, a male deceased, who upon his death has left irĩ (that which yields, i.e. 'livestock', 'gardens' but also 'sustenance', 'substance', and 'prosperity') for his offspring. Such a person never really dies. His progeny constantly turn to him for guidance in times of crisis. The language of Matigari's casting as a revered spirit stems from the world of Gĩkũyũ traditional religion where the rhythm of life is organically bonded with the sacred. This image recuperates the indigenous notion of community as a polity that includes not just the living but also the transcendental ancestors, the living dead. As such, Matigari not only shows his children what is wrong with their community but also shows them what they must do to correct the situation. Indeed in the idiom of the folktale on which the novel is modelled, Matigari the mythical figure who frequently indulges in the paranormal ends up metamorphosing into the elusive healer for what is essentially a public malaise.

Matigari Ma Njirũũngi's indigenous poetics do not, however, restrict its scope of relevance. On the contrary, the novel's democratic character serves to open up the field of its possible associations. The journey motif links Ngũgĩ's novel to the picaresque novel in world literature, and to one of its greatest examples – *Don Quixote* (1613) by Miguel de Cervantes (trans. Rutherford, 2001). Ngũgĩ's vision is akin to the Spanish writer's humanistic ideas embedded in the broad canvases of people's life in the novel which expose to the public gaze the tyranny, exploitation of the masses and moral hypocrisy practised by the official Spain of Cervantes' time. Another counterpart of *Matigari Ma Njirũũngi* is Nikolay Nekrasov's *Who Can Be Happy and Free in Russia?* (1864–1877) (trans. Soskice, 1970). As seven ordinary Russians criss-cross their motherland in an elusive search for happiness, this epic poem turns into a brilliant indictment of tsarist Russia. Matigari can also be seen as a kind of a 'contemporary Nasreddin Hodja' (Kotlyar, 2010: 16). Although the typical setting of a Nasreddin tale is an early Middle Eastern village, reminiscent of Matigari's Trampville, his populist philosophy transcends time and space and serves to reassure and inspire those who are on the side truth and justice. These masterpieces are bound by generic links born out of the democratic traditions which they are heir to and which they continue.

WORKS CITED

De Cervantes, Miguel. *Don Quixote de la Mancha*. Translated by John Rutherford and introduction by Roberto González Echevarría. New York: Penguin, 2001.

Gikandi, Simon. *Ngugi wa Thiong'o*. Cambridge: Cambridge University Press, 2000.

Gurnah, Abdulrazak. 'Matigari: A Tract of Resistance', *Research in African Literatures* 22 (4), 1991: 169-72.

Jackson, Rosemary. *Fantasy: Literature of Subversion*. London: Routledge, 1981.

Julien, Eileen. *African Novels and the Question of Orality*. Bloomington and Indianapolis: Indiana University Press, 1992.

Kabira, Wanjiku. *The Oral Artist*. Nairobi: Heinemann, 1983.

Kortenaar, Neil T. 'Fictive States and State of Fiction in Africa', *Comparative Literature* 52 (3), 2000.

Kotlyar, E. S. 'The National Sources of Contemporary African Prose Fiction: Ante-novelistic and Pre-novelistic Forms'. In Nikiforova, I. D. (ed.) *The History of Novelistic Forms in African Literature* [in Russian]. Moscow: Russian Academy of Sciences, 2010.

Lovesey, Oliver. '"The Sound of the Horn of Justice" in Ngũgĩ wa Thiong'o's Narrative'. In Gallagher, Susan V. (ed.) *Postcolonial Literature and the Biblical Call for Justice*. Jackson: University of Mississippi Press, 1994.

———. 'The Post-colonial "Crisis of Representation" and Ngũgĩ wa Thiong'o's Religious Allegory'. In Scott, Jamie S. (ed.) *Religion and in Post-colonial Cultures*. Amsterdam: Rodopi, 1996: 184.

Nekrasov, N. A. *Who Can Be Happy and Free in Russia?* Translated by Juliet M. Soskice. New York: AMS Press, 1970.

Ngũgĩ wa Thiong'o. *Weep Not, Child*. London: Heinemann, 1964.

———. *The River Between*. London: Heinemann, 1965

———. *Petals of Blood*. London: Heinemann, 1977.

———. *Caitaani Mũtharaba-inĩ*. London: Heinemann, 1980.

——. *Matigari*. Translated by Wangũi wa Goro. London: Heinemann, 1989.

——. *Re-membering Africa*. Nairobi: East African Educational Publishers, 2009: 95.

Ngũgĩ wa Thiong'o and Mĩcere Mũgo. *The Trial of Dedan Kimathi*. London: Heinemann, 1976.

Nkosi, Lewis. 'Ngugi's *Matigari*: The Novel of Post-Independence'. In Cantalupo, Charles (ed.) *The World of Ngũgĩ wa Thiong'o*. Trenton, N.J.: Africa World Press, 1995.

Ogude, James. *Ngũgĩ's Novels and African History: Narrating the Nation*. London: Pluto Press.

Vambe, Maurice T. *African Oral Story-telling Tradition and the Zimbabwean Novel in English*. Pretoria: University of South Africa Press, 2004.

Wilson, William A. 'Herder, Folklore and Romantic Nationalism', *Journal of Popular Culture* 6 (4), 1973: 823; 1999: 13-14.

Abiku in Ben Okri's
Imagination of Nationhood

A Metaphorical Interpretation of
Colonial-Postcolonial Politics

IKENNA KAMALU

> A literary text may serve to remind us of what of the past has never
> been past. In this, it may not be just a crypt but an abiku and, as such, a
> way of rethinking the relation between past and future. Literature may
> be both crypt and abiku.
> (Rooney, 2000: 114)

Literature, like other semiotic regimes such as sculpture, painting
photography and film, can and has been used to present individual
and group experiences. Artists have utilized all of the modes
mentioned above, with varying degrees of success, to engage with
such social and political issues as colonialism, politics, religion,
corruption and underdevelopment. Thus, the role of art, besides
its traditional functions of entertainment and education, includes
the provision of a critique of the life and experiences of participants
involved in social interaction. The postcolonial African literary text
has been used to provide an appraisal of ideology, identity, power
relations and inter-group relationships in Africa. Literary and
linguistic analysts have also tried to explore whether the resources
of art can be harnessed to provide a good interpretation of life
situations and function as an instrument for shaping and reshaping
of the socio-political direction of the society.

Colonialism is one historical experience the full impact of which
generations of African scholars have yet to fully unravel. Besides the
physical balkanization of the continent to serve imperial interests,
there are issues of economic and human exploitation, cultural
and linguistic distortions, negative representation/presentation of
Africa, its people, and its values by the West. The West invented
reasons to justify its acts of aggression as a rescue mission that was
in the best interest of Africa. To them, Africa should be grateful for
their timely intervention because it was a dark continent – without

language, culture, system of government, philosophy or human dignity, prior to its colonization. Even when the colonialists and their apologists acknowledge the existence of these basic forms of humanity in Africa, they still downgrade and fetishize the peoples as barbaric, primitive, crude and evil. This epistemic assumption which forms the basis of Western configuration of the other has been contested by African writers such as Chinua Achebe, Wole Soyinka, Ayi Kwei Armah, and Ben Okri. In the realm of philosophy, scholars Robin Horton, Kwame Anthony Appiah and Kwasi Wiredu have advanced sound arguments to counter imperial discourses that seem to denigrate and disparage the originality of African thought in religion and philosophy.

Our chief concern in this study is to explore how Ben Okri uses his art to foreground the cultural values of Africa which imperialism tried to annihilate or downgrade. Working within the framework of Critical Metaphor Analysis (CMA), therefore, this study will focus more on those portions of texts that support the rhetoric that colonialism was a form of predation. We shall also endeavour to justify the argument that the current socio-political upheavals in postcolonial Africa are part of the burdens of our colonial inheritance. The data for textual analysis is drawn from Ben Okri's book of poetry: *An African Elegy* (AAE, henceforth); and the trilogy: *The Famished Road* (TFR), *Songs of Enchantment* (SOE) and *Infinite Riches* (IR). The texts under consideration, as a corpus, constitute a formidable counter discourse to Western epistemological perceptions and assumptions about Africa. In exploring the theme of politics and social justice in Ben Okri's works, we shall approach the study from the following perspectives: Abiku as cultural metaphor; theoretical orientation;metaphor analyses; and then draw some conclusions.

Abiku, as *cultural metaphor* in Yoruba ethnography, refers to a stubborn spirit-child that maintains a cycle of dying and being reborn. The belief in the existence of the spirit-child is pervasive in African culture and worldview. The concept of man-spirit ambivalence is central to Africa's perception and expression of its cultural reality and identity. In Nigeria particularly, the belief in the existence of the spirit-child, 'child-god' (Osundare, 1988), 'strange unnatural child' (Cooper, 1996), is quite popular and still subsists in our everyday socio-cultural experiences. Ato Quayson (1997: 122) posits that 'the belief in the abiku phenomenon is widespread in southern Nigeria with the name "abiku" being shared by the

Yorubas and Ijos while the Igbos refer to them as ogbanje.' Children who manifest features of half-human, half-spirit are known as abiku and ogbanje in Yoruba and Igbo respectively. Chinua Achebe and Niyi Osundare therefore believe that a good understanding of the indigenous belief system is crucial to grasping the nebulous nature and manifestation of the spirit-child. This, according to Asakitikpi (2009: 70), is because the belief in the abiku/ogbanje myths is already 'engrained in the belief system of the people, and they shape their cosmology and ultimately their social behaviour'. Osundare (1998) observes that the abiku myth stretches its 'cultural scope beyond the pale of Yoruba experience'. He contends that 'what Soyinka, acting within the context of memory and experience, of Yoruba culture and language, calls "Abiku" is a mythic equivalent of what Achebe and Nzekwu, acting within the context of memory and experience of Igbo culture and language, express as "Ogbanje" respectively in *Things Fall Apart* and *Blade Among the Boys*' (94). This confirms the assumption that the abiku myth also exists in other African cultures. The abiku myth emanated from the traditional belief of the Yoruba in reincarnation. Ato Quayson describes it as a 'constellar concept' (1997: 123) because it embraces various beliefs about predestination, reincarnation and the relationship between the real world and that of spirits. Again, Osundare argues that since the abiku myth is situated within the manifold complex of Yoruba cultural behaviour, not in isolation from it, its interpretation, therefore should involve 'an examination of that aspect of Yoruba, nay African belief from which "Abiku" takes its root' (93).

This study is not primarily on abiku as a cultural token per se, rather, we are interested in the phenomenon as part of what George Lakoff and Mark Johnson (1980: 22) regard as cultural metaphor because metaphors are culturally motivated. They argue that some of the metaphorical constructions of our experiences are 'deeply embedded in our culture' and 'which metaphors we have and what they mean depend on the nature of our bodies, our interactions in the physical environment, and our social and cultural practices' (247). Similarly, Jonathan Charteris-Black (2005: 30) states that metaphor 'draws on the unconscious emotional associations of words, the value of which are rooted in cultural knowledge'. Thus, to understand the abiku phenomenon the way and manner Okri uses it in his texts means we must make use of the cultural information and culturally based conceptual frames at our disposal. Elsewhere, George Lakoff (1993: 241) posits that there are great ways in which conventional metaphors can be made real. According to him, conventional metaphors 'can be realized in obvious imaginative products such as cartoon, literary works, dreams, visions, and myth'. In this study, therefore, we examine how the abiku myth is metaphorically exploited in Ben Okri's texts to frame the image of the nation and its political conditions.

As far as *theoretical orientation* is concerned, the conceptual theory of metaphor, which is widely associated with George Lakoff and Mark Johnson (1980), explains that metaphor is at the heart of inference. Conceptual metaphor allows inferences in sensory-motor domains to be used to draw inferences about other domains. According to Lakoff and Johnson, metaphor involves the mapping of one domain of knowledge (source domain) on another (target domain). Thus, we use our knowledge of one domain of experience to understand another. Jonathan Charteris-Black (2004: 13) states that in mapping, 'the structure of concrete source domains is mapped onto that of abstract target domains. The aim of the mapping is therefore to represent the structural identity between two domains.' Zoltan Kovecses (2010: 4), therefore, defines metaphor as 'understanding one conceptual domain in terms of another conceptual domain'. The conceptual domain from which we draw metaphorical expressions to understand another conceptual domain is known as the *source domain* while the conceptual domain that is understood this way is the *target domain*. Conceptual metaphor takes the form A is B (for example, LIFE IS A JOURNEY) – that is, conceptual domain A is conceptual domain B. Thus, Kovecses explains that LIFE, ARGUMENT, LOVE, THEORY, IDEAS, SOCIAL ORGANIZATIONS, and others are target domains, while JOURNEYS, WAR, BUILDING, FOOD, PLANTS, and many others are source domain. The target domain is the one we try to understand through the use of the source domain (ibid.: 4).

The *critical metaphor analysis* (CMA) approach which this study adopts aims at showing how metaphor helps us to understand and interpret the underlying ideology in a literary discourse. Charteris-Black, who developed this approach, argues that it aims to bring together perspectives from critical discourse analysis, corpus analysis, pragmatics and cognitive semantics. According to him, 'I will refer to the integration of cognitive semantic and pragmatic approaches that is based on corpus evidence as critical metaphor analysis' (2004:13). The approach canvasses for the integration of linguistic analysis with cognitive understanding and social insights in textual analysis. He contends that metaphor can only be fully explained by taking into consideration its semantic, pragmatic and cognitive dimensions. Based on the above, he defines metaphor as:

> a linguistic representation that results from the shift in the use of a word or phrase from the context or domain in which it is expected to occur to another context or domain where it is not expected to occur, thereby causing semantic tension. It may have any or all of the linguistic, pragmatic and cognitive characteristics. (ibid: 21)

Charteris-Black identifies 'semantic tension' as a criterion for the identification of metaphors in discourse contexts. Thus, the occurrence of metaphors is expected to generate semantic tension because metaphors occur in unexpected contexts or domains. As a linguistic phenomenon it does possess pragmatic and cognitive characteristics. This explains why any word form can be a metaphor if the context makes it so. Charteris-Black further identifies the linguistic criteria of metaphor as *reification, personification,* and *depersonification.* Reification is referring to something that is abstract using a word or phrase that in other contexts refers to something that is concrete; personification refers to something that is inanimate using a word or phrase that in other contexts refers to something that is animate; while depersonification refers to something that is animate using a word or phrase that in other contexts refers to something that is inanimate. The pragmatic characteristic is that metaphor is motivated by the underlying purpose of persuading; and that this purpose is often covert and reflects speaker intentions in context; while the cognitive characteristic is that a metaphor is caused by, and may cause a shift in the *conceptual system.* This involves a psychological association between the attributes of a linguistic expression in its *original* source domain context and those of the referent in its *novel* target domain context (21).

Charteris-Black (2004: 42) describes CMA as 'a way of revealing underlying ideologies, attitudes and beliefs – and therefore constitutes a vital means of understanding more about the complex relationships between language, thought and social context.' There are three stages to the approach: first metaphors are identified, then interpreted and finally explained. This correlates with Norman Fairclough's three stages for critical discourse analysis, which are identification, interpretation and explanation. The crucial importance of CMA approach is that it enables the analyst to establish the ideological and rhetorical motivations that underlie language use in context. As Charteris-Black (2004: 42) puts it, 'metaphor analysis can be employed to explore ideology.'

In examining metaphor, our analyses will explore Okri's use of its resources to create new frames, categories and semantic domains that reveal colonial and postcolonial experiences. The frames and schemata, created through the resources of metaphor, will enable us to have a better understanding of how the metaphor of abiku is used to construct politics, ideology, identity and inter-group relationship in Okri's world. The constraints of space will not permit us to explore many of the frames deployed by Okri to project politics and social justice within the framework of postcolonial discourse.

Since nations are considered in this study as metaphorical children this part of the analysis investigates the rhetorical description of analogous metaphorical frames that involve the mapping of the ontology of the spirit-child on that of a nation in Ben Okri's fiction and poetry. It is important because several studies on Okri's texts that feature the abiku phenomenon have either focused on his use of magical realism as a generic style, or on his social criticism. Some of these studies have focused essentially on his artistic presentation of social disjuncture in postcolonial Nigeria. Some have also traced the intertextual relationship between Okri and Wole Soyinka, Chinua Achebe, J.P. Clark and Amos Tutuola in the presentation of the image of the spirit-child and the phantasmagoric world. But none of these studies has attempted, in a rigorous and conscious manner, to examine Okri's use of the magical realist or animist mode to desecularize the discourse on nationhood and present the interlocking relationship between the socio-political and religious experiences of the participants in social discourse.

Charteris-Black (2005) and Kovecses (2010) recognize myth as one of the non-linguistic realizations of metaphor. Kovecses notes that conceptual metaphors in myths may be realized in a variety of ways, one of which is when a metaphor functions as a key element in a myth; while another is through the characters of myth themselves (66). Okri uses the abiku myth to conceptualize nations and nationhood as the two excerpts below reveal:

> Our country is an abiku country. Like the spirit-child, it keeps coming and going. One day it will decide to remain. It will become strong. (TFR, 478)

> In his journeys Dad found that all nations are children; it shocked him

that ours too was an abiku nation, a spirit-child nation, one that keeps being reborn and after each birth come blood and betrayals... (TFR, 494)

Metaphorically, Okri wants the reader to comprehend the concept of nationhood using their knowledge of a child (spirit-child). And because he conceptualizes a nation as a child (spirit-child) he maps the ontological features of the child (spirit-child) onto that of a nation. Thus, the mapping evokes the following frames in the reader:

(i)   a nation is conceived as a child
(ii)   a nation is given birth to (or born) as a child
(iii)   a nation is nurtured as a child
(iv)   a nation can be a normal child or a spirit-child
(v)   a normal and healthy nation prospers like a normal and healthy child
(vi)   a spirit-child nation is always sick and problematic, and destined to die again and again
(vii)   the spirit-child nation cannot live until a propitious sacrifice is made by a medicine man
(viii) even a propitious sacrifice by a medicine man may not stop the spirit-child nation from dying
(ix)   Nigeria is an abiku nation – sick and problematic and needs the services of a *strong* medicine man to live and be strong
(x)   the spirit-child nation can only live if it chooses to, like Azaro (TFR, 487)
(xi)   Nigeria as an abiku nation can live if it chooses to (like Azaro), and with the support of a *strong* medicine man

Okri in 'Political Abiku' (AAE), as in his fiction, relates the abiku phenomenon to the image of the nation. We can therefore argue that Okri uses the myth to communicate a negative evaluation about the Nigerian nation. The ideological and rhetorical motivation that underlies its deployment is to encourage the reader to perceive the country as being as sick and problematic as a spirit-child, and also to offer a justification as to why it is not doing well like other healthy economies. Metaphors appeal to emotions and arouse certain feelings in the hearer or reader. The abiku myth evokes emotions of fear, sorrow and fatality in those who understand its nature. Its deployment is to activate the unconscious feelings of fear and hopelessness that we usually associate with the spirit-child. The text also wants the reader to know that the country is in dire need of the services of a strong medicine man if it is to live. Here, the text reveals a covert negative evaluation of Nigeria's political leadership. It presupposes that it has, all this while, engaged the services of weak so-called medicine men. This explains why the crisis of its abiku nature appears intractable. We can therefore infer that Okri is advocating a change in the country's leadership structure. The charismatic, focused and goal-oriented leadership he advocates for the country is framed in the image of a strong medicine man. The Valiant Leader Myth is one of the political myths identified by Edelman. According to Charteris-Black (2005: 25), this is one in which the political leader is benevolent and effective in saving people from danger by displaying qualities of courage, aggression and the ability to overcome difficulties. The abiku myth is used to remind the nation of the type of political leadership to which it should aspire.

Metaphor as a cultural product functions effectively when the listener or reader has a good understanding of its cultural sources. Thus the understanding of a metaphor is both cognitively and contextually (cultural and situational) dependent. The spirit-child is the product of human parents. It is the responsibility of its parents to see that it survives and overcomes pressing challenges to become strong like other children. It is therefore a sign of bad or poor parenting when a sick child is abandoned on account of its health conditions. Okri uses the abiku myth to negatively evaluate the colonial parents of Nigeria for giving birth to a sick and problematic child, whom they eventually abandon to its own fate. Nigeria is a colonial creation with multiple socio-political, cultural and religious challenges. Okri's rhetoric covertly indicts the colonial West for developing Nigeria for Western selfish interests, and for abandoning it at times of need. In the prevailing scenario, Okri urges his compatriots to be ready to make 'propitious sacrifice' for the survival of the nation and to display serious 'intent to bear the weight of a unique destiny' (TFR, 494).

Within the context of 'King is a monster/devourer metaphor', the myth of King of the Road is used by Okri to frame oppression and exploitation. (See TFR 258-61 for full text). Dad told Azaro the story to explain the several 'whys' that people ask about the road and nature. It is the story of the 'King of the Road'. The King of the Road was a giant who used to live in the forest. When the forest could no longer satisfy his huge appetite, he decided to relocate to the road. He had a huge stomach and was never satisfied. For a long time people made sacrifices to him so that he would allow them to pass on the road. They never complained because 'they found him there when they came into the world. ... People believed that he had lived for thousands of years and that nothing could kill him and he could never die'. However, when he became a terror to the people of the world, they decided to either make peace with him or kill him. The first two peace delegations sent to him were all eaten up by him, so the people of the world decided to kill him. They directed all human beings to come with the most potent poison at their disposal to a crucial gathering. They complied but 'While the different people travelled with poison some of it spilled over and that is why some plants can kill and why there are places in the forest where nothing ever grows'. The story has it that the King of the Road also ate up the third delegation that took the poisoned food to him. Dad informs that 'Only one person escaped. And that person was our great-great-great-grandfather. He knew the secret of making himself invisible.' Dad says that after the King of the Road had eaten up the delegation together with the poisoned food he became hungrier and because he could not find anything more to eat, he began to eat up himself until 'only his stomach remained'. A terrific rain that lasted seven days started that night and washed off his stomach and dissolved it into the ground:

> What had happened was that the King of the Road had become part of all the roads in this world. He is still hungry, and he will always be hungry. That is why there are so many accidents in the world.

The narrator explains that there are so many reasons why people still make him sacrifices which include: so that he can let them travel safely, to remember that the monster is still there, and a form of prayer that his type should never come back again to terrify our lives. The tale ends with an admonition from the narrator 'That is why a small boy like you (Azaro) must be very careful how you wander about in this world.' It is interesting to note that all the explanatory clauses begin with the adverbial clause of reason '*that is why...*' or '*so that...*'

The next task is to find out the rhetorical and ideological motivation behind Okri's creation of the myth. Drawing from social and cultural contexts of the text we can infer that the metaphor of the king of the road is used to frame the dominance and exploitation which are best expressed in colonialism. A close reading of the text reveals that colonialism has all the features of the king of the road. Let us consider some of them here. The colonial authority made claim to possessing a long historical and cultural existence and hegemony that entitled it to be revered and served by others. Like the king of the road, it exploited the people of Africa and exhibited an insatiable appetite for their wealth and other resources. The poisonous trees and infertile portions of the earth are the permanent damages inflicted on Africa by colonialism. The delegates that were eaten up were African nationalists who lost their lives trying to fight against colonial oppression, or negotiate for freedom. The metaphorical death of the king of the road is the flag independence attained by most African countries. However, the text reveals that flag independence has not freed the colonized nations from the economic and political control and manipulations of their erstwhile masters. It appears that colonialism has become even more powerful than ever before. The narrator says that the king of the road has become a part of all the roads in the whole world and has continued to claim lives through accidents. More frightening is the fact that it is still hungry and always will be.

Okri uses the myth to remind his readers that colonialism still exists in diverse forms and is now aided by advanced technologies like the Internet and the cable network – which have become sources of mind control; economic, socio-political, cultural, and linguistic dominance. This also explains why there are so many accidents in the world. The term, accident, is a euphemistic expression of exploitation – social, economic and political victims of colonialism and neocolonialism. The underlying ideology of the metaphor shows that many colonized nations, for many reasons, still make sacrifices to their former colonial masters. Okri uses the resources of reification and personification to tie the cognitive and ideological dimensions of the narrative. Colonialism, an abstract entity is expressed through concrete images like road and kingship. Again, road, an inanimate entity is personified as human through the deployment of the pronoun 'he'. In all, Okri wants his readers to conceptualize colonialism as beast/monster with a rapacious appetite for destruction and exploitation. Colonialism facilitated the creation of what Okri, in *Infinite Riches*, calls 'new sprits which fed the bottomless appetite of the great god of chaos' (IR, 128). It is the West he frames as the great god of chaos with a bottomless appetite – an image that ties with that of the king of the road in *The Famished Road*. Dad's advice to Azaro, is Okri's warning to dependent nations, to be wary of their relations with the West because the latter is a devourer.

Okri uses the Governor-General as a metonymic configuration of group identity. George Lakoff (1987:13) describes this as 'reference-point reasoning', or 'metonymic,' reasoning which is the idea that a part of a category (that is, a member or subcategory) can stand for the whole category in certain reasoning process. The Governor-General is used to frame colonial injustices against Africa. In *Songs of Enchantment* Okri laments the deliberate distortion of African values and the denial of its accomplishments by 'the dominant history of the short-sighted conquerors of the times' (SOE, 160). The Governor-General, knowing that colonial rule will soon end, spends several days destroying all incriminating records that reveal colonial atrocities and injustices in Africa, including those that contain 'notes about dividing up the country' and 'the new map of the nation' (IR, 38). The destruction of incriminating documents is to evade justice. We are told that when he 'completed the destruction of all incriminating documents relating to the soon-to-be-created nation', he proceeds to 'rewrite our history' (IR, 125). The Governor-General rewrites history to favour the West. He distorts Africa's past and makes it to suit colonial ideology; 'he rewrote our past, he altered our present' (IR, 127, 128). Even time is altered. He makes his longer and ours shorter. African names, rivers, mountains, towns, geography, etc. are changed and distorted. According to Okri:

> He changed the names of places which were older than the places themselves. He redesigned the phonality of African names, softened the consonants, flattened the vowels. In altering the sound of the names he altered their meaning and affected the destiny of the named. ...The Governor-General in rewriting our history, deprived us of language; of poetry, of stories, of architecture, of civic laws, of social organization, of art, science, mathematics, sculpture, abstract conception, and philosophy. He deprived us of history, of civilization and, unintentionally, deprived us of humanity too. Unwittingly, he effaced us from creation. (IR, 126)

In poems like 'Lament of the Images', 'The Cross is Gone' and 'Little Girl' (AAE) Okri laments the demonization, alteration and destruction of African cultural values by colonial forces. 'Lament of the Images' accuses the West of stealing images from Africa and destroying those that did not appeal to their taste. According to him, 'They took the painted bones/The stones of molten kings/The sacred bronze leopards....They burned/All that frightened them.../They burned them all/They burned them in heaps/They burned them in alien piety.' Besides stealing and destroying items of rich cultural value in Africa (see pp.125-30 for more of the African values that suffered colonial distortion), the Governor-General 'made our history begin with the arrival of his people on our shores' (IR, 126). He reminds the West that it is we Africans:

…who bear within us ancient dreams and future revelations. Who began the naming of the world and all its gods… who fertilized the banks of the Nile with the sacred word which sprouted the earliest and most mysterious civilization, the forgotten foundation of civilizations …whose secret ways have entered into the bloodstream of the world-wonders silently. (IR, 127)

The thrust of Okri's rhetoric is to rearticulate and reposition Africa in world civilization and culture. His is a counter rhetoric to Western claims to legitimacy, rationality and cultural superiority. The reference to the 'Nile' and the 'foundation of civilization' activates the historical knowledge frame that attributes the origin of modern civilization to Egypt – Africa. The text therefore interrogates Western hypocrisy that accepts Africa as the cradle and foundation of civilization but still downgrades it and turns 'our philosophies into crude superstitions, our rituals into childish dances, our religions into animal worship and animistic trances, our art into crude relics and primitive forms …' (IR, 127). In the light of the above, Okri demands social justice in the lamentation below:

'The white people turned our children into slaves/In broad daylight/ …we didn't even threaten them with death/And they haven't been taken to any court on earth or in heaven/So now we suffer/In broad daylight….And our case unheard in any court/On earth or in heaven/ And the great injustice forgotten/On earth and in heaven…' (IR, 311)

Okri is asking for a redress of the colonial injustices against Africa. In 'ruler for state' metonym, conceptual metonym and conceptual metaphor are blended to activate a schema for a ruthless dictator who relishes in dehumanizing and exploiting the other in favour of self. Okri equally criticizes his African forebears whom he calls '…our lily-headed ancestors/How they betrayed us: /How we betrayed ourselves' ('Stammering on Bedrock', AAE). He also directs his attack on the political leadership of the postcolonial era for sustaining the culture of violence introduced by the colonial powers. Politicians use 'political masquerades', which is a 'perversion of traditional masquerades to scare us into voting for them' (SOE, 71). This explains why he conceptualizes politics in

Nigeria as madness and describes politicians and their agents as 'madmen of our history' (TFR, 193).

In conclusion, this study shows that metaphor can be a critical tool in the exploration of the rhetorical and ideological motivations behind language use in a literary discourse – it is used in the texts under consideration to express evaluative meanings, covertly and overtly. The study also shows that metaphor is important in influencing our underlying political and social beliefs. Okri uses the abiku rhetoric as a metaphor for social justice by the oppressed and exploited. Okri's reinscription of spirituality into the discourse of Nigeria's nationhood is a confirmation of the crucial importance of the literary imagination and its linguistic analysis in the project of creating deeper understanding about identity, inter-group relationships and the humanistic pursuit of the common good.

WORKS CITED

Achebe, Chinua. *Things Fall Apart*. Ibadan: Heinemann, 1958.

——. *The World of the Ogbanje*. Enugu: Fourth Dimension Publishers, 1986.

Asakitikpi, A. E. 'Engaging in Life's Dialogue: A Sociological Interpretation of the Notion of Abiku in the Works of Soyinka, Clark and Okri'. In *Re-Visioning Humanistic Studies*, A.E. Eruvbetine and Udu Yakubu (eds). Lagos: Cultural Institute, 2009: 65-79.

Charteris-Black, Jonathan. *Corpus Approaches to Critical Metaphor Analysis*. New York: Palgrave Macmillan, 2004.

——. *Politicians and Rhetoric: The Persuasive Power of Metaphor*. New York: Palgrave Macmillan, 2005.

Cooper, Brenda. *Magical Realism in West African Fiction*. London: Routledge, 1998.

Fairclough, Norman. *Critical Discourse Analysis: The Critical Study of Language*. London: Longman, 1995.

Kovecses, Zoltan. *Metaphor: A Practical Introduction*. New York: Oxford University Press, 2010.

Lakoff, George. *Women, Fire, and Dangerous Things: What Categories Reveal about the Mind*. Chicago: University of Chicago Press, 1987.

Lakoff, George. 'The Contemporary Theory of Metaphor.' In *Metaphor and Thought*. A. Ortony. (ed.). New York: Cambridge University Press, 1993: 202-51.

Lakoff, George and Johnson, Mark. *Metaphors We Live By*. Chicago: The University of Chicago Press, 1980.

Nzekwu, Onuora. *Blade among the Boys*. Ibadan: Heinemann, 1972.

Okri, Ben. *The Famished Road*. London: Jonathan Cape, 1991.

——. *Songs of Enchantment*. London: Vantage, 1993.

——. *African Elegy*. Ibadan: Heinemann, 1993.

——. *Infinite Riches*. London: Orion Books Ltd, 1998.

Osundare, Niyi. 'The Poem as a Myth-linguistic Event: A Study of Soyinka's Abiku' in *African Literature Today* 16. London: James Currey, 1998: 91-102.

Quayson, Ato. 'Ben Okri'. In *African Writers*. Ed. C. Brian. Cox. New York: Simon & Schuster Macmillan, 1997: 599-608.

Rooney, Caroline. *African Literature, Animism and Politics*. London: Routledge, 2000.

Refracting the Political

Binyavanga Wainaina's
One Day I Will Write About This Place

RACHEL KNIGHTON

As Kenya's best-known writer of his generation, Binyavanga Wainaina is recognized not only for his literary output, but also for his theoretical approach to current African writing. Enhanced by his role as founding editor of *Kwani?*, the literary journal, Wainaina's voice as pioneer of a new literary movement has been cultivated through his numerous interviews and articles published online. His internationally acclaimed satirical article 'How to Write About Africa' (2005) in particular, exemplifies not just Wainaina's literary stature, but his movement away from the prevailing narratives concerning Africa.[1] While Wainaina's focus is on stereotypical Western representations of the continent, his article also illustrates a drive towards a new way of conceptualizing an Africa free of images of subjection and subjugation. In stating his reluctance to 'manipulate myself to suit the postcolonial situation', Wainaina instead positions himself as an author occupied by multiple concerns, including politics.[2] Asserting that 'I'm far more interested in texture, in aesthetics, in word play', Wainaina's stress on the literary in addition to the political is indicative of his narrative engagement with politics in *One Day I Will Write About This Place*.[3]

Wainaina's approach to the political resonates with wider critical debates surrounding recent African writing. Moving away from canonical postcolonial writers, literary scholars are increasingly preoccupied with exploring the new directions African literature is taking. Politics or social commitment, as characteristic features of postcolonial writing, are therefore treated as subjects of contention. This is particularly evident in current African writers' perceptions of their own work. Mukoma wa Ngugi, for example, dispels the reading of 'African fiction as fulfilling a political and cultural function', arguing for the importance of 'questions of aesthetics'

33

in literary criticism.[4] Whilst Mukoma's article highlights the need to read African literature for its form as well as content, it also registers a concern over the place of politics in recent writing.[5] Politics is presented as becoming a stereotypical feature of African writing that new writers aim to make more complex.[6] The multiple focuses of Wainaina's memoir and his refusal to 'fulfil any kind of "theme"', makes *One Day I Will Write About This Place* exemplary of this emerging tradition.[7] Politics nevertheless plays an important role within the text, and it is Wainaina's strategies of narrating the political that I will examine further here.

Reading Wainaina's memoir alongside Ato Quayson's theory of political representation, this article examines the techniques of refraction operating within Wainaina's work. In his *Postcolonialism*, Quayson's chapter, 'Literature as a Politically Symbolic Act', provides a useful framework through which to examine *One Day I Will Write About This Place* because of its focus on the political. Arguing that 'the discursive network in African life [...] can always be read as ultimately political', he describes literature in particular as performing a '*liberatory politics*' (his italics), where techniques of 'defamiliarization' and 'perspectival alienation' are central to literary representations of the political.[8] Highlighting literature's ability 'to refract social reality', Quayson underlines the importance of 'defamiliariz[ing] existing [social] categories' in order to intervene or transcend them.[9] Whilst the concept of alienation is vital in examining Wainaina's narrative strategy, it is employed in a different way to Quayson's assessment of it. I contend that Wainaina's text contains features of refraction with regards to the political not as a consequence of the political project of the narrative, but as a result of the contesting themes at play within his writing.

Preoccupied with language and sound, Wainaina's portrayal of the political moment in contemporary Kenya is filtered through an exposition of the sensory, which in turn is used to convey his consciousness as a child and his sensibility as a writer. As a memoir, therefore, *One Day I Will Write About This Place* combines the personal, aesthetic and political as a method of writing about the self. Wainaina's aesthetics are, importantly, centred around his creation of the language of childhood experience. Statements such as 'I was trying to do something new and adventurous with the language I was using' and 'I wanted to create a vehicle that captured the imagination of childhood', illustrate Wainaina's focus on conveying the sensory through words and act as a key component in the writing of his life-narrative.[10] Beginning with an analysis of the centrality of the sensory to Wainaina's narrative strategy, what follows is an examination of its presence within several political events depicted in the text.

As emphasized by a number of Wainaina's early reviewers, 'sensory experience' and the 'sensual' form a major strand of *One Day I Will Write About This Place*.[11] Jennifer Acker's comment on Wainaina's 'prismatic method of telling', including reference to 'sensory experience' , provides a useful model for textual analysis. However, the primacy of the sensory merits further enquiry.[12] Describing his growth as a writer, Wainaina positions the sensual as a vital component of his authorial skill. In an epiphanic moment midway through the text, realizing his vocation as a writer, he writes: 'It is clear – so clear. All this time, without writing one word, I have been […] watching people, and writing what I see in my head, finding shapes for reality by making them into a book'.[13] Wainaina's claim to watching people; translating their movements and sounds into text, mirrors his narrative strategy within his memoir, where he finds a language to convey sensory experience. Drawing explicit attention to his 'own sensual comfort' (143), Wainaina not only communicates his orientation as writer, but locates the source of his intellectual stability within the mapping of the sensory. Specifying 'thirst' as something 'I will talk about' (ibid.), Wainaina connects this moment to an earlier episode in the text, where he dramatizes his effort to 'know' (ibid.) or explicate the sensation of thirst as a child.

Wainaina uses thirst – and its incomprehensibility – in order to convey the subjectivity of his seven-year-old self. Asking, 'What is thirst? The word splits up into a hundred small suns' (5), thirst becomes a similar site for imaginative exploration to his preceding perception of the sun refracted through the trees. Focusing specifically on thirst as a 'word' (ibid.), Wainaina positions the linguistic as a key component in his character's understanding of the senses. The young Wainaina's inability to drink or to physically find a 'Thirst Resolution' (ibid.) like his older sister, whose 'glass [is] already empty' (ibid.), is mirrored in his difficulty to define the word 'thirst'. Stating that '[t]his word, *thirst, thirsty*. It is a word full of resolution' (ibid.), Wainaina is nevertheless presented as unable to pin it down. The text recreates his thought process as he tries to come to terms with it: 'Thirst is… is… a sucking absence' (7). Longing 'to be certainly thirsty' (6) but being left 'so uncertain and speculative' (ibid.) by the word 'thirst',

Wainaina uses this sensation not simply to convey the limitations of his childish awareness of the sensory. His aspirations towards certainty also point to a characteristic uncertainty that surrounds Wainaina's presentation of himself.

Wainaina's investigation of the sensory in this passage is used to outline the chaos surrounding his constructed persona that resonates throughout the text. Stating that: 'Words, I think, must be concrete things. Surely they cannot be suggestions of things, vague pictures: scattered, shifting sensations?' (5), Wainaina uses the vagaries of thirst as a metaphor for his own uncertainty. Whilst '[o]ther people have a word world' where 'words like *thirsty* have length, breadth and height' (6), the unfixed nature of Wainaina's conception of thirst mirrors the blurring of lines between his physical and imaginative presence. Asserting that '[m]y patterns are always tripping on each other in public' (4), Wainaina's movements are presented as unstable because of his frequent retreat into his imagination. Describing a game of football at the start of the memoir, for instance, he writes that 'I am lost. Arms and legs and ball are forgotten', as he imagines that '[t]he thousand suns are breathing' (ibid.). Portrayed later in the text as 'mixed up' (160), conscious of his 'dreaminess and absent-mindedness' (159), Wainaina's quest for 'certainty' 'in defiance of chaos' (111) is presented as achievable through the writing process. Articulating the sensory through language, writing enables Wainaina to find 'shapes for reality' (143) that would otherwise elude him. Wainaina's understanding of the world around him as illustrated is therefore seen alongside his ability to put words to events, a strategy that impacts his narrative engagement with the political.

The sensory, therefore, is central to Wainaina's narrative strategy through his identification of it as a prominent feature of his writing. Each person or event described within his memoir is shaped in relation to a depiction of the sensory through language. The sensory is also a vital part of Wainaina's narrative strategy because it enables him to convey his own subjective consciousness surrounding the events he portrays. Wainaina's concern for the sensory illustrates his imaginative capacity as a child, centring on the imagination as the locus of his individual subjectivity. Wainaina's ability to convey the sensory through words is also used to represent his growth as both a person and a writer, acting as a reminder of the importance of the personal in his autobiographical account. It is through the sensory, then, that Wainaina brings together the personal, political and aesthetic concerns of the text in a series of refractive processes. This is particularly evident in Wainaina's depiction of the Madaraka or Independence Day ceremony examined below.

Early in his memoir, Wainaina recounts his experience of watching the 'Independence Day ceremonies on television' (44). Focusing on the sensory in his portrayal of this moment, Wainaina uses sound to communicate the impact of the event on his twelve-year-old self. Centring on '*Mp* and *mpr* words' (ibid.), Wainaina employs these sounds to convey the order and gravity of the political ceremony as it appears to him; a ceremony attended by President Moi and based on marches and 'dances [...] in rows and columns' (45). He intersperses descriptions of the activities on-screen with words such as 'Imprint. Impress' (44) and 'Proud. Pretty. Prim. Promising' (45), using the resonance of these hard syllables to reinforce the formality of the event. He also includes the sounds of the 'many whistles' made by 'Boy Scouts' (44), using an extended '*Mprr*' (ibid.) to represent the 'order' (ibid.) imposed by Baden-Powell and also on the missionary movement in colonial Kenya. Employing sound in this way, Wainaina demonstrates the strength of his imagination as a child. The portrayal of the political is, in this case, mediated through the re-creation of Wainaina's childish perceptions, as Wainaina reconstructs the language of his childhood experience.

Wainaina's preoccupation with sound is extended through the representation of his babysitter, Wambui. Transcribing her 'broken English, slangy Kiswahili, Gikuyu inflections' (49), Wainaina's impersonation of her is juxtaposed with his presentation of the Madaraka Day ceremony. As she 'turns down the volume' (47) of the television, the reader is confronted with her singing to 'the livers of mBabylon...' (48). This passage not only provides a humorous, contemporary offshoot to the political that highlights the shifting ambience of Wainaina's childhood. It once again illustrates Wainaina's imaginative engagement with language and the scaling of the political as a result. Personifying the different letters of the Gikuyu-sounding alphabet – '*A, mbi, ci*' (ibid.) – Wainaina presents them as interspersed with the action of the ceremony. He writes: 'Policemen circle them; the president pauses. *N* starts to agitate, standing there in straight colonial lines' (48). Language, here, is portrayed as interrupting the ceremony in the same way that Wainaina's focus on the linguistic disrupts the narrative's political trajectory.

Language, as well as refracting the political, is also employed by Wainaina to make a political point. Wainaina focuses on Wambui and her use of language in order to comment on the political dynamics that have shaped Kenya to the present day. After dwelling on Wambui's singing – 'mangled in her Subukia accent' (48) – Wainaina moves into a description of her lineage: 'She is a market woman. A (L)Rift Valley girl. Third generation' (49). Connecting her dialect to her ancestry in this way, Wainaina examines the history behind her Gikuyu accent. He writes: 'Wambui is Gikuyu by fear, or Kenyatta-issued title deed' (ibid.), going on to claim that '[t]hey all became Gikuyu after Independence, for the president was Gikuyu' (ibid.). Through reference to language, Wainaina looks back to Kenya's post-independence politics, highlighting the power structures operating under Kenyatta's rule. Further on in the text, Wainaina also uses languages to represent Kenya's political fragmentation. Describing 'Urban Kenya' as 'a split personality' (125) comprised of English, Kiswahili and 'our mother tongues' (ibid.), Wainaina anticipates his engagement with Kenya's 2007 post-election violence; a subject I will analyse in more depth later in this article.

To return to the portrayal of Madaraka Day, Wainaina's use of the sensory represents a further level in the refraction of the political for autobiographical and artistic concerns. As I have already discussed, Wainaina's ability to convey the sensory through words is also used to represent his growth as a person and a writer. The uncertainty surrounding his ability to describe this particular event is, therefore, indicative of his difficulty to comprehend and articulate what he experiences as a result of his young age. Writing that '[w]ords must surround experience [...] sucking all this up and making it real', Wainaina declares that 'I do not have enough words for all this' (53). Whilst his 'mind and body' are presented as 'quickening' (ibid.) to the sounds around him, 'lagging behind is a rising anxiety of words' (ibid.). Wainaina pictures himself here as unable to find words for the sensory. He underlines instead his chaotic impression of events by stating: 'My new word *bureaucrat* is running around my mind in a panic' (52). Affirming that 'one day I will arrange the words right for this strange night' (53), Wainaina looks forward to a future moment of comprehension and explication. Analysed in isolation, this episode is constructed to convey the scrambled and confused subjectivity of Wainaina's twelve-year-old self.

Wainaina draws on the sensory as a method of conveying his own uncertainty at an earlier point in the text. Recounting the death of President Kenyatta, Wainaina's portrayal of the political is once again refracted through personal and aesthetic concerns as he communicates his awareness as a child. The description of the 'grainy old reels of traditional Gikuyu dancers singing for Kenyatta' (22) shown on television, is soon displaced by a focus on the 'shaking, shapeless sounds' (24) emanating from the '*nyatiti*' – 'a traditional Luo musical instrument' (ibid.). Wainaina dwells on this instrument as a symbol of his own incomprehension. Contrasted against his 'yellow mouth organ' (24) with its 'clear separate sound' (25), he underlines the 'chaos' (24) of the nyatiti's notes as it resembles the 'many unrelated sounds and languages' (25) of the people on-screen. Connecting sound with the people in this way, Wainaina employs the sensory to convey his own political consciousness. The '[g]libberish' of the '*harambee* sounds of people in the many costumes of Kenya'[14] defies the order of 'do, re, mi, fa, sol, la, ti, do-' (ibid.), creating a new, alternative Kenyan vocality that Wainaina, who 'speak[s] only English and Kiswahili' (12), is apparently unfamiliar with. Through this passage, then, Wainaina positions language and sound as vital components in the presentation of political cohesion and comprehension within the text.

The construction of the term '*Ki-may*' (25) in this passage is also used to indicate the young Wainaina's confusion surrounding the political event he witnesses. Used to signify uncertainty, this term epitomizes – perhaps paradoxically – the importance of the linguistic in ascertaining the level of Wainaina's character's comprehension within the text. Representing 'any language that I cannot speak' (ibid.), Wainaina employs the word *ki-may* to reflect the multiple, incomprehensible sounds he hears on the television. ' "*Kimay*", he writes, 'is the talking jazz trumpet: sneering skewing sounds, squeaks and strains [...] bursting to say something, and then not saying anything at all' (ibid.). Kimay, therefore, becomes an expression of Wainaina's inability to come to terms with the sensory, whilst also replicating this incomprehension through its own sound. The texture of the word itself signifies uncertainty: '*Ki-maaay*. It calls at the most unexpected moment. Certainty loses its spine, and starts to accordion' (ibid.). Wainaina's creation of this word not only illustrates a preoccupation with the linguistic or aesthetic that foregrounds his childish imagination and confused consciousness within the political. Representing the various languages of Kenya that he cannot speak – 'Ki-kuyu, Ki-Kamba, Ki-Ganda, Ki-sii [...]' (25-6) – kimay also acts as a measure of Wainaina's political awareness; a strategy that I will analyse for its effect within the concluding pages of the text.

Wainaina's use of the term kimay at the end of his memoir combines the personal, aesthetic and political in a final process of refraction. Recording his experience of watching a documentary on *benga* as an adult,[15] Wainaina writes of the inclusion of the 'nyatiti', which 'sounds fine. No kimay. […] The music is coherent and complicated' (251). This change from confusion to understanding over the complex sounds of the nyatiti can be seen to signify Wainaina's analytic growth as a result of his maturity. The sound of the nyatiti does not produce 'scattered, shifting sensations' (5), but rather has become concretized and comprehensible. Without the presence of kimay, Wainaina is no longer pictured as uncertain, and this clarity is also representative of his growth as a writer. Describing the nyatiti as 'a literary form' (252) that 'maintain[s] the integrity of the story' (253), Wainaina's understanding of it as an instrument or sound also mirrors the resolution of the text, as his life-narrative comes together to achieve coherence. Focusing on the 'singer' (253) or 'storyteller' (252) that plays the nyatiti, Wainaina draws attention to his role as writer, and his ability to finally narrate or 'write about this place' (164).

Whilst kimay carries significance for the representation of his growth as both a person and a writer, Wainaina also uses it for political resonance. Defining it as 'the guitar sounds of all of Kenya speaking Kenya's languages' (253), Wainaina employs kimay as a metaphor for national unity, envisaged through the linguistic. Representing the many languages used within Kenya – 'Ki-kuyu, Ki-Kamba, Ki-Ganda, Ki-sii […]' (25-6) – kimay posits a democratic view of Kenyan society through its emphasis on the polyphonic. With language presented by Wainaina as a major indicator of ethnic division, kimay is used as a term of resistance to political fragmentation. In his portrayal of the lead-up to Kenya's 2007 post-election violence, for instance, he centres on language as a defining feature of social fracture. In the wake of Kibaki's inauguration as president, for example, Wainaina describes a *matatu*-conductor's ability to 'change from language to language' as 'an excellent way to diffuse our present political tensions' (193). He also records, a few years into Kibaki's presidency, that 'there is a national conversation taking place, and this conversation is happening in Gikuyu, for Gikuyu, and of Gikuyu' (210), conveying his concern over Kenya's political hegemony constructed along ethnic lines.

Wainaina amalgamates the personal and political resonance of kimay in the final paragraph of his memoir to communicate a political message. Wainaina's portrayed certainty over kimay is employed here to convey sentiments of national stability. 'If *kimay* brought me uncertainty', he writes, 'it was because I simply lacked the imagination to think that such a feat was possible' (253). Acker puzzles over the significance of kimay in her review of the text, yet it is clear that Wainaina is pointing to the possibility of the harmonious existence of diverse sounds and languages that kimay represents.[16] Wainaina's position is given further weight through its connection to wider Kenyan society. Asserting that '*kimay* was part of a project to make people like us certain of our [uncertain] place in the world' (253), Wainaina uses his new awareness of kimay to forge a sense of national unity and solidarity. He writes: 'Right at the beginning, in our first popular Independence music, [...] Kenyans had already found a coherent platform to carry diversity and complexity in sound' (253). Referring to the nyatiti, Wainaina employs it as a trope that resists political fragmentation, pointing in particular to the conflict surrounding Kenya's 2007 post-election violence.

Several important points regarding Wainaina's narrative strategy emerge from this pivotal passage on kimay. The first is the use of the sensory – through kimay – to bring together the personal, aesthetic and political strands of the narrative. To summarize this technique as it operates here, Wainaina's portrayed certainty over kimay is used to signify his personal and authorial growth, as well as his growing political awareness. Focusing on the latter category, Wainaina's presentation of the political is again refracted through personal and aesthetic concerns. His growth in awareness over the possibility of political unity is, crucially, envisaged through sound and the sensory. His message of Kenyan political stability is also seen alongside his own progression from uncertainty to certainty, bringing together the personal and political within his life-narrative. Taking a step back, the text's final passage on kimay marks a transition from the earlier political moments examined in this chapter. Wainaina's emphasis has shifted significantly from the personal and aesthetic to the political as his narrative comes to a close. I want to mark this transition by mapping Wainaina's engagement with the 2007 post-election violence, and the dual political-personal emphasis his memoir carries as a result.

Helon Habila, in his review, describes *One Day I Will Write About This Place* as 'simply commentary and critique' after 'the section where he grows up'.[17] This can be attributed, in part, to Wainaina's engagement with Kenya's political fragmentation in the post-Moi years, and the increased politicization of the text as a result. We have seen that Wainaina makes several references to the Kenyan political scene in the early part of his memoir, including highly politicized remarks concerning Bob Geldof and the aid culture of the West.[18] Wainaina's most sustained political analysis is, however, in his depiction of the build-up to Kenya's 2007 post-election violence. Centring on his opposition to the ethnic division exacerbated by the election between Mwai Kibaki and Raila Odinga, Wainaina uses his memoir to underline the impact of this political breakdown. He writes of 'the poisonous election' (237) and his disenchantment with Kenyan politics, stating: 'I do not want to vote for a better Gikuyuland. I want to vote for a better Kenya' (234). His portrayal of the 'election collapse' (244) is especially written to evoke a response through its use of the second person. Wainaina states that: 'For days there is no news'; 'You will all sit stunned and watch as your nation [...] is taken over by young men with sharpened machetes and poisoned bows and arrows' (245).

Wainaina's commitment to recounting the turbulence of the post-election violence brings together the personal and the political within his memoir. His journey – as depicted in the text – assumes communal significance as Wainaina acts as a mouthpiece for the political turmoil surrounding the election in 2007. He situates his own life-narrative alongside a wider concern for his country. Wainaina's politics within *One Day I Will Write About This Place* coincide with his earlier work for *Kwani?*, where he was involved in the 'Coalition of Concerned Kenyan Writers' to produce texts addressing the election conflict.[19] To return to his memoir, the final paragraph on kimay and Wainaina's message of the possibility of political unity is therefore read in the context of his engagement with the post-election violence. For all its political impact, however, the last sentence of the text centres the narrative once again on Wainaina's refractive technique. Stating that: 'We fail to trust that we knew ourselves to be possible from the beginning' (253), Wainaina's line can be read for its personal, aesthetic and political resonance. The use of the first person plural indicates a collective, political significance. It could also point to Wainaina's success in achieving a state of psychological certainty, as well as his own authorial accomplishment as he reaches the end of his narrative.

Wainaina's technique of refracting the political resonates with two recent analytic models: the 'cryptopolitical' and 'parapolitical'. Brendon Nicholls defines the term 'cryptopolitical' with reference to Dambudzo Marechera's fiction, which he argues 'address[es] its historical referents via the displacing and condensing mechanisms of the psyche and via the pleasure-giving transports of story'.[20] Applying this model to *One Day I Will Write About This Place*, Wainaina's 'displacing and condensing mechanisms' appear as the personal and aesthetic concerns of his memoir.[21] The personal is manifested through Wainaina's construction of a childish consciousness and the shaping of a characteristic uncertainty. The aesthetic is located in Wainaina's preoccupation with the sensory and the linguistic. Wainaina's politics, unlike Marechera's however, are not created by these 'ambivalent' categories, but are shaped by and seen alongside them.[22] Nevertheless, such a strategy does produce a cryptic effect on readings of the political. Kimay, the most politically symbolic feature of the text, for example, is never at once straightforwardly political, but must also be read for its aesthetic and personal signification.

Turning to the 'parapolitical', Gerald Gaylard describes it as a 'new understanding of politics as hidden, multiple, shifting and momentary'.[23] He argues that instead of politics being all-pervasive, 'contemporary African writing finds or wrests meaning from fragments through relative location'.[24] I have established that Wainaina's major political focus within his memoir is his stress on national unity in the face of ethnic division. This is conveyed in the latter pages of the text through the depiction of kimay. Applying Gaylard's theory to Wainaina's work, the text's political message can indeed be seen as masked by the narrative's emphasis on the sensory. Political cohesion and harmony is presented through sound. Wainaina's political message can also be seen as gaining significance through the 'relative location' of 'fragments'.[25] As argued above, Wainaina's emphasis on Kenyan unity is read in connection with his earlier engagement with the post-election violence. Reading for the political therefore entails a piecing together of interrelated moments. It also requires a sifting through of the symbolic matrices of the text, locating the political amongst the personal and aesthetic strands of the memoir.

Wainaina's methods of refraction between the personal, aesthetic and political complicate the text's trajectory, demonstrating the multifocal, contrapuntal nature of his work. *One Day I Will Write*

About This Place is never focused on one singular theme, and this in turn affects Wainaina's approach to narrating the political. Through the use of refractive techniques, Wainaina's text recasts Quayson's theory of political representation, locating itself within the more recent tradition of the movement away from politics as an unequivocal postcolonial concern. Wainaina's literary politics instead centre on the importance of the personal and the artistic, recalibrating theoretical notions of the politicization of African autobiography.[26] Politics, however, does form an integral part of Wainaina's memoir, and his engagement with Kenya's 2007 post-election violence speaks to the kinds of recent political conflicts that new and emerging African writers are addressing.

NOTES

1   Binyavanga Wainaina, 'How to Write About Africa', *Granta*, 92 (2005) <http://www. granta.com/Archive/92/How-to-Write-about-Africa/Page-1> [accessed 21 August 2013].

2   Binyavanga Wainaina, interviewed in 'Playing with Language' by Melissa de Villiers, *Times Live* (13 November 2011) <http://www.timeslive.co.za/lifestyle/ books/2011/11/13/playing-with-language> [accessed 21 August 2013].

3   Wainaina, cited by de Villiers, *Times Live*.

4   Mukoma wa Ngugi, 'Wanted dead or alive: Happy African Writers!', *Africa Review* (19 August 2011) <http://www.africareview.com/Arts+and+Culture/Wanted+dea d+or+alive++Happy+African+Writers/-/979194/1221726/-/rbs75rz/-/index.html> [accessed 21 August 2013].

5   See Mukoma wa Ngugi, *Africa Review*.

6   See also Helon Habila, 'We Need New Names by NoViolet Bulawayo – review', *The Guardian* (20 June 2013) <http://www.theguardian.com/books/2013/jun/20/need-new-names-bulawayo-review> [accessed 24 August 2013].

7   Wainaina, cited by de Villiers, *Times Live*.

8   Ato Quayson, 'Literature as a Politically Symbolic Act', in *Postcolonialism: Theory, practice, or process?* (Cambridge: Polity Press, 2000), pp. 76-102, (p. 85; 95; 93).

9   Quayson, p. 93; 95.

10 Wainaina, cited by de Villiers, *Times Live*.

11 Jennifer Acker, 'Kimay: One Day I Will Write About This Place by Binyavanga Wainaina', *The Common* (17 January 2012) <http://www.thecommononline.org/reviews/kimay-one-day-i-will-write-about-place> [accessed 21 August 2013]; Zoe Norridge, 'One Day I Will Write About This Place, by Binyavanga Wainaina', *The Independent* (9 December 2011) <http://www.independent.co.uk/arts-entertainment/books/ reviews/one-day-i-will-write-about-this-place-by-binyavanga-wainaina-6274032. html> [accessed 21 August 2013].

12 Acker, *The Common*.

13 Binyavanga Wainaina, *One Day I Will Write About This Place* (Minneapolis: Granta, 2011), pp. 142-3. Page numbers cited within the text hereafter.

14 *harambee* – defined by Wainaina as a 'pulling together', *One Day I Will Write About This Place*, p. 13.

15 *benga* – a genre of popular Kenyan music that evolved between the late 1940s and the 1960s.
16 See Acker, *The Common*.
17 Helon Habila, 'One Day I Will Write About This Place by Binyavanga Wainaina – review', *The Guardian* (4 November 2011) <http://www.theguardian.com/books/2011/nov/04/one-day-write-binyavanga-wainaina-review> [accessed 21 August 2013].
18 Wainaina's opposition towards stereotypical representations of Africa is a widely recognized aspect of his work. See *One Day I Will Write About This Place*, p. 86; 90; pp. 232-3. See also Wainaina, 'How to Write About Africa'; Alexandra Fuller, 'A Writer's Beginnings in Kenya', *The New York Times* (12 August 2011) <http://www.nytimes.com/2011/08/14/books/review/one-day-i-will-write-about-this-place-by-binyavanga-wainaina-book-review.html?pagewanted=all> [accessed 21 August 2013]; de Villiers, *Times Live*.
19 See *After the Vote* (Nairobi: Kwani Trust, 2008).
20 Brendon Nicholls, 'Postcolonial Narcissism, Cryptopolitics, and Hypnocritique: Dambudzo Marechera's *The House of Hunger*', p. 28. Draft article under consideration by *Postcolonial Text*.
21 Nicholls, 'Cryptopolitics', p. 28.
22 Nicholls, 'Cryptopolitics', p. 27.
23 Gerald Gaylard, *After Colonialism: African Postmodernism and Magical Realism* (Johannesburg: Wits University Press, 2005), p. 242.
24 Gaylard, p. 250.
25 Gaylard, p. 250.
26 See Sidonie Smith and Julia Watson (eds), *De/Colonizing the Subject: The Politics of Gender in Women's Autobiography* (Minneapolis: University of Minnesota Press, 1992), p. xviii; xxi; Roger A. Berger, 'Decolonizing African Autobiography', *Research in African Literatures*, 41.2 (2010) <DOI: 10.1353/ral.0.0250> [accessed 29 October 2012] (p. 34).

WORKS CITED

Primary Source
Wainaina, Binyavanga, *One Day I Will Write About This Place* (Minneapolis: Granta, 2011).

Secondary Sources
Acker, Jennifer, 'Kimay: *One Day I Will Write About This Place* by Binyavanga Wainaina', *The Common* (17 January 2012) <http://www.thecommononline.org/reviews/kimay-one-day-i-will-write-about-this-place> [accessed 21 August 2013].
Berger, Roger A., 'Decolonizing African Autobiography', *Research in African Literatures*, 41.2 (2010) <DOI: 10.1353/ral.0.0250> [accessed 29 October 2012].
Dawson Varughese, E., *Beyond the Postcolonial: World Englishes Literature* (Basingstoke: Palgrave Macmillan, 2012).
—— 'Man of the House' and Other New Short Stories from Kenya, edited by Emma Dawson (Nottingham: Critical, Cultural and Communications Press, 2011).
Fuller, Alexandra, 'A Writer's Beginnings in Kenya', *The New York Times* (12 August 2011) <http://www.nytimes.com/2011/08/14/books/review/one-day-i-will-write-about-this-place-by-binyavanga-wainaina-book-review.html?pagewanted=all> [accessed 21 August 2013].

Gaylard, Gerald, *After Colonialism: African Postmodernism and Magical Realism* (Johannesburg: Wits University Press, 2005).

Githire, Njeri, 'New Visions, New Voices: Emerging perspectives in East African fiction', *Transition*, 102 (2009) <DOI: 10.1353/tra.0.0125> [accessed 2 November 2012].

Habila, Helon, '*One Day I Will Write About This Place* by Binyavanga Wainaina – review', *The Guardian* (4 November 2011). <http://www.theguardian.com/books/2011/nov/04/one-day-write-binyavanga-wainaina-review> [accessed 21 August 2013].

—— '*We Need New Names* by NoViolet Bulawayo – review', *The Guardian* (20 June 2013) <http://www.theguardian.com/books/2013/jun/20/need-new-names-bulawayo-review> [accessed 24 August 2013].

Kahora, Billy, Kwani Editor, *After the Vote* (Nairobi: Kwani Trust, 2008).

Kurtz, J. Roger, *Urban Obsessions, Urban Fears: The Postcolonial Kenyan Novel* (Oxford: James Currey, 1998).

Moore-Gilbert, Bart, 'A Concern Peculiar to Western Man? Postcolonial Reconsiderations of Autobiography as Genre', in *Postcolonial Poetics: Genre and Form*, edited by Patrick Crowley and Jane Hiddleston (Liverpool: Liverpool University Press, 2011), pp. 91-108.

Muhoma, Catherine, 'Versions of Truth and Collective Memory: The Quest for Forgiveness and Healing in the Context of Kenya's Postelection Violence', *Research in African Literatures*, 43.1 (2012) <DOI: 10.1353/ral.2012.0021> [accessed 23 November 2012].

Mukoma wa Ngugi, 'Wanted dead or alive: Happy African Writers!', *Africa Review* (19 August 2011) <http://www.africareview.com/Arts+and+Culture/Wanted+dead+or+alive++Happy+African+Writers/-/979194/1221726/-/rbs75rz/-/index.html> [accessed 21 August 2013].

Nicholls, Brendon, 'Postcolonial Narcissism, Cryptopolitics, and Hypnocritique: Dambudzo Marechera's *The House of Hunger*'. Draft article under consideration by *Postcolonial Text*.

—— Review of *After Colonialism: African Postmodernism and Magical Realism* by Gerald Gaylard, in *Postcolonial Text*, Vol. 3, No. 2 (2007)

Norridge, Zoe, '*One Day I Will Write About This Place*, by Binyavanga Wainaina', *The Independent* (9 December 2011) <http://www.independent.co.uk/arts-entertainment/books/reviews/one-day-i-will-write-about-this-place-by-binyavanga-wainaina-6274032.html> [accessed 21 August 2013].

Quayson, Ato, *Postcolonialism: Theory, practice, or process?* (Cambridge: Polity Press, 2000).

Smith, Sidonie and Julia Watson, eds, *De/Colonizing the Subject: The Politics of Gender in Women's Autobiography* (Minneapolis: University of Minnesota Press, 1992).

Villiers de, Melissa, 'Playing with Language', *Times Live* (13 November 2011) <http://www.timeslive.co.za/lifestyle/books/2011/11/13/playing-with-language> [accessed 21 August 2013].

Wainaina, Binyavanga, 'How to Write About Africa', *Granta*, 92 (2005) <http://www.granta.com/Archive/92/How-to-Write-about-Africa/Page-1> [accessed 21 August 2013].

Ayi Kwei Armah's
The Resolutionaries
Exoteric Fiction, the Common People & Social Change in
Post-Colonial Africa – A Critical Review

EDWARD SACKEY

The Resolutionaries (2013) is Armah's eighth novel. The word 'resolutionary' is his neologism and refers to a group of people who resolve to do things which always remain frozen as resolutions. Specifically, the word signifies Africa's political leadership and intellectuals who make extensive and serious discussions of subjects in speeches or writings without translating them into realities. They are indefatigable talkers, not doers – innovators. Copycatting is their expertise, sad to say; they are seriously lacking in creativity.

In Armah's highly provocative autobiographical novel – *Why Are We So Blest?* (1972) – Solo Ankonam, a translator, an artist and Armah's second self, subjects himself to an intensive critical meditation on the role of art and the artist in post-independence Africa in the context of Africa's 'deep destruction, the most criminal' by the colonial enterprise (230). Consequently, Armah has resolved to deform the Western novel form in the mode of Solo Ankonam's resolution to serve the revolutionary interest of contemporary Africa. All things considered, Solo Ankonam firmly resolves:

> Why not simply accept the fate of an artist, and like a Western seer, close my eyes to everything around, find relief in discrete beauty, and make its elaboration my vocation? Impossible. The Western artist is blest with that atrophy of vision that can see beauty in deliberately broken-off pieces of a world sickened with oppression's ugliness. I hear the call of that art too. But in the world of my people that most important first act of creation, that rearrangement without which all attempts at creation are doomed to falseness, remains to be done. Europe hurled itself against us—not for creation, but to destroy us, to use us for creating itself. America, a growth out of Europe, now deepens that destruction. In this wreckage there is no creative art outside the

47

destruction of the destroyers. In my people's world, revolution would be the only art, revolutionaries the only creators. All else is part of Africa's destruction. (231)

He resolves to commandeer absolutely his expertise in fiction writing to the total liberation of Africa from its wreckage by Western colonialism. My perspective on all of this is that it is in the context of *Why Are We So Blest?* – Armah's aesthetic theory in particular, and the corpus of his writing in general, that *The Resolutionaries* is best appreciated and understood. The reason is that Armah's writing is organic in the sense that it consists of different books that are all connected to each other. It is an organic whole and *The Resolutionaries* absolutely mirrors it by showing its links with the other novels; its siblings, so to speak. It is true that *The Resolutionaries* is brand new, but it has obvious connections with the Armah novels we already know: *The Beautyful Ones Are Not Yet Born* (1968, 2008), *Fragments* (1969, 2006), *Why Are We So Blest?* (1972), *Two Thousand Seasons* (1973, 2000), *The Healers* (1978, 2000), *Osiris Rising* (1995) and *KMT: In the House of Life* (2002). Reading these novels closely, it appears, for Armah, history is the present, that is to say the present-present, and the past in the present, gathered into one single instant of consciousness, moving back and forth diachronically in time, or transporting itself from time present into time past. This is the impression one gets reading Armah's writing as a body; and I would say he wishes to be read on those terms.

Not only is *The Resolutionaries* a rich seam of knowledge about pre-colonial and post-colonial or contemporary Africa; it is also an attempt to push back the frontiers of the novel to accommodate African perspectives. Which is also part of the revolution in African literary production proposed in the resolution of Solo Ankonam; and this is an idea which is an integral part of Armah's novelistic production. The message Armah puts out in his writing is as important to him as the literary devices and strategies he deploys. A careful study of his writing reveals that it is evolutionary in concept and practice and that he burns himself out as a creative writer. The Western novel, for example, which has developed in a totally different cultural and historical context, which is the import of Solo Ankonam's revolutionary resolution, cannot adequately express the experiences of the African people. It does not speak to them because it is nourished from the sources of Western history and thought. The context of the Western novel is Western. That's all. Armah has never made the Western novel the model for his African project, and thus reflect the mentality of a Westernized novelist unable to tear himself away from the Western Europe of his education. What his memoir – *The Eloquence of the Scribes* (2006) – shows decisively is how, from his earliest days, he has always conceived of himself as fully situated in an African context with African obligations and commitment to Africa's future. That commitment is fully consistent with his literary vocation. Subsequently, he has embarked upon the project of a radical restructuring of his novels to invest in them African ideological content. This is loudly manifested in the narrative of *The Resolutionaries*.

Armah's novelistic restructuring, the budding of the oral tradition with the written tradition which is seeded in *The Beautyful Ones Are Not Yet Born* in a stealthy fashion, flowers and becomes easily detectable in *Two Thousand Seasons*. Now the blossoming of orality in this novel has brought into sharp focus the use of language for the ear; presumably the birth of the speaking voice in African fiction. *The Resolutionaries* clearly continues with the idea of the speaking voice in African fiction and this is insinuated in what Armah describes as 'A Conversation with the Reader,' thereby suggesting the speaking voice in this novel. It is interesting to note an observation Robert Fraser, an astute reader of Armah, made in his book *The Novels of Ayi Kwei Armah* (1980). He writes, among other things:

> If the performance of twentieth-century writers is anything to go by, the usual direction of change is towards greater complexity and a more opaque texture. Armah presents us with a marked exceptional rule. His work has in no sense become harder. He is not one of those artists – James Joyce might serve as an example – whose work becomes more hermetic or convoluted as it develops. Rather the opposite: Armah's prose style has become increasingly transparent, the amount of ambiguity, for example, Having notably declined. . . . Armah has evidently become increasingly concerned with the democratic basis of his art. There has been a marked effort to reach out beyond the confines of the literati and the university intelligentsia to the potential reading public , and hence hopefully to recapture some of the wider ancestral appeal of the oral artist.... The direction which his style and narrative manner have taken can hence be viewed, not so much as the result of pressures which have accumulated within the art itself, as the product of a growing awareness of the social context within which the professional artist in Africa must operate. (Preface, ix-x)

What flows from the preceding statements is that Armah absolutely shares the perspective that philosophies, concepts, institutions and structures always carry with them the umbilical cords which connect them to the societies that produce them. In the same way, there cannot be any universal grammar valid for all languages because grammar is always evolved by individuals who speak and write one, two or three languages, but not a universal language. Language, either spoken or written, always carries with it an umbilical cord which connects it with the speaker or reader who, using words taken from the common store, always colours them with the strains of his own affectivity and psychic structures. My view is that it is the same principle that Armah applies to his practice of fiction writing. He literally cultivates his practice of fiction writing in the cultural soil of Africa; he consciously critically incorporates the African worldview in his novelistic practice, in his conversations with Africa. For him, the novel genre is an effective tool for social communication. Listen to him:

> I use fiction for the presentation of information not because I consider it, as a genre, superior to academic hierophantic forms, but because I am temperamentally more at ease in the exoteric role of storyteller than in the exalted roles of an academic repository of knowledge, or of a priestly mystagogue. Academic professors enlighten gatherings of disciples come to learn at their feet. Hierophants work in the tradition of preachers of divine truths. I claim neither the expert knowledge of the professional academic nor the divine insight of the inspired hierophant.
>
> As a writer, I do not consider myself a teacher or a possessor of knowledge. I am a curious spirit seeking information ancient, modern and future, ready to share the path with like minded companions. A novel, to my way of thinking, offers the possibility of a conversation between author and reader, in the kind of hetarchical relationship I would work in if I found companions to do research with, face to face. Unable to work in that ideal mode, I come to fiction as a reasonable surrogate form. That is the spirit in which I offer this book—as a conversation with the reader.

A devoted democrat and an anti-Resolutionary, Armah in reality loves to relate to his readers in the way Jesus Christ treated his disciples. As co-equals. He blended in with his disciples to the extent that if Judas Iscariot had not betrayed him, the Roman soldiers could not have recognized him. Similarly, in the narrative of *The Resolutionaries* Armah's presence is muted in a polyphonic narrative arrangement. The novel's protagonist and focalizer is not an individual; rather, he is a perfect blend of four closely related people: Jehwty, Benga, Sali, and Nefert – the co-ordinator of the narrative. It is not, therefore, far-fetched to compare the novel to music. Indeed, one of the fundamental principles of the great polyphonic composers is the equality of voices. No one voice dominates and none serves as mere accompaniment. Such is the polyphonic narrative arrangement of *The Resolutionaries*; none of the four protagonists is a mere accompaniment. They sing the African song in unison. The novel comprises twelve chapters. These are composed in such a way that the reader follows the narrative as a flame follows a stretch of burning cordite: each chapter ignites the next, so that a continuous flame runs from chapter to chapter, right to the end, illuminating the reader's mind, who through this light, makes up his or her own experience of the reading which, once completed, becomes an unforgettable part of his or her ethos. It smooths the flow of the narrative, making it very pleasant reading.

The words one reads in *The Resolutionaries* carry with them the marks of the affectivity and the mind of the protagonists – Jehwty, Benga, Sali, and Nefert – the authors of the narrative. The novel is composed in an order that aims at the knowledge and expression of what ought to be done to change Africa's social realities for the better. This is a novel that is set up to communicate with Africans, specifically by appealing to what they know – the neo-colonial structure of economics, education, and history in post-colonial Africa – through actual experience to be the way things are in contemporary Africa, emphasizing the need to reverse this trend by reverting to African-centred solutions. It is an exoteric social realistic writing meant to communicate a vision of experience, successfully I think, which comes out as a community of devoted Africans working selflessly to change the social realities of Africa for the better. Thus between the protagonists and the reader, there exists in *The Resolutionaries* a body of shared knowledge – concerning reality and necessity, possibility and freedom, personality and value system – along with a body of feelings, both rational and irrational, which arise from the particular circumstances of contemporary Africa. The point is to raise the contemporary African's consciousness to a revolutionary level and arouse positive change in post-colonial Africa.

The polyphonic narrative arrangement of *The Revolutionaries*, bringing about the equality of voices in the novel, is a loud statement of Armah's position on the question of authorship. Moreover, 'A Conversation with the Reader' embeds a set of literary theoretical positions which Armah holds and defends jealously. And these are given artistic expression in the nature of *The Resolutionaries*. They include the function of the author, Armah's theory of fiction, and the role of the novelist in the African revolution. I would say that they are not new in the scheme of Armah's writing, but *The Resolutionaries* represents them in a dramatic form. In the African oral tradition, the source of Armah's poetics, literary criticism is an integral part of the business of literary creativity; it is not an afterthought; something that is clearly demonstrated in the craft of *Two Thousand Seasons* – an intelligent simulation of the cooperative African storytelling tradition. Obviously, Armah's practice of the business of fiction writing is informed by cooperation. Needless to say, PER ANKH, the publisher of Armah's books since 1995, is 'a cooperative publisher funded by an international group of friends, . . . interested in accurately researched information on Africa.' Such a strictly cooperative consciousness is factored into the world of *The Resolutionaries*, effectively drowning individualism. Therefore, the question of the author as the source of the meaning of the work – a God-like figure is debunked. Armah, in fact, makes this point clear in the last two paragraphs of 'A Conversation with the Reader', absolutely rejecting the savant syndrome arrogantly displayed in academia. However, this is not to deny the importance of the author as the historical subject who made the text; rather, it is to free both author and reader from the stronghold of a misconceived interpretive authority. So, yes, Armah's role as the author of *The Resolutionaries* can be compared to that of Nefert, the coordinator of the narrative. The point is that the narrative of *The Resolutionaries* is revolutionary both in form and discursive ideology. And it is in consonance with the resolutions contained in *Why Are We So Blest?*. Interestingly, Armah's experiment in fiction writing, especially as demonstrated in *The Resolutionaries*, appears to be a synthesis of the fictive novel and the non-fiction novel to achieve his pet project of exoteric social realism in his fiction. I think Armah's project of restructuring the novel gains momentum in the narrative of *The Resolutionaries* thereby opening up new ground in African fiction.

In his essay 'The Storyteller: Reflections on the Works of Nikolai Leskov,' Walter Benjamin (1968) writes:

[t]he earlier symptom of a process whose end is the decline of storytelling is the rise of the novel at the beginning of modern times. What distinguishes the novel from the story (and from the epic in the narrower sense) is its essential dependence on the book. The dissemination of the novel became possible only with the invention of printing. What can be handed on orally, the wealth of the epic, is of a different kind from what constitutes the stock in trade of the novel. What differentiates the novel from all other forms of prose literature – fairy tale, the legend, even the novella – is that it neither comes from oral tradition nor goes into it. This distinguishes it from storytelling in particular. The storyteller takes what he tells from experience – his own or that reported by others. And he in turn makes it the experience of those who are listening to his tale. The novelist has isolated himself. The birthplace of the novel is the solitary individual, who is no longer able to express himself by giving examples of his most important concerns, is himself uncounseled, and cannot counsel others. (87)

That is to say, the novel as a literary form is not community-oriented; it is solipsistic by nature. So when Armah tells the readers of *The Resolutionaries* in 'A Conversation with the Reader' that 'I am temperamentally more at ease in the exoteric role of storyteller than in the exalted roles of an academic repository of knowledge, or of a priestly mystagogue,' definitely, he prefers a community-oriented genre as an effective tool of communication. As Walter Benjamin points out, 'the storyteller takes what he tells from experience – his own or that reported by others. And he in turn makes it the experience of those who are listening to his tale.' He continues further that 'the novelist has isolated himself [and that] the birthplace of the novel is the solitary individual, who is no longer able to express himself by giving examples of his most important concerns, is himself uncounseled, and cannot counsel others.' This is certainly at variance with the make-up of *The Resolutionaries*; it is at variance with the kind of novelist Armah is striving for. He does not in any way want to isolate himself from the African people. He lives among Africans and works among them. There is a sense, therefore, in which Armah could be described as the 'organic intellectual' with apologies to the Italian Marxist critic Antonio Gramsci.

Armah's avowed transparency in fiction writing as opposed to esoteric fiction writing – fiction that is likely to be understood or enjoyed by only a few people with a special knowledge or interest – is motivated by his desire to reach as many people as possible;

the common people. By all standards, *The Resolutionaries* is a clear expression of exoteric fiction targeted at the common people. I presume the point is to attract as many people as possible to reading the novel. It appears, for very good reasons, I believe, Armah is confident that the common people are in touch with his writing; and that his message is seeping down to them. However, such a claim might be regarded with a certain amount of scepticism in the light of the people's attitude to reading. But isn't that bibliophobia among Africans becoming a thing of the past?

One issue this novel exudes profusely is the effective solution to 'our language problem' (Armah, 29 April 1985). Armah yearns for Africa to have a language and a literary form or forms that would consort with African experience, including the traumatic experience of having no common language. Like *Two Thousand Seasons*, *The Resolutionaries* bears the impress of the recognition that Africa must find its own language or be doomed to quote itself as a stereotype in a language that belongs to 'slaveraiders'. Until now, Armah held the position that one of the most effective ways of triumphing over Africa's inherited colonial languages is to use them, for in so doing they undergo a torsion that wrenches them from their own context and replaces them in the context of the writer who uses them. Though it is certainly not an effective solution to 'our language problem', but it is intended to last for only a short time until something more permanent is found. Hitherto, the general feeling among African intellectuals is that inventing a common language for Africa is an impossibility. Armah thinks the opposite is the truth. As the group of devoted African intellectuals in *The Resolutionaries*, who have dedicated their lives to working assiduously to change Africa's social realities for the better, say:

> We can create that language out of the many shreds of our common consciousness, just as out of the forty-two ethnic tongues of Kemet, one language grew to serve a united people. What our ancestors were able to do, we can in our turn achieve. But first we need to turn away from our obsessive efforts to turn the contempt of enemies into respect. It is a waste of time to seek respect from Europeans. We have to grow beyond seeking the approval of those who hate us, and concentrate instead on working with each other. (380)

Additionally, a character claims:

> Ancient Egypt scholars knew the value of a common language. It was one key to the creation of a cohesive society, and that was the

core secret of Egypt. Unity. Their official language, *ro en Kemet*, was a synthesis of all the ethnic languages that came together in the unified society. If today we're interested in a unifying language, we can proceed rationally, from a core of indispensable words, syntax, and idiomatic structures. Words like sun, earth, moon, star, planet, river, animal, soil, sand, sea, you, me, us. Relational structures for expressing connection, rupture, movement, stasis, change, direction. For these we could select the most euphonious expressions from the ancient Egyptian language. (388)

The Resolutionaries thus makes a strong case in support of the possibility of devising a *lingua franca* for Africa, provided African intellectuals put their shoulders to the wheel of unrelenting research work. The novel, a work of social realism and intelligence, insists the idea is not utopian and that it can be done. What arouses the reader's curiosity in the narrative of *The Resolutionaries* is the spectre of Ancient Egypt, a spectre which has consistently haunted Armah's memory and writing – specifically from *Osiris Rising* to *The Resolutionaries*. Armah is one African novelist who is convinced that the solutions to the social problems of contemporary Africa are in the archives of Ancient Egypt and that they are ours through history. He leads beyond the deafening disavowal of the Africanness of Ancient Egypt today, a disavowal he sees as a Western conspiracy to deny Africa of its past. What, then, is the basis of Armah's vested interest in Ancient Egypt?

Historically, Ancient Egypt is the antecedent of modern Africa. Following the Arab invasion of Ancient Egypt and the subsequent colonization of modern Africa by Western Europe, post-colonial Africa has lost its real identity; its culture and cultural values. This has created a disconnect between our cultural values and national orientation and, according to Kwame Gyekye (2013), 'this can be put down to the fact that our indigenous cultural values were during the colonial interregnum disregarded in the creation of institutions, such as political institutions, in favour of European values and institutions.' He adds that, 'it can be put down also to the failure on our part, even in the post-colonial times, to attend to and exploit the strengths of the culture to guide the creation of institutions' (160). Gyekye states further that

> national orientation must take its rise from – and must be guided by – the cultural values of the nation. Cultural values are those forms of behavior, practice or thought that are nurtured by a culture and held, cherished and maintained by the users of the culture as most

worthwhile and desirable, as having sufficient importance and relevance for their lives. There is a dynamic relation between national orientation and the cultural values of a people. It would be correct to say that the dynamic relation between cultural values and national orientation would naturally exist for a nation whose cultural and political evolution has been uninterrupted and whose cultural values have, consequently, influenced, in fact, determined the direction in which that nation has developed and organised its affairs. However, this dynamic relation between cultural values and national orientation cannot be expected to exist in its completeness in a formerly colonized nation, such as Ghana, the cultural and political evolution of which, due to colonial rule, did not have the chance to maintain a steady, undisturbed progress. Thus, there was, or is, a disconnect, in many ways, between the cultural values of a colonized people and their national orientation. (159-60)

Flowing from Gyekye's brilliant submission, no one needs to be told that post-colonial Africa requires a critical cultural re-engineering to change its continental orientation. One African novelist who champions this *cause celebre* is Ayi Kwei Armah. Armah's African project, which is a cultural project to be precise, seeks to draw cultural strengths from Ancient Egypt and modern day Africa to change the Western-oriented post-colonial African cultural values and the continental orientation of Africa. He is of the considered view that the answer to the developmental problems of post-colonial Africa can be found in the cultural experience of the people of Ancient Egypt.

The Resolutionaries is a vibrant work of art. The life and energy one experiences reading this novel is derived from its mode of characterization. Additionally, the novel is dialogue-heavy. The characters, especially the four protagonists, interact with each other to the extent that the reader forgets that the people he or she is reading about are Armah's creation. These characters stubbornly assume a life of their own as Armah himself confesses in 'A Conversation with the Reader'. Practically speaking, Armah the author has, willingly I would say, given up control over the work. And therein lies his greatness as a novelist. As Robert Fraser says in the above excerpt, 'Ayi Kwei Armah has been seen as a startling writer, a fearless and unpredictable enfant terrible at drastic odds with the literary establishment.' Indeed, the poetics of *The Resolutionaries* vindicates Robert Fraser. Armah's writing occurs by pushing the boundaries of fiction writing and socio-cultural norms, by reconfiguring what post-colonial Africans see and know. His artistic innovation and revolution is incremental. He is one African writer who is not afraid to break the rules of craft; he does not tread the familiar paths. He makes great effort to blaze new ground and the more he writes the greater his transgressions. And since the man is alive and writing, we should brace ourselves up for more of such groundbreaking works. He kicks what he calls esoteric writing (e.g. *Why Are We So Blest?*) out of fiction, making it simple and accessible. The interesting thing about Armah is that he doesn't just break the rules of the craft of fiction; evidently, he knows them very well. His writing is serious, thoughtful and daring, and time will tell if it will continue to endure. He is worthy of the attention of the African intellectual community, the African political leadership, the planners of our education system and our teachers in particular. Armah is worthy of our attention NOW!

WORKS CITED

Armah, Ayi Kwei. *The Beautyful Ones Are Not Yet Born.* Popenguine, Senegal: 1968, 2008.
——. *Fragments.* Popenguine, Senegal: Per Ankh, 1969, 2006.
——. *Why Are We So Blest?* Garden City, New York: Doubleday & Company, Inc., 1972.
——. *Two Thousand Seasons.* Popenguine, Senegal: Per Ankh, 1973, 2000.
——. *The Healers.* Popenguine, Senegal: Per Ankh, 1978, 2000.
——. 'Our Language Problem,' *West Africa* 29 April, 1985: 831-2.
——. *Osiris Rising.* Popenguine, Senegal: Per Ankh, 1995.
——. *KMT: In the House of Life.* Popenguine, Senegal: Per Ankh, 2002.
——. *The Eloquence of the Scribes.* A memoir on the sources and resources of African Literature. Popenguine, Senegal: Per Ankh, 2006.
——. *The Resolutionaries.* Popenguine, Senegal: Per Ankh, 2013.
Benjamin, Walter. 'The Storyteller: Reflections on the Works of Nikolai Leskov,' *Illuminations* Essays and Reflections. trans. Harry Zohn. New York: Schocken Books, 1968: 83-109.
Fraser, Robert. *The Novels of Ayi Kwei Armah.* London: Heinemann, 1980.
Gyekye, Kwame. 'Our Cultural Values and National Orientation', *Philosophy, Culture and Vision.* African Perspective. Accra: Sub-Saharan Publishers, 2013: 159-81.

In Quest of Social Justice

Politics & Women's Participation
in Irene Isoken Salami's *More than Dancing*

H. OBY OKOLOCHA

Nona Odaro, presidential candidate of United People's Liberation Party (UPLP) in Irene Salami's 2003 play *More than Dancing* (MTD) summarizes the problem the author tackles in this play. She states:

> The political playing field is uneven and not conducive to women's participation. Women who enter politics find the political, cultural and social environment often unfriendly and even hostile to them. The low level of women's representation in the decision making arm of the government is a violation of their fundamental democratic rights and as such of their basic human rights.... (87)

The play opens with Madam Bisi Adigun, women's leader UPLP, angry and protesting that women are dancing to entertain party members at a convention. In agitation, she stops the dancing women, 'Enough of the dancing! Enough is enough!! Year in, year out, primaries come and party elections go, all we do is dance. Is dancing all we can do? Is that all we are meant for?' (1). She calls their attention to the fact that the party hierarchy is dominated by men, safeguarded by men and that all the worthwhile positions – chairman, vice chairman, treasurer, secretary, financial secretary, welfare officers, members of the board of trustees, public relations officers and so on are occupied by men. The only things women do in political parties are dance, feed the men and vote for them for pathetic rewards such as bags of rice, salt and clothes. Mabel Evwierhoma, critic and literary writer, confirms the situation Salami portrays:

> Erstwhile political parties are structured in such a way that women were seen and heard when dancing troupes were needed to entertain party faithful or they were to be fed. At other times, oblivion welcomed them in the women's wing where they had no influence over the goings on in the party mainstream' (34).

Contextual and in-text evidence illustrate a long-standing history of gender-based inequality in politics and public governance. Thus, Salami resourcefully employs historification – the use of material drawn from history and periods in the past – to show that the norm of excluding women and marginalizing them in political processes is an area of social injustice which women have battled for generations. The struggle to empower women politically – to increase their involvement in leadership roles and participation in the formation of public policy, and to maintain gender equity in the management of national resources – continues to be a major issue in contemporary times. Salami's re-enactment of women's historical struggle for political relevance situates the contemporary quest for political justice as a continuation of past struggles. The continuing constitution of Nigeria's political arena as a male territory is the social injustice that Salami contests in *MTD*.

This chapter provides a critique of gender inequality in the structure of political power in Nigeria. It interrogates the structures that obstruct women's participation in politics and governance as they are depicted in *MTD* and identifies patriarchy and 'self' – a problem created by patriarchy – as the major obstacles denying women justice in political participation. Economic inequity and formal education are mentioned cursorily as some of the other problems militating against women in politics but they are not discussed in detail because they are well known problems with clear-cut solutions. The paper evaluates the playwright's recourse to historification as a weapon to advocate women for leadership and offer suggestions for redressing the existing injustice in politics.

Issues dealing with social justice and equality for women in political participation have come to the fore globally. Like most concepts in the humanities and social sciences, the concept of social justice is subject to a wide variety of interpretations depending on usage and context. Iain McLean and Alistair McMillan assert that social justice is the application of the 'foundational character of justice in social life' (499). They point out that social justice goes beyond the design of legal constitutions, to critical perspectives on economic theories and organizations, to theories of civil obedience and other interactions and also necessarily refers to 'just' conditions of social living (ibid.). David and Julia Jary see social justice as the principle of 'social fairness' tailored to the concept of justice, which consists of the recognition and protection of individual and social rights. For them, inequality is unacceptable (345). These opinions enable the conclusion that social justice means that all conditions of social interaction in society should be subjected to the principles of justice; which is a fair and proper balance between all the members of a social group. This balance, absent in the Nigerian political arena depicted in *MTD*, ignites the quest for justice.

Victoria Onuoha (2008) writes that justice 'means the scope or opportunity for seeking (equity) in the determination of rights and obligations through the legal system' (2). She explains that in 'just' societies, all human beings are born free and equal and are therefore, entitled to the same rights and privileges. 'However', she observes, 'deficient or discriminatory justice systems or other political, systematic, economic, socio-cultural or religious impediments can undermine this basic human rights principle' (ibid.), and create situations of marginalization and social injustice. Justice is therefore, social when it is not individualistic, when its object and form involve the application of equity in dealing with others, and it entails working together to accomplish justice in a civil society. Social justice therefore, demands that the principles of justice must be applied to all interactions, in all areas of social life. It requires that Salami's protagonist, Nona Odaro, university professor and top member of United People's Liberation Party in *MTD*, and all those who are capable, must be given equal opportunities and advantages in political spaces.

The Nigerian government, like others, has responded in some measure to these international developments. The Nigerian government duly guarantees the rights of women by introducing the principle of nondiscrimination against any citizen in Section 2 of the Nigerian constitution of 1999 and several other laws. Ostensibly, gender equality in political participation is enshrined in the Nigerian constitution, in its principle of non-discrimination, and this suggests that this international stance on women is actually being domesticated in Nigeria. Gender equality is also embedded in the practice of democracy but disparities on account of sex remain pervasive in Nigeria. Nona insists: 'If the hallmark of a democratic society is plurality of expressed opinions and contributions by those living within it, then the participation of women in leadership positions ought to be valued and encouraged' (5), but the principle and practice of democracy in Nigeria has not been able to close the gap of gender inequity. Major characteristics of democracy are justice and equity. This means that all segments of the population must be justly represented and must participate in the processes of governance. Unfortunately, women continue to contend with formidable obstacles in politics and other areas of social interaction, 'even when' Onuoha (2008) notes 'the Nigerian society is ostensibly founded on the principles of democracy and social justice' (2).

Onuoha further points out a cardinal reason why women continue to be in the background of political activity:

> Nigerian women now have not only the fundamental rights available to their male counterparts, but also special survival, participation and protection rights afforded to them by some gender-specific domestic and international laws. These laws…are meant to cure the disabilities… that women are subjected to… The problem now appears not to be the paucity of women's rights law, but of the capacity and opportunities to access the benefits of these laws…' (4-5)

She rightly pinpoints that the problem is the inability of women to position themselves to access the benefits of these laws or take advantage of the opportunities granted by them. This suggests that if women do not feature significantly in political processes, they may not have made sufficient effort to participate or access reform, so the injustices continue. Nigerian literature amply depicts this existing situation.

Indeed, Nigerian literature illustrates that in spite of the inter-national and domestic laws discussed earlier, social inequities in politics continue; depictions of political leadership in all genres of Nigerian literature identify the disparity in the participation of men and women in political processes and leadership spaces. In Osadebamen Oamen's *The Scar* (2005) the protagonist Isehakhe, returns to Omanekhui, armed with Western education and the zeal to represent her people in politics. In congress, she declares her intention and the following reaction follows:

> **First Politician:** (Stands up and adjusts his agbada). A woman must not be allowed to represent us or given any leading role in our society, no matter how bad it is, the head should always remain a man…. How can a woman referred to as the weaker sex govern the affairs of a people? Even in the absence of men, who will give a woman that privilege? To me, a crippled man is better than an able-bodied woman when it comes to politics and administration …. Women are meant to manage homes on behalf of men. (16-17)

Most men in the gathering agree. This myopic reaction is evidence that, in the Nigerian context, leadership is a closely guarded male domain. Oamen seeks to change this situation, so he positions his protagonist, Isehakhe to break into the field of politics in spite of male opposition – a major achievement for a woman in the context of the play. .

Like Oamen's *The Scar*, Harry Iyorwuese Hagher's *Mulkin Mata* (1991) depicts a significant political revolution. In the play, African women are aggrieved at the perennial gross mismanagement and bad governance of the nation by its male leaders. The men loot the nation's resources in the manner of armed robbers and leave it impoverished. Women of Africa unite, seize power to save the continent from collapse and within a short time, Women Revolutionary Government (WRG) actually succeed in reversing the destruction the men have orchestrated. The men strongly resist WRG which they see as an overthrow of the 'usual order'. Significantly, Hagher's play rectifies gender inequity forcibly. Women themselves orchestrate and achieve the much needed socio-economic revolution, indicating the author's confidence in the leadership abilities of women.

Women writers also advocate the forcible dismantling of male monopoly of politics. In *The Reign of Wazobia* (1992), Tess Onwueme, like Hagher, also seeks to dismantle the monopoly forcibly. The playwright positions a female king – Wazobia – against the wishes of men in the community. Onwueme's quest for justice for women in the political arena is evident in her support of Wazobia's tyrannical hold on power at the expiration of her tenure as regent. Onwueme suggests that Wazobia is the messiah that will rescue society from the ravage of bad male leaders. *The Reign of Wazobia* instigates women to break into this male domain by force when necessary. Similarly, *MTD* advocates that women should break into politics. Salami shows that the heroines of history, whose examples she holds up for contemporary women to emulate, have always had to break into political spaces by force. Hence Nona in *MTD* (2003) gets the warning: 'You have to work hard at getting the right keys to open the gate or you may have to break in' (86).

In her works, Irene Isoken Salami consistently provides female protagonists who make significant contributions to their societies as leaders. *Idia: the Warrior Queen of Beni* (2008), dramatizes a memorable period of Benin history when Queen Mother Idia succeeded in putting an end to the age-long Benin tradition of killing queen mothers when their sons were enthroned as monarchs.

As the mother of the newly enthroned Oba Esigie, Queen Mother Idia has a limited time to live but she is determined not to go the way of those before her (2). She resolves to 'speak for all to hear, …[and to be] silent no more' (5). Analysing the play, Akosu Adeiyongo remarks: 'With this declaration, the stage is set for a major constitutional dispute which is later to change the course of history in Benin Kingdom' (168). Idia speaks out in protest and the law on the killing of queen mothers, a destructive tradition, is abolished. Salami also highlights Idia's bravery and competent leadership. At the threat of attack from outside forces, the Oba and his chiefs cannot strategize a defence; they shy away from the need to prepare for war. In contrast, Idia resolves: 'I will fight the battle myself and bring down Chief Oliha and his allies'… Accordingly, she takes over the role of leadership in Benin Kingdom, mobilizes and leads soldiers to war and emerges victorious from the battle. Queen Idia liberates women from untimely death and turns them into a formidable force in patriarchal society.

Salami's mission to advocate for women participating in political processes becomes more pronounced in *MTD*. Tse Andera Paul posits: 'Salami's *More Than Dancing* is an attempt to rekindle the revolutionary consciousness of the Nigerian woman to rise up to the challenges of her time. The playwright has made a political statement with the play that Nigerian women are capable of doing greater than merely dancing at party rallies' (117). Evwierhoma observes that Nona, the protagonist in *MTD* has 'woken from the slumber of political ineptitude…' (34). Salami's *MTD, Idia…,* and *Emotan,* like Onwueme's *The Reign of Wazobia*, are feminist manifestos for women's participation in politics.

THE STRUCTURES OF POLITICAL DISLOCATION

Jean O'Barr comments on the situation of African women in politics: 'After a global survey of women in politics, most African countries register five percent or less of women at every level, in every sphere of government' (1986: 154). O'Barr's survey indicates that women in all societies of the world are marginalized in the area of politics; however, the degree of this marginalization is highest in African societies. Reacting to the political and socio-economic imbalance between men and women, Kate Millet, an acclaimed feminist avers that this inequity is a result of the patriarchal organization of life in most cultures of the world (1970: 30-34). This patriarchal social system is operative in *MTD*.

In *More Than Dancing*, the men face a serious crisis. Women team up and present Professor Nona Odaro as their own presidential candidate for the forthcoming elections. In outrage, the men react:

> OHIO: What did you say? Pres...what? Not senator, not deputy governor, not governor, not vice-president. P-R-E-S-I-DENT. These women must be very ambitious...
> SANI: ...America, the champion of democracy and women liberation movement, has never had a female president.
> MADU: You see, all women are good for is to dance at party rallies, not to rule! They have no place in politics! Not in African politics or decision making process!
> SANI: When America produces a female leader, then Nigeria will be ready to produce one. Until then, tell Prof. Nona Odaro to go home and cook for her husband, period! (30)

The men's reaction illustrates their myopia and traditional views. It makes it clear that patriarchal societies are reluctant to embrace change and that men consider the public sphere of politics as their domain and the private/domestic sphere of the home as that of the woman. It also illustrates the gender imbalance in patriarchal social systems. Millet's proscriptions on patriarchy explain Sani's opinion that a female Professor should be at home, cooking for her husband. Millet states:

> Patriarchy's chief institution is the family. It is both a mirror of and a connection with the larger society; a patriarchal unit within a patriarchal whole. Mediating between the individual and the social structure, the family effects control and conformity where political and other authorities are insufficient. As the fundamental instrument and the foundation unit of patriarchal society, the family and its roles are prototypical. Serving as an agent of the larger society, the family not only encourages its own members to adjust and conform, but acts as a unit in the government of the patriarchal state which rules its citizens through its family heads. (33)

Millet's remarks indicate that though the family, society, and state are separate entities, but they interrelate and depend on each other. For example, the family's major contribution to society and state is to socialize their youth into prescribed models of conduct, role, work, and even temperament. Thus, the family socializes women into private (domestic) roles and men into public (leadership) roles. Cooperation between the family, society and state is in this manner assured. In patriarchy, women do not participate in the public areas of societal life, and are governed by the state through the men in the family.

This patriarchal conditioning is so deep rooted that it defies rank and education. The members of UPLP – a political party in the play – are highly educated men yet the greater majority cannot conceive of a woman as president. In a satirical effort to show how unsuitable a woman would be for the position, Madu presents a ludicrous scenario:

> Imagine the senate has asked the president to come and defend the budget. Her maids would phone the senate president, 'Hello, my madam is in labour, her husband has just taken her to the maternity ward'. We do not want a leader that would be controlled by the dictates of her mood when she is experiencing her monthly period, or take off from crucial meetings because her husband is demanding his lunch. (39)

A negligible few like Hakeem argue: 'Taking into cognizance the gendered perspective and involving women and men in decision-making process is a hallmark of any genuine democratic framework. This is why democracy, by definition cannot afford to be gender-blind' (37). Without a doubt, Hakeem is Salami's mouthpiece.

Ambassador Uyi Odaro, Nona's husband, starts out strongly in support of his wife; he refuses the tempting offers of five and twenty million naira to convince his wife to step down, and he rejects the nomination for vice-president which was offered to him as a way of forcing his wife out of the race, but he becomes worried when he perceives a threat to his traditional position as the man and head of his home. When money and high office fail, Terna and Madu, his peer politicians, point out the personal consequences of supporting his wife's presidential ambition:

> You see, before long, people will refer to you as 'that man, the husband of Prof. Nona, the daughter of Honourable Chief Ode'. Your identity will be subsumed in hers…you will become insignificant in the scheme of things. You will decrease while she increases, flying on the wings of her father's fame and glory, not yours. (57)

Remarkably, the offer of money and office do not entice Uyi or make him withdraw support for his wife but the specter of a possible threat to his ego, the image and identity of himself as a man hit home. For a while, his attitude becomes difficult and obstructing but he gets over it and resumes support for his wife. This patriarchal attitude where men find it difficult to accept women in public areas of interaction is also illustrated in Onwueme's *The Reign of Wazobia*.

Wazobia calls a meeting of the entire Ilaa community; (men and women, young and old) to share 'thoughts on the rules of governance' (1992: 27). The men resist the involvement of women in political matters because: 'Serious matters of state concern are too heavy for the brittle heads of women and children...that of the youth is even better' (ibid.). No logical reason is given for judging the youths as better than the women in political matters, but the men believe it strongly, making it clear that patriarchal gender biases are often irrational and fallacious. These biases are so deeply entrenched that they underlie the actions of both men and women in the community. In *MTD*, the male politician Sani, is unrelenting: '...the day a woman becomes the president of the Federal republic, I will cross over to Chad. A woman will not rule me. Allah forbid' (38). That Allah is beseeched never to allow a woman rule is a reminder that religious doctrines are characterized by prejudices against women. For example, the Koran asserts male superiority when it states that 'woman is inferior to man and is his subject' (5 Wat 7). In the Bible, 'the head of everyman is Christ; the head of every woman is man' (1 Cor.11:3). These assertions demonstrate that religious belief is another factor that breeds the male views and attitudes in *MTD*. Clearly, religion backs up gender relations predicated on the inequalities of power and upholds relationships of domination and subordination between the sexes. Julie Okoh articulates the heart of the problem in the plays above: 'The men cannot see themselves being governed by women no matter how intelligent, how industrious, and how progressive they may be. As far as the African man is concerned, it is the prerogative of men to rule and women to carry out instruction' (114-15). Patriarchal systems breed a gendered political culture.

Unfortunately, patriarchy originates other obstacles that obstruct women from political participation. Trailing in the wake of patriarchy is a huge problem which Molara Ogundipe-Leslie identifies as 'the mountain of self', which is deeply personal, operates invisibly, and is therefore difficult to locate and rectify. Ogundipe-Leslie identifies six mountains on the back of the African woman: oppression from the outside (colonialism and neocolonialism), traditional structures, her backwardness, man, her colour/race, and herself (28). The last mountain – herself –

which Ogundipe-Leslie judges to be 'the most important' (36) is the focus here. She explains:

> Women are shackled by their own negative self-image, by centuries of the interiorization of the ideologies of patriarchy and gender hierarchy. Their own reactions to objective problems therefore are often self-defeating and self-crippling. Woman reacts with fear, dependency complexes and attitudes to please and cajole where more self-assertive are needed. (36)

This demonstrates that 'self' is an offshoot of patriarchy, operating extensively and independently, its effects reaching further and doing more damage than patriarchy. Ogundipe-Leslie considers 'self' as the most important of the obstacles hindering women from functioning effectively in the political arena. This is because 'self' consists of the anxieties deeply embedded in the psyche of women; silent and unobtrusive, the anxieties cannot be addressed by tangible measures such as legislation. Consequently, the solution to 'self' is intensely individualized, meaning that every woman needs to solve the problem in her own way. The truth of these assertions is adequately illustrated in Salami's *MTD*.

Women members of the United People's Liberation Party meet to discuss their actions of yesterday. They have told the men that they will dance no more; they want more meaningful involvement in politics – they want political positions, key positions in political party organizations, votes for themselves as contestants, equal benefits for men and women in the party. Women discuss their next line of actions now that they have taken a stance; they decide to introduce their own presidential candidate, but some of the women have serious misgivings about what seems to be an unduly bold step. Minika voices her apprehension:

> I have reservations about this so-called "positive step in the right direction." Which direction are we going? UPLP is a man's party. Men basically started it, they funded it; we cannot displace them in their own party. We have to be content with whatever they offer or drop on us for now. Any contrary move now may lead to disaster. Let us reason well before we start…We are women under authority. Must we break our homes simply because we want political liberty? (2003: 7-11)

Minika represents a large segment of the women in whom the idea that politics is not a woman's domain is so deeply entrenched that it would be much easier to pass laws and change public policies in favour of women than to change their mindset. Her statement reveals that 'self' is the major problem here; she lacks confidence in the ability of women and fears that women will not stand a chance to compete in the public sector of men. She would prefer the women clamouring for equality to be content with whatever crumbs the men allow them to have. This mindset manifests the deeply ingrained inferiority complex which underlies her thought processes and decisions. This negative self-image operates unobtrusively, often unconsciously, and remains unidentified; and is therefore more difficult to tackle than a visible lack of formal education or economic inequity.

As Millet (1970) explains, this negative self-image, created by years of indoctrination from family and state, manifests itself as fear in two broad areas: the woman's fear of her own inabilities and fear of losing her marriage. In patriarchal systems, the home is the woman's greatest source of respect, status and validation. The fear that opposing the men might lead to the ultimate consequence, a broken marriage, cripples action and leads to an acceptance of the status quo. Fortunately, women are beginning to question the principles holding them down, hence another woman asks Minika: 'Have our husbands broken up their homes because they are engaged in political activities?' (MTD, 11). Nona summarizes the mountain of self as it operates in the play: 'Most of them [women] lack confidence in themselves. They have imbibed the traditional belief that men are the "born" leaders and as such they do not stand a chance against them at the polls so "why bother to contest?" they ask. There is this culture of fear that prevents them from contesting elections' (86), or even having an interest in politics. The fear is so deep seated that it doesn't go away at just a swipe.

Salami turns the stumbling block of fear into a source of encouragement by revealing that gender culture can be a hoax. The underlying irony is that while a large number of the women feel constrained by insecurity and fear, the men ironically also harbour fear; they doubt their own inabilities and fear losing their marriages – the same things women are afraid of. MTD shows that men are actually afraid of the emergence of women in politics. Sani reminds party members: 'I warned you about nominating a wise woman like Madam Bisi as woman leader. That woman is too intelligent for us. Now, see what we are faced with; she is turning the table against us'. He despairs that the women have all 'become so wise that it is very difficult to use them now. They are awake from their long slumber' (31–2). Sani admits that men recognize and fear women's political ability. Unwittingly, he agrees that women have the intellect and ability for leadership if they have the opportunity; he also recognizes that the ability has always been there but has remained unexploited because women have been in a slumber induced by patriarchal indoctrination. The men are afraid that women might indeed make better leaders and demystify the superiority of men. Women therefore constitute a political threat that makes it imperative for men to keep them in the background or out of politics entirely.

Men harbour other fears too. Nona's husband is an ambassador situated at the peak of socio-political hierarchy, yet Uyi Odaro is afraid of becoming insignificant in his home. He is terrified by the thought that he 'will decrease' while Nona increases (57). Money and political position are not as important as his need to remain 'her husband and the lord of my home' (ibid.). Apparently, 'self' also operates in men but in the opposite direction. It manifests as a superiority complex and breeds the need to protect the status of superiority. Thus, 'self' operating in both men and women is paradoxically a platform for oppression; the platform from which the men maintain oppressive superiority over women and the platform from which women compliantly accept injustices. Consequently, one can argue that some of the differences which the women have been taught to respect, and which hold them down, are actually non-existent. Salami highlights the fact that the men fear the women too; highlighting this gives women the courage and the wisdom to conquer 'self'.

To boost women's self-confidence, Bisi reminds them of the heroic exploits credited to a few women in the history of Nigeria. She points out that to eliminate women's prevailing political powerlessness, women must be prepared to discard fear and inferiority complex, make painful sacrifices, or remain sidelined for ever. She states: 'For any group to move ahead, they must be prepared to pay a price' (11). In this case, women must liberate their minds from the shackles of inferiority complex, lack of self-confidence, dependency and fear of the unknown. Salami makes it clear that to access equality in political processes, women must begin by unveiling the blindness of the mind – Ogundipe-Leslie's mountain of self – erase the indoctrination that men have more leadership prowess, and discard the belief that women have no place in public politics and governance.

Nona, Bisi, and the other women who are prepared to sacrifice for the emergence of women in politics symbolize a new consciousness and the surmounting of 'self' that women need to break into the gates of politics and governance. Nona stands up for justice and motivates other women to break out of the prison of 'self'; she is firm in her conviction: 'We cannot say we are a democratic party until people see in practical terms, a radical turn around in the conditions of women generally and that they have been empowered to have access to all aspects of governance as equal partners with other members of the society...' (4). Nona's firm stand demonstrates that even in acts of collective resistance and courage, the individual must have self-confidence to participate meaningfully in the group.

Hakeem, a UPLP member agrees with Nona. Hakeem recognizes that women contribute significantly to national development, although their contributions are rarely acknowledged publicly. Unrelenting in his support of the women, he reminds male members of the party that women play important roles in campaigning and mobilizing support for the party and the men, so it is unfair to consider them novices and unsuitable for political offices (34). In another instance, he implores the men: 'Gentlemen, let us be reasonable. These women have been our strongest political allies. If they now desire to contest, let us lend them our support too. What difference does it make whether a man or a woman rules anyway? The important thing is for us to have a good leader. Let us give them a chance to rule. They probably may be better than us' (69-70). Hakeem is a man who has broken free of his patriarchal conditioning; his mind is open to the growth of new ideas and the transformation of undesirable attitudes. When he suggests that women might turn out to be better political leaders than men, the absence of 'a male ego' is significant. A human rights advocate, he emphasizes the right of every man or woman to exercise his or her political power (69).

In the same vein, Tse Andera Paul argues:

> The exclusion of women from politics and the decision making process in this country has caused the nation more harm than good. How much have Nigerian men who have ruled in the past fifty years tried to better the lot of ordinary Nigerians? It is possible that if women were allowed to partake in the decision making process, maybe Nigeria would have been better today... (2010: 120)

Andera Paul and Hakeem, recognize women's capacity for leadership and the disadvantages of excluding them. Evwierhoma is quite right when she remarks: 'The play's cogent message is the statement by Hakeem, the gender sensitive party faithful' (Evwierhoma 2011: 35). Hakeem tries to convince the other men: 'Mr. Terna, whether you like it or not, the continued exclusion of women from the decision-making positions in the nation will slow down the pace of development of the democratic process and stunt the economic growth of the nation...' (35). He is the voice of equality and justice in political processes which the playwright's seeks for women in the play.

Other obstacles militating against women in politics include the absence of economic power and formal education. Women are largely domiciled at home and have not been exposed to the economic opportunities which the men have had; hence they do not have economic strength. This is important because Nigerian politics depicted in *MTD* is a game of huge economic resources. Sani mockingly reminds women to 'remember that politics costs money' (2003: 3). Another party stalwart, Femi, is sure that women cannot gather or amass the kind of money required for participation in politics. He is sarcastic: 'I will love to see a good display of money as women come out to contest for positions...' (ibid.). Women prove him wrong, and show that a redefinition of self and a firm conviction will make the way for the acquisition of economic power.

The absence of formal education contributes significantly to keeping women politically ignorant and inactive. This situation of ignorance is detrimental in several ways; the worst is that it brings about a compliant acceptance of inequity and injustice. Women, who have emerged successfully as social reformers in the past and present, have been, in most cases, educated or at least socially and politically aware. Nona and Madam Bisi are examples; in fact, Sani had warned the men that Madam Bisi was too intelligent to be a subservient woman leader (31). Education removes ignorance, dismantles biases, makes women aware of their own abilities and opens their eyes to possibilities to explore. It also creates awareness of inequities, eliminates naivety, gives the courage to question the logic of existing social attitudes, enables reappraisals and makes compliant acceptance of unjust situations difficult. As is well documented, education is a revolutionary weapon of self-liberation and liberation from social injustice. However, these factors have received consistent attention in text and in context, and are addressed in domestic and international laws.

HISTORIFICATION

Literary writers resort to history to nourish their work for a wide variety of reasons. In *Things Fall Apart* and *Arrow of God*, Chinua Achebe used historical resources to affirm aspects of culture which have suffered misrepresentation. In *Hopes of the Living Dead*, history serves as the platform from which Ola Rotimi canvasses for the human rights of disadvantaged persons in society. Similarly, Salami's *MTD* dredges out the heroic exploits of historical women such as Queen Amina of Zaria, Moremi of Ife, Emotan and Idia of Benin, Funmilayo Ransome-Kuti and Madam Tinubu of Lagos, Kambasa of Bonny and others who were victorious in male- dominated spaces. Salami uses the trials and triumphs of historical women as a method of showing the avenues through which women can correct the prevailing political inequality. She highlights qualities which have enabled the heroic women in history to break the stronghold of gender inequality. Attributes and attitudes such as resocialization, collective resistance, perseverance, and sacrifice stand out as the author's suggestions for a breakthrough. These qualities are presented as the weapons with which women in all ages have conquered marginalization and accessed social justice.

Queen Amina of Zazzau established the Hausa empire in the sixteenth century; she conquered cities, expanded her territories, led migrations, opened trade routes; she was a woman 'as capable as a man…a trailblazer' (*MTD* 17), whose skill on horseback is as established as her exploits. Amina was a tireless warrior who also had patriarchal attitudes to contend with. In a flashback, Salami recalls an instance when Amina wanted the army ready to go to war and Waziri, a male commander in her army, cautioned: 'Your Majesty, life is not all about expansion of kingdoms and empires… Every three months, you are in the battlefield. When will you rest? You are a woman, you know? You need to get yourself a husband so you can have children…' (59). Amina did not tolerate the patriarchal impunity of thinking that her rightful place in society is as a wife and mother. She insisted: 'I will not be encumbered with marriage. I hate being bossed around by any man. Waziri, go ahead, get the men ready' (*MTD* 59). Queen Amina of Zazzau, was like Queen Idia of Benin, a warring Queen who mobilized warriors and went to the battlefield herself. Idia successfully defended Benin kingdom from the Igalas, at a time when the men were too cowardly to defend the kingdom against invaders. Akosu Adeiyongu maintains that Idia decided to go to war herself when she identifies the vacuum created by the incompetence and insensitivity of leadership (171). To be victorious in warfare, Amina and Idia discarded the yoke of patriarchal conditioning and the thinking that a woman's significant value is only as a wife and mother. Amina made what must have been the ultimate sacrifice in the context of her traditional society; she chose not to have a home and children, because she regarded them as encumbrances that would not permit the life of leadership and conquest that she had chosen. Idia faced the possibility of death on the battlefield but that did not deter her. The lessons from history are clear; the struggle for gender equality in politics needs courage, perseverance, sacrifice and the dismantling of Ogundipe-Leslie's mountain of 'self'.

In a flashback which the playwright structures as a dream, Moremi of Ife recounts to Nona: 'I rescued my people from persistent Igbo raid. I...allowed myself to be captured by the Igbos, I discovered their secrets while living in their midst. As I escaped, I let out this secret to my people. My people defeated them in their next raid at the cost of my son, my precious son Oluorogbo's life' (*MTD* 19). Moremi pays a price too; the life of her son is lost in the process. Funmilayo Ransome-Kuti – a revolutionary teacher, proprietress, leader and organizer of women – appears to Nona: 'I headed an advocacy group on the right of women to vote and stand for election...campaigned tirelessly for suffragette causes in Northern Nigeria, ...faced challenges from many governments...' (*MTD* 24-5). Ransome-Kuti suffered so many trials that she died from the stress. Women from Aba, Ibibioland, Calabar and Ogoni, representing heroines of the 1929 women's war popularly tagged Aba women's riot, give account of their united revolt against colonial government's taxation and marginalization. Their protest was 'well established' and involved women of South Eastern Nigeria in complete solidarity; they were relentless in their pursuit, and the result was that colonial government felt their impact enough to react inappropriately with the senseless murder of unarmed women (*MTD* 23-4). Historification is used to advise that social change has to be pursued collectively and relentlessly, and that success necessarily involves huge sacrifices.

The past heroines whose exploits are showcased share a number of attributes in common. Each one had a vision and purpose that was communal, reaching beyond the individual to embody advantages for the larger society. The issues in contention affected all women; hence the heroines of the past had the strong support of other women for the various causes they had to fight. Their resistance was collective, and they persevered in their struggles till they achieved victory. The social vision, the passion to brave stiff opposition and face the possibility of death meant that these mothers of our past had re-socialized themselves to conquer their patriarchal indoctrinations – they had all conquered 'self' – to emerge in public politics. Salami applauds these historical heroines and implies that the attributes which enabled them to access the ranks of political power remain prerequisites for success in contemporary politics.

History shows that women in different generations have had different obstacles to surmount. Mama Nigeria, a grand historical personage in *MTD*, recognizes that in each generation, women have 'fought gallantly and kept the faith'. They have been 'undaunted in the face of challenges of your time…The important thing to know is that for each of these challenges, there is a strategy. Strategies vary from generation to generation'(25). The perseverance of past heroines is encouragement to contemporary women to persevere in the face of tribulations. Notably, all the instances in which women have been successful in politics have required tremendous courage, and perseverance in the face of awesome obstacles. As Mama Nigeria warns Nona: 'You have to realize that no one will throw open the gates of leadership for you to drive in unrestricted. You have to work hard at getting the right keys to open the gate or you may have to break in. No battle is ever won on a platter of gold. You have to keep fighting until you succeed' (86). Thus, whenever Prof. Nona becomes discouraged and tempted to give in, Salami employs the dramatic device of causing her to sleep, which enables past heroines to appear to her in the form of flashback. These appearances in which they recount their own struggles and obstacles energize Nona not to give up the fight. They give her hope that persistence in the struggle is the only way to succeed. In one of these appearances, Mama Nigeria encourages Nona: 'My daughter, don't give up… Don't be discouraged when many are not following. Let nothing distract you from your focus' (89-90). Historification is therefore the dramatic strategy used to proffer solutions in this play.

CONCLUSION

The Nigerian social, cultural and justice systems depicted in Irene Salami's *More Than Dancing* are such that women are severely disadvantaged by longstanding patriarchal practices and biases which deny them access to political power and consign them to the margins of political activities – an undeniable situation of social injustice. The play reveals that men have conspired to keep women out of politics because of fear that the women will surpass them in competence and unravel the myth of male superiority, but women have been collaborators with men in their own marginalization. Emanating from *MTD*, is the argument that politics and governance continue to be male spaces because women have not been able to break free of the strong hold of 'self'. Pertinently, women in history who have conquered strongholds to emerge triumphant in political spaces have done so through an undeniable process of self-awareness, a conscious reappraisal of circumstances, a strong conviction and decision to rewrite their own political identities. They have been women who have conquered 'self'. *MTD* illustrates that contemporary women are becoming increasingly self-aware; they are redefining their identities, and are in Marxist terms, taking up arms against situations of injustice in politics. The play encourages women to persevere in confronting the challenges of each generation by revealing that patriarchal gender culture is often fallacious and some of the differences that hold women down are actually non-existent.

   MTD employs the device of history in a number of ways. Historical precedents show that men 'naturally' occupy leadership positions in all cultures; they are protagonists and pioneers, hence 'his-story' which constrains and marginalizes women, has been the norm. Salami turns history into a weapon by focusing on female historical protagonists who have emerged significantly in political spaces. By recounting the challenges each heroic woman in history had to surmount to rewrite 'her-story', the playwright teaches the virtues of self-definition, re-socialization, collective resistance, and persistence in the struggle. These examples of heroines who left spectacular footprints in the political arenas of their societies are used to energize women of the present in their struggle. Historification demonstrates that the quest for political justice has been a battle in every generation, a continuous battle from which women cannot relent; 'it is a commitment that must be renewed and preserved by each generation of Nigerian woman' (87) until they access justice in political matters permanently.

WORKS CITED

Evwierhoma, Mabel. 'The Rising Profile of Irene Isoken Salami and the New Nigerian Women-Centred Drama'. *African Women: Drama and Performance*. Ed., Irene Salami-Agunloye. Boston: Evergreen Books, 2011: 30-37.

Hagher, Iyorwuese Harry. *Mulkin Mata*. Ibadan: Heinemann, 1991.

Jary, David, and Julia Jary. *Unwin Hyman Dictionary of Sociology*. 2nd ed. Glasgow: Harper Collins, 1999.

McLean, Iain, and Alistair McMillan. *The Oxford Concise Dictionary of Politics*. New York: Oxford University Press, 2003.

Millet, Kate. *Sexual Politics* [1970]. Urbana: University of Illinois, 2000.

Oamen, Osedebamen. *The Scar*. Benin City: Forthspring, 2005.

———. *Women of Orena Are Wiser Than the Gods*. Benin City: Forthspring, 2009.

O'Barr, Jean. 'African Women in Politics'. *African Women South of the Sahara*. Eds, Margaret Jean Hay and Sharon Stichter. New York: Longman, 1986: 144-60.

Ogundipe-Leslie, Omolara. *Re-creating Ourselves: African Women and Critical Transformations*. Trenton NJ: Africa World Press, 1994.

Okoh, Julie. *Theatre and Women's Human Rights in Nigeria*. Port Harcourt: Pearl, 2002.

Onuoha, Victoria E. 'The Nigerian Society and Issues of Justice for Women'. *Nigeria Education Law Journal (NELJ)* Vol 9, No 1. Ibadan: Golden-Gems, 2008: 1-15.

Onwueme, Tess. *The Reign of Wazobia*. Ibadan: Heinemann, 1992.

Salami-Agunloye, Irene. *Idia: the Warrior Queen of Benin*. Jos: Saniez, 2008.

Salami, Irene Isoken. *More Than Dancing*. Jos: Saniez, 2003.

Tse, Andera Paul. 'Towards an Improved Political Participation by Nigerian Women: An Evaluation of Irene Salami's *More Than Dancing*'. *Jos Journal of Humanities*, Vol 4, No 1. Jos: Faculty of Arts, University of Jos. 2010: 115-26.

Breaking the Laws in J.M. Coetzee's
The Childhood of Jesus

Philosophy & the Notion of Justice

LAURA WRIGHT

Did you think you were … a creature beyond the reach of the laws of
nations? Well, the laws of nations have you in their grip now … the
laws are made of iron.

Coetzee, *Life & Times of Michael K*, 1985

COETZEE, THE LIMITS OF THE LAW,
AND (IN)ACTIVIST GUILT

Through their free indirect discourse and dialogic nature,[1] many
of J. M. Coetzee's novels ask explicit and literal questions of the
reader, as, for example, the question put to us of David Lurie in
Disgrace (1999): after his daughter is raped and David tries to
imagine her experience, the narrator asks, 'does he have it in him
to be the woman?' (160). In that they ask such questions, Coetzee's
novels require engagement with the debate that such questioning
engenders, and while such dialogism might prepare the way for
some sort of activist change, most of Coetzee's characters remain
only ever on the edge of change, about ready to change, but unable
to enact change. In his recent work, *The Childhood of Jesus* (2013),
however, Coetzee refuses to allow us to remain in the space of
dialogic philosophy; the child at the heart of the narrative – David,
not Jesus – asks question after question, 'why' after 'why,' until his
questions, most of which bring to the fore the artificiality of various
laws, become unanswerable for his sometimes guardian Simón, a
man who ultimately believes that 'there are higher considerations
than obeying the law, higher imperatives' (299). Faced with the
prospect of losing David, Simón must act instead of answer, and he
breaks the law to leave Novilla with David and Inés, the woman to

whom Simón has "given" David to mother. After an exploration of the nature of law-based limitation that characterizes his previous novels, this essay posits that *The Childhood of Jesus* offers an affront to previous readings of Coetzee's work as demonstrative of the impossibility of any action that lies outside of 'the man-made rules' (289) that exist in a 'universe . . . ruled by laws' (291).

Coetzee's works, in particular *Elizabeth Costello* (2003), *Summertime*, and *The Childhood of Jesus*, wrestle with the concept of what it means to be good within the confines of the various institutionalized laws and posit that if it is possible for one to act in the service of goodness as defined as existing outside of the law – or perhaps more appropriate to Coetzee's work, if one is to come close to approaching action – one must constantly renegotiate, via philosophical inquiry, one's position within the confines of unjust laws in order to arrive, instead, at a personal conception of justice. In this conception, then, goodness is less dependent upon action than upon questioning the mechanisms that inhibit it; goodness is the recognition of the need for action, even in the face of forced inaction, and it is necessarily based on the dialogic questioning at the core of Coetzee's literary project. In *The Childhood of Jesus*, David refuses to conform to a world that demands that he 'tell the truth' (262) as through his actions and questions he challenges the veracity of any objective notion of the law, a position that forces the other characters in the novel to move from blind obeisance towards activist conceptions of justice. When David's teachers want to send him to a special school because of his failure to adhere to the laws of mathematics, Simón's friend Eugenio asserts that

> Once [David] begins to feel more secure in his surroundings, once it begins to dawn on him that the universe – not just the realm of numbers but everything else too – is ruled by *laws*, that nothing happens by chance, he will come to his senses and settle down. (291, my emphasis)

Such an assumption is at odds with David's response to being told to tell the truth: he says, 'I am the truth' (263), a claim that positions individual activism against hegemonic conformity to a universe supposedly ruled by laws.

***

I want to begin this exploration by commenting on the consistent critical attempt to codify Coetzee's body of work even as his work and his characters seek to defy codification – and to posit that such resistance constitutes a kind of activism. For example, it may be inaccurate to refer to Michael K, the eponymous character of Coetzee's 1983 novel *Life & Times of Michael K*, as an activist although he does not conform to the laws of nations (particularly the laws of apartheid era South Africa). Such laws are, if not utterly unjust, completely arbitrary and at odds with K's singular attempt to first care for his mother and, after her death, avoid the mechanizations of war. Here as in much of his oeuvre, Coetzee's characters seek to occupy space outside the iron grip of the law, but are always reinscribed within it. K's attempt to be 'out of all the camps at the same time' (182) is indicative of his perhaps unconscious adherence to an ethical imperative to embody an impossible space that exists both outside of and in opposition to the law, a position for which there is no legal codification, and this question of what happens to one in the absence of classification within the law is a primary theme in much of Coetzee's fiction. As a result of his attempts to remain outside of all the camps, the 31-year-old K is constantly misclassified and recodified.[2] Similarly, in the codified analysis Coetzee's oeuvre, there is a consistent attempt to place his work within the confines of specific camps – South African, postcolonial, allegorical, or postmodern, for example – even as certain terms inscribe the very ways his work resists such categorization.

The first such term is 'limits'. Anker (2011), Clarkson (2009), and Marais (2006), for example, all chronicle the ways that Coetzee's work confronts or reinforces various barriers, whether to action, speech, imagination, or representation. Marais, for example, notes the ways that the genre of the novel attempts to address violence: 'my contention is that realism's inattention to the interplay between subjective violence and symbolic violence impairs the ethical efficacy of the emotion with which this mode of writing has traditionally sought to counter violence, namely sympathy' (2006: 94). Anker notes that the dominant mode of discussing Coetzee's 2003 *Elizabeth Costello* is via animals rights,[3] but that 'liberal articulations of rights are . . . afflicted by deep liabilities,' as they are often 'exclusionary and premised on gendered, racialized, class-based and other hierarchies and divisions' (2011: 169). Clarkson focuses on *Waiting for the Barbarians* and *Disgrace* to 'explore the ways in which Coetzee's texts confront the difficulty of bringing meaningfully into linguistic range that which appears without precedent in given language' (2009: 106). There are other such pieces. Durrant examines the 'Limits of the Sympathetic

Imagination' in *Elizabeth Costello* (2006); Baker explores the 'Limits of Sympathy' in *Age of Iron, Lives of Animals,* and *Disgrace* (2005); Buelens looks at the 'Limits of Responsibility' in *Disgrace* (2009); and Titlestad explores the 'Limits of Allegory' in *Dusklands* (2008).

A second and related term prevalent in the criticism of Coetzee is 'guilt,' and in his work, guilt results from a failure to overcome systemic boundaries – limits – to action, as those boundaries are codified in apartheid era law, the militarized production of empire, dietary norms with regard to meat production and consumption, and familial obligations. Robinson (2012) examines that way that 'Coetzee has wrestled in his writing with a sense of anguished moral entanglement in his country's crimes against humanity', and many other critics examine guilt in Coetzee's writing, particularly with regard to *Disgrace*'s engagement with various kinds of specifically South African guilt. These include Horrell (2008), Diala (2001-2) and Van der Elst (2006) Taken as a whole, what the prevalence of such analyses – as well as the analyses themselves – indicate is the way that Coetzee's oeuvre functions to open a discursive space for recognition of the ways that conception and enforcement of the law, political, social, and 'natural,' particularly in South Africa, and more generally predicated always on the enforcement of rights-based mandates, forecloses the possibility of goodness or ethical action outside of the law.

ELIZABETH COSTELLO AND THE PROBLEM OF PHILOSOPHY

Most, if not all, of Coetzee's novels end with characters having changed only through their acquisition of negative knowledge,[4] or, perhaps even more problematically, by virtue of their realization that they haven't changed essentially, haven't acted or have had, as the result of the law, their actions nullified, coopted, or misread. At the end of *Waiting for the Barbarians*, for example, the Magistrate finds himself on 'a road that may lead nowhere' (1980: 156); at the end of *Life & Times of Michael K*, Michael, without a home and nearly starved to death by his attempts to stay outside of the fictional South African civil war that rages around him, imagines subsisting on teaspoons of water taken from the earth. *Disgrace* is Coetzee's most famous work, a novel that examines the life of white South African former literature professor David Lurie's downfall after his questionably consensual sexual relationship with a female student, his daughter Lucy's subsequent gang rape, and David's service in the disposal of the corpses of unwanted euthanized dogs. The novel ends with David, burned, robbed, and jobless, 'giving up' a crippled dog to the needle. One way to read such endings is to concede that change – that action – is impossible, that within the confines of 'society,' one will always encounter the 'limit,' the boundary that makes attempts at action both futile and subject to consistent criticism, misreading, and reinscription.

Philosopher Robert Pippin (2010) notes that 'any human social world is obviously finite, limited in resources and space, and it comprises agents whose pursuits of individual ends unavoidably must limit what others would otherwise be able to do,' and the space wherein human societies grapple with their nature as at once 'deeply conflictual and competitive . . . [and] . . . cooperative and communal' is 'commonly known as the political' (19). This political space establishes the boundaries – the social norms, the unspoken rules, and the codified laws – that seek to make sense of human interactions, and, as Pippin notes, such rules, in that they oppress and champion certain groups at certain historical moments, make 'philosophical abstraction' – as opposed to action – 'both understandable and problematic' (21). But the problem with philosophy is the very problem raised by Coetzee's character, Elizabeth Costello, who argues against philosophy, noting the inadequacy of language that it provides her with regard to her activism on behalf of animals. That language, as she puts it:

> Is the language of Aristotle and Porphyry, of Augustine and Aquinas, of Descartes and Bentham, of, in our day, Mary Midgley and Tom Reagan. It is a philosophical language in which we can discuss and debate what kind of souls animals have, whether they reason . . . . I have that language available to me. (66)

While she notes that she could 'fall back on that language' of reason, 'both reason and seven decades of life experience tell [her] that reason is neither the being of the universe nor the being of God' (67); therefore, she refuses to bow to it.[5]

And despite this critique of philosophy inherent in the text, philosophy is the camp into which the Costello lectures are inevitably placed and the lens via which they are often critiqued, even as the character of Costello explicitly seeks to remain, like Michael K, outside that camp. In response to the language of philosophy, Costello makes a dialogic plea for the empathetic imagination as a more appropriate mode of active engagement, asking, 'why on earth should we not be capable of thinking our way into the life of a bat?' (77), an entreaty to empathize with the reality of animals and therefore to act on their behalf because of our very human ability to imagine their reality. This is not the stuff of philosophy; it is the stuff of the heart. In the ways that Costello is challenged by members of her audience at fictional Appleton College, by her philosophy professor daughter-in-law Norma, and by any number of actual critics who have written about this work, to appeal from the heart is to be considered less than serious and to invoke both ire and disdain.[6]

Within the context of 'Lives', Costello compares the treatment of animals in contemporary industrialized societies to the treatment of Jews in Nazi Germany, and this analogy generates outrage among members of her audience at Appleton, as such an assertion, in any context, is apt to do. At the end of 'Lives,' Costello says to her son John,

> I no longer know where I am. I seem to move around perfectly easily among people, to have perfectly normal relationships with them. Is it possible, I ask myself, that all of them are participating in a crime of stupefying proportions? Am I fantasizing it all? I must be mad! Yet everyday I see the evidences. The very people I suspect produce the evidence, exhibit it, offer it to me. Corpses. Fragments of corpses that they have bought for money. (114)

When she mentions the 'crime of stupefying proportions,' Costello is, of course, speaking of the treatment of animals in the industrialized world, but within the context of the United States (where she is speaking), the laws pertaining to livestock animals fail to afford them any significant ethical consideration, and in South Africa (the country from which the work originates), as Lucy Lurie notes in *Disgrace*, 'on the list of the nation's priorities, animals come nowhere' (73). To commit a 'crime' per se, a law would have to be in place that is being broken; as there are no such laws that prohibit the slaughter and consumption of animals, 'crime' in this instance is a completely subjective entity. Costello's assertion that a crime has been committed is not only reflective of Costello's conception of a lived social justice but also about the possibility of action and of whether any individual action can shift the political space that enables and supports injustice, whether towards another species or towards another group of human beings, when such perceived injustice is not legally considered a 'crime.'

Here is the essential dilemma put to Coetzee's audience in *Elizabeth Costello* by Costello herself: 'is it possible, I ask myself, that all of them are participating in a crime of stupefying proportions? Am I fantasizing it all? I must be mad!' (114). If there is no law against our participation, how can we be implicated in a crime of stupefying proportions, or is Costello 'mad' as she asserts? And then follows a second question. Costello says to her son John, 'calm down, I tell myself, you are making a mountain out of a molehill. This is life. Everyone else comes to terms with it, why can't you? *Why can't you?*' (115). If this is only life, and everyone else seems comfortable enough with uncomfortable, even unconscionable truths, then what do we make of those who do not sit comfortably by but who take action? What about those people?   John answers – quite unsatisfactorily – 'there, there . . . there, there. It will soon be over' (115). And then in a metafictive moment, it is over, as 'The Lives of Animals' ends with this statement. It's over; we don't have to deal with Costello's uncomfortable positions any more. On to 'The Humanities in Africa,' the section that follows, unless, of course, we want to talk about Costello's dilemma and, in turn, about the larger issues with regard to our ethical consideration of and action in response to the plight of the Other.

THE CHILDHOOD OF DAVID: WWJD (WHAT WOULD JOHN (COETZEE) / JESUS DO?)

Prior to *Childhood*, Coetzee's work has engaged with, and criticism of his work has been characterized, by limitations to action and the guilt engendered by such limitation. Despite this, however, some of Coetzee's more recent works, particularly *Disgrace*, *Elizabeth Costello*, and *Summertime* (and others that fall outside the scope of this essay), offer – even require – dialogic engagement between text and audience via the presentation of a dilemma. Such dilemmas, in that they engage specifically with questions of ethics and the law, however one might choose to define the law (as natural or man-made), require either action or justification for inaction in the face of issues posited within his texts as unjust or, as Elizabeth Costello contends, as 'crime.' Engaging with Coetzee's work via philosophical inquiry allows us to provide such justification, but the empathetic imagination championed by Elizabeth Costello requires action. Why can't we 'think [our] way into the existence of a bat' (80)? Only because philosophy allows us not to and allows us to engage in the dialogic debate without reaching the infamous limit of the debate, the place where there is no longer an acceptable counter to the dilemma except for action.

In the present moment of Coetzee's fiction, we have *The Childhood of Jesus* (2013), a novel that depicts the absurdity of characters who endlessly philosophize about absolutely everything, even the 'pooness of poo' (159) or the 'chairness' of chairs (144). Everything amounts to a 'philosophical disagreement' (140) between characters, with even Simón's fellow colleagues, all stevedores, taking a course on philosophy. *Childhood* is located in the Spanish speaking non-place of Novilla, in one sense 'no villa,' or 'no village' – or literally, 'heifer' in Spanish – a space occupied by a young boy recently renamed David and his guardian Simón, a space that reviewers claim is a city 'run on drably utopian and vaguely socialist lines' (Markovits), an 'invented, indeterminate location' (Talt, 2013), and 'a kind of heaven' (Lytal, 2013);[7] Simón calls it 'limbo' (*Childhood* 28). When Simón and David arrive, 'the man at the gate points them towards a low, sprawling building in the middle distance' (7). Indeed Novilla is liminal, a place beyond the gate, a place in 'the middle' of seemingly nowhere – the space of dilemma –where late in the novel Simón tumbles into a literal void, the crack ...

> between the quay and the steel plates of [a] freighter. For a moment, he is held there, gripped so tightly that it hurts to breathe. He is intensely aware that if the ship has to drift only an inch and he will be crushed like an insect. The pressure slackens and he drops feet first into the water. (274)

If the space of Novilla is a space in limbo, then such limbo exists between philosophy about action and actual action, a space characterized by Simón's consistent belief that he is in 'no position to challenge the law' (271) and to disagree only philosophically prior to his plunge into the water. After the fall, however, Simón finds reading a philosophical text about 'chairs and their chairness' (144) to be unbearable, wanting instead a different kind of philosophy 'that shakes one. That changes one's life' (278). The novel begins with the man and boy's arrival in Novilla from Belstar, the boy having become separated from his mother at some point prior; they have been given new names, and they are encouraged to lose 'interest in old attachments' (28), even as the man seeks to find the boy's mother. Ana tells Simón, 'people here have washed themselves clean of old ties. You should be doing the same; letting go of old attachments, not pursuing them' (29). David's questions begin almost immediately: 'why are we here?' (25), to which Simón responds, 'there is nowhere else to be but here' (26).

Benjamin Lytle states that 'Coetzee's title, *The Childhood of Jesus*, will seem like a provocation,' particularly as the novel is not about the biblical Jesus in any concrete way. It is, however, about a child 'who appears stuck in the 'why?' stage that most kids have passed through by school age' (McGillis 2013). These 'whys' are asked in response to the seemingly more mundane accepted laws that govern everyday life than those posed by Elizabeth Costello, but like Costello, the boy questions the ethics of the rules that govern human behaviour. When Simón tells the boy that he has a duty to practise chess since he is 'blessed with a talent', David asks why, and Simón responds, 'Why? Because the world is a better place, I suppose, if each of us can excel at something' (57). In another instance, after Simón has explained that 'coins come from a place called the Mint' (198), Simón asks, 'why don't you just go to the Mint' (199) to get money as opposed to getting it from the paymaster at the docks. Simón answers, 'because the Mint won't just give us money. We have to work for it. We have to earn it.' The boy again asks, 'Why?' Simón responds in exasperation, 'Why? The answer to all your *Why? Questions*, past, present and future is: *Because that is the way the world is*' (199). But David is not dissuaded from continuing to ask why about everything from the laws of mathematics (why, for example, can't 888 be greater than 889?), to the laws regarding what Simón refers to as 'the human condition' (203). The boy, in his refusal to adhere to laws that make no sense to him, ultimately forces both Simón and Inés to question their own adherence to them. According to Lytle (2013),

> Towards the end, Simón sides … sides with David against his school-teachers. Perhaps David is a mathematical genius, and 2 + 2 = 5. … Why should David listen to his teachers 'when a voice inside him says the teacher's way is not the true way?' One of Simón's friends accuses him of schoolboy philosophizing – as in 'What if the mad are really sane and the sane are really mad?' But Simón, in siding with David/Jesus, has turned his back on Western philosophy.

This marks the narrative shift from philosophical abstraction to action. It is the place from which the narrative of a Jesus capable of Costello's empathetic imagination can be constructed; this is the moment when the philosophy 'that shakes one. That changes one's life' (278) – presumably the 'philosophy' of empathy and salvation practised by the biblical Jesus that David is poised to become.

If David is somehow the child who will become the Jesus of Christian mythology – and there are many hints in the text to indicate that this is the case – then that mythology has reinscribed him as a vastly different being from Coetzee's David. Coetzee's prequel, as it were, forces us to reread the biblical story of Jesus backwards and as a radical makeover: the biblical Jesus is then a misreading, a man renamed and made older; he is more like the empathetic Costello than this spoiled child of Novilla. Near the end of the novel, Simón tells David, 'we all have fathers, it's a law of nature' 302), and again, as in much of Coetzee's fiction, we find ourselves grappling with how fathers signify within his work. *Summertime*, the third instalment in 'Scenes from a Provincial Life,' Coetzee's *autre*biography,[8] ends with a dilemma that lays out in stark opposition the nature of choosing ethical responsibility over personal gratification with regard to the concept of the father and fatherland – or, to look at the problem differently, to choose one ethical imperative over another – which is, after all, what is always at stake in the endless tug-of-war between competition and communalism that characterizes human social existence and shapes and limits our ability to act outside those parameters. John Coetzee, having moved back to South Africa from London during the 1970s to care for his father, encounters a country where the papers chronicle 'tales from the borderlands, murders followed by bland denials.' John 'reads these reports and feels soiled' (4), while his father views 'Africa' as 'a place of starving masses with homicidal buffoons lording it over them' (ibid.). When his father becomes ill with cancer of the larynx and is rendered unable to speak or to work, John is faced with the burden of responsibility for him. Of John, the narrator says, 'he is going to have to abandon some of his personal projects and become a nurse' (265), and one can assume that his 'personal projects' constitute his writing. But 'alternatively, if he will not be a nurse, then he must announce to his father: I cannot face the prospect of ministering to you day and night. I am going to abandon you. Goodbye' (266). The novel ends on the horns of a dilemma: 'one or the other: there is no third way' (ibid.).

WWJD: What would John do? Does he stay and forego his art (and would that choice constitute the more ethical choice anyway)? Or does he leave the father(land) and his presumed obligations to it (for example, to confront and protest those aforementioned 'murders in the borderlands') to become a Nobel Prize winning novelist, or, in the case of Jesus, the Christian saviour of humankind? The answer would seem obvious, except that this is fiction, and the John Coetzee represented within it both is and is not the J.M. Coetzee who wrote *Summertime* and *The Childhood of Jesus*. If to abandon the father within Coetzee's oeuvre is to abandon the law (as is the case in *Life & Times of Michael K* where K considers his father as 'the list of rules on the door of the dormitory' (104) of Huis Norienius, the institution where he lives as a child), then in *Summertime*, it is also to abandon the fatherland – South Africa – which Coetzee has done by moving to Australia and becoming an Australian citizen. Such action places him, like Michael K, outside of the camps as well, those that would define his being and his work as 'African' or postcolonial and, as a result, necessarily responsible for literary engagement with the apartheid law or for 'real' action on the part of its legacy. The issue of any or enough action is of central concern in Coetzee's work, whether, as we have seen, such action is taken (or not taken) on behalf of animals, of political prisoners, or of one's own family. At the end of *Childhood*, the 'family of David' (304) has left as well, abandoned the laws 'to start a new life' (324) that will, presumably, allow for action beyond philosophy; this novel does not leave us on the horns of a dilemma.

In *Childhood*, initially when Inés tries to convince Simón that they must take David out of the special school where he has been placed to learn to stick to the rules, he says, 'but those people have the law behind them, and we are in no position to challenge the law.' Inés counters, 'even if the law is bad?' and Simón responds, 'it is not a question of good or bad, Inés, it is a question of power. If you run away then [they] will send the police after you and the police will catch you' (271). Ultimately, however, he chooses to leave Novilla with David and Inés anyway, realizing that 'there are higher considerations than obeying the law, higher imperatives' (299). The so-called family leaves, and after he is blinded by a magnesium flash, David demands not to be called David any longer: 'you must call me by my real name' (318). This is the moment of escape from the inaction of philosophical debate, the abandonment of the notion that one cannot care about that which one does not care about. The persistence of the dialogic 'why,' and the requirement that the why be answered, continually leads in *The Childhood of Jesus* to a place where the only answer is simply another tautology: such and such *is* because *it is*. One cannot *care* because one *does not care*. Neither position is satisfactory; both require action beyond such simplistic truisms. And the boy has predicted this moment all along, claiming early in the narrative when Simón says that David cannot fall into a crack in the pavement, 'I can! You can! Anyone can! You don't know' (47). In reading *Don Quixote*, David tells Simón that 'a hole will open up . . . between the pages' (195), and then, for the first time in Coetzee's fiction, that space does open, as Simón tumbles into the crack between the boat and the dock, between philosophy and action, and then crosses from one side to the other.

NOTES

1   I have written about Coetzee's dialogism in "Does he Have it in Him to be the Woman?': The Performance of Displacement in J. M. Coetzee's *Disgrace*,' *Ariel* 37.4 (2006): 83-102, and elsewhere.

2   For example, on the charge sheet at the hospital where he is admitted, Michael is listed as Michael Visagie, age 40 (70), and the medical officer who treats him later in the narrative consistently calls him 'Michaels' (131). Furthermore, despite the fact that Coetzee's audience knows otherwise, within the text, K is believed to be an 'arsonist . . . running a flourishing garden . . . and feeding the local guerrilla population' (131).

3   The focus on animal rights in *Elizabeth Costello* is dependent on the fact that the two sections in that novel that constitute *The Lives of Animals* were published as that text in 1999, after Coetzee presented the two as the 1997-1998 Princeton Tanner Lectures.

4   In other words, they learn that they cannot learn. Take, for example, the Magistrate in *Waiting for the Barbarians* whose narrative ends with his proclamation that 'this is not the scene I dreamed of. Like much else nowadays I leave it feeling stupid' (156).

5   According to Cora Diamond, in the case of Costello, 'philosophy characteristically misrepresents both our own reality and that of others, in particular those 'others' who are animals,' and 'the philosopher's understanding is deflected; the issue becomes deflected, as the philosopher thinks it or rethinks it in the language of philosophical skepticism' (11-12).

6   Norma, Costello's daughter-in-law, 'gives a sigh of exasperation' (76) during Costello's lecture; Abraham Stern, a poet in the English Department at the college where she speaks writes to tell her that he did not attend the dinner in her honour because of the comparison she makes between the treatment of animals and the suffering of Jews during the holocaust (94); and any number of critics have engaged via philosophy, as I am doing now, with Costello's empathetic sensibility.

7   At the time of writing, an MLA database search pulls no results in scholarly criticism of *The Childhood of Jesus*. All of my citations for this novel are book reviews.

8   For Coetzee's discussion of the concept of autrebiography, see *Doubling the Point*, ed. Attwell p. 394.

WORKS CITED

Anker, Elizabeth. 'Elizabeth Costello, Embodiment, and the Limits of Rights'. *New Literary History* 42.1 (2011): 169-92.

Attwell, David (ed.) *Doubling the Point, Essays and interviews, J.M.Coetzee*. Harvard University Press, 1992.

Baker, Geoffrey. 'The Limits of Sympathy: J. M. Coetzee's Evolving Ethics of Engagement'. *Ariel* 36.1-2 (2005): 27-49.

Buelens, Gert. 'Catastrophe, Citationality and the Limits of Responsibility in *Disgrace*', in *The Catastrophic Imperative: Subjectivity, Time and Memory in Contemporary Thought*. Eds, Dominick Hoens et al. New York: Palgrave, (2009): 154-70.

Clarkson, Carrol. 'J. M. Coetzee and the Limits of Language'. *Journal of Literary Studies/ Tydskrif vir Literatuurwetenskap* 25.4 (2009): 106-24.

Coetzee, J. M. *Disgrace*. New York: Penguin, 1999.

—— *The Lives of Animals*. Princeton University Press, 1999

—— *Elizabeth Costello*. New York: Penguin, 2003.

—— *Life & Times of Michael K*. New York: Penguin, 1985.

—— *The Childhood of Jesus*. Melbourne: Text, 2013.

—— *Summertime*. London: Harvill Secker, 2009.

—— *Waiting for the Barbarians*. New York: Penguin, 1980.

Diala, Isidore. 'Nadine Gordimer, J. M. Coetzee, and Andre Brink: Guilt, Expiation, and the Reconciliation Process in Post-Apartheid South Africa'. *Journal of Modern Literature* 25.2 (2001-2002): 50-68.

Diamond, Cora. 'The Difficulty of Reality and the Difficulty of Philosophy'. *Partial Answers: A Journal of Literature and the History of Ideas* 1.2 (2003): 1-26.

Durrant, Sam. 'J. M. Coetzee, Elizabeth Costello, and the Limits of the Sympathetic Imagination'. in *J. M. Coetzee and the Idea of the Public Intellectual*. Ed. Jane Poyner. Athens: Ohio UP, 2006: 118-34.

Horrell, Georgina. 'Postcolonial Disgrace: (White) Women and (White) Guilt in the 'New' South Africa'. in *Bodies and Voices: The Force-Field of Representation and Discourse in Colonial and Postcolonial Studies*. Eds, Merete Borch et al. Amsterdam: Rodopi, 2008: 17-31.

Lytal, Benjamin. 'Coetzee's Jesus'. *Newsweek* 18 March 2013. Web. 1 June 2013.

Marais, Mike. 'Death and the Space of the Response to the Other in J. M. Coetzee's *The Master of Petersburg*'. in *J. M. Coetzee and the Idea of the Public Intellectual*. Ed., Jane Poyner. Athens: Ohio UP, 2006: 83-99.

—— 'Violence, Postcolonial Fiction, and the Limits of Sympathy'. in *Studies in the Novel* 43.1 (2011): 94-114.

Markovitz, Benjamin. Review of *The Childhood of Jesus*. *Guardian* 2 March 2013. Web. 1 June 2013.

McGillis, Ian. 'Childhood of Jesus: Savior in a Strange Land'. *Montreal Gazette* 10 May 2013. Web. 11 June 2013.

Pippin, Robert. 'The Paradoxes of Power in the Early Novels of J. M. Coetzee.' *J. M. Coetzee and Ethics: Philosophical Perspectives on Literature*. Eds, Anton Leist and Peter Singer. New York: Columbia UP, 2010: 19-41.

Robinson, Forrest G. 'Writing as Penance: National Guilt and J. M. Coetzee'. *Arizona Quarterly* 68.1 (2012): 1-54.

Talt, Theo. Review of *The Childhood of Jesus*. *Guardian* 27 February 2013. Web. 1 June 2013.

Titlestad, Michael. 'Unsettled Whiteness: The Limits of Allegory in Three South African Novels'. *Authority Matters: Rethinking the Theory and Practice of Authorship*. Eds,

Stephen Donovan et al. Amsterdam: Rodopi, 2008: 223-56.

Van der Elst, Jacques. 'Guilt, Reconciliation and Redemption: *Disgrace* and its South African Context.' *A Universe of (His)stories: Essays on J. M. Coetzee.* Ed. Liliana Silkorska. Frankfurt: Peter Lang, 2006.

Wright, Laura. '"Does He Have it in Him to be the Woman?" The Performance of Displacement in J. M. Coetzee's *Disgrace*', *Ariel* 37.4 (2006): 83-102.

The Rhetoric & Caricature of Social Justice in Post-1960 Africa

A Logical Positivist Reading of Ngũgĩ wa Thiongo's *Matigari*

ERIC NSUH ZUHMBOSHI

Most literary pundits agree that a literary work is not created *ex nihilo*. In other words, it is a reflection of a particular society in space and time. The writer's immediate socio-political context is regarded as the material cause of the text since the raw material for his literary productivity comes from his society. Diana Laurenson and Alan Swingewood, in *The Sociology of Literature*, write: 'Literature, because it delineates man's anxieties, hopes, and aspirations, is perhaps one of the most effective sociological barometers of the human response to social forces' (1971: 17).

This mimetic capacity of literature is the source of the debate on the role of the writer in African literature, in particular and post-colonial literature in general. Established African writers and critics such as Chinua Achebe and Wole Soyinka have argued that the African writer should play a functional role in his society; he should be the voice of the voiceless and the visionary of his time. Wole Soyinka, in 'The Writer in a Modern African State' contends thus: '[...] the time has now come when the African writer must have the courage to determine what alone can be salvaged from the recurrent cycle of human stupidity' (1969: 19). The African writer, according to Soyinka, should perform the role of the gadfly of his society and also a compass to show the society which direction to go in. In other words, he should be the harbinger of truth and a firebrand crusader against social injustice and all forms of exploitation of his people. This justifies Soyinka's argument that 'When the writer in his own society can no longer function as conscience, he must recognise that his choice lies between denying himself or withdrawing to the position of a chronicler or post-mortem surgeon' (19-20).

91

This article seeks to carry out a critical discourse of Ngũgĩ wa Thiong'o's *Matigari* to show that post-colonial writers are in a constant search for justice and socio-political equality in their different socio-political contexts. The article, therefore, justifies the premise that nation-building and national harmony in post-colonial societies are impossible without conscious policies laid down by the ruling political elite to institute justice and equality in their political and juridical societies. Therefore, the constant friction and social revolt in post-colonial societies comes about through the lack of social justice and equality among the ruling elite and the entire citizenry.

For the sake of conceptual clarity, it is important to define the concept of social justice, a concept that has been very intricate in its definition even within the circles of erudite and celebrated philosophers. In *The Republic*, Plato treats the idea of justice and finally defines it as giving to each person or individual what he or she deserves based on the person's character traits which include his ability, virtues and vices. The above definition shows that Plato situates justice within the confines of meritocracy – where an individual is given only what he or she merits.

Aristotle pushes the debate further and tackles the concept of justice from an egalitarian perspective. In *The Politics*, he opines that '[…] justice in a community means equality for all. This is not inconsistent with the theory of justice which I explained in my Ethics, for it involves the same principles – that justice is related to persons and that equality must be equal for equals' (1962: 128). A synthesis of both the Platonic and Aristotelian perspectives of justice shows that it is a concept that has to do with meritocracy and equality. Justice, within the purview of this paper, is the aggregate of decisions and its results taken by those who wield political and administrative power in society to determine what constitutes fair treatment under the law.

The theory adopted for the purposes of this paper is logical positivism. Also known as logical empiricism, logical positivism began as a philosophical movement that arose in Vienna in the 1920s. Proponents of this movement argue that true knowledge is one that is verifiable. Consequently, any body of knowledge which cannot be verified by the scientific method is meaningless and should be discarded. It is in this connection that exponents of this theory reject all forms of metaphysical truths since such truths cannot be verified following the principle of verifiability.

One of the major disciples of this theory is A.J. Ayer. In his book, entitled *Language, Truth, and Logic* (1935), Ayer eloquently defends the doctrine of logical positivism by proving that real knowledge is factual knowledge and not metaphysical knowledge. This explains why, in connection to the verifiability principle, he argues that:

> The criterion which we use to test the genuineness of apparent state-ments of fact is the criterion of verifiability. We say that a statement is factually significant to any given person, if, and only if, he knows how to verify the proposition as being true or reject it as being false. If, on the other hand, the putative proposition is of such a character that the assumption of its truth, or falsehood, is consistent with any assumption whatsoever concerning the nature of his future experience, then, as far as he is concerned, it is if not a tautology, a mere pseudo-proposition. (6)

The above views of Ayer allude to the fact that the principle of verifiability is very important in determining whether a statement is true of false. Ayer's approach to logical positivism has been adapted as the theoretical framework of this paper, and the analysis of *Matigari* will therefore take into consideration not only the intrinsic nature of the text, but also the extrinsic in order to see whether the fictional or imaginary society in the text has a relation with the society out of the text.

The quest for an alternative politics, through the practice of social justice and equality, has been one of the preoccupations of African writers of the post-1960 era. In fact, these writers do not see their functions as having ended with political independence; they still see their role as very relevant in the post-independence period as they are geared towards exposing and commenting on the socio-political conditions of the Africans masses and their relationship with the ruling political elite. Chinua Achebe, in *The Trouble with Nigeria* (1983), argues thus:

> I realised after independence that they and I were now on different sides because they were not doing what we agreed they should do. So, I had to become a critic. I found myself on the side of the people against their leaders – leaders this time being black people. (88)

These writers depict the post-colonial African state as one which is bedevilled with injustice and inequality orchestrated by the ruling political elite. This implies that the post-independence African leader and politician is not too different from the colonial master. In other words, the writers see them as reincarnations of their colonial masters – since these elites are committing the same ills and atrocities as their white colonial masters including the oppression and exploitation of the masses..

In this connection, therefore, *Matigari* could be read as a political discourse on the absence of social justice and equality in post-colonial or post-1960 African societies. What is very peculiar about this novel is that, unlike Ngũgĩ's previous novels that have specific social settings, *Matigari* does not have any particular social setting. In a preface to the novel, Ngũgĩ wa Thiong'o affirms that the novel is set nowhere and he gives the reader the liberty to determine where he/she thinks the events of the novel are taking place. The writer is indirectly articulating that the situation in *Matigari* fits any post-colonial society in the world – whether within Africa or beyond Africa. Just like *Devil on the Cross*, the novel *Matigari* was first published in 1985 in the Kikuyu language and in 1989 it was translated into English. This was the author's method of revolting against Western imperialism and to assert his philosophy that for African literature to regain it prestige and esteem, it must be written in an African language.

The novel cuts across two historical periods in the history of Africa and other post-colonial societies: the colonial period, which is seen through the use of the flashback technique, and the post-independence period. In the colonial society, the protagonist, Matigari, runs into a fierce battle with the colonialist Settler Williams because of the latter's exploitative tendencies. This is evident in the text as Matigari constructs his house, cultivates his plantation, but it is the colonialist who sleeps in the house and reaps the produce of this plantation. Matigari and his family instead sleep outside, on the veranda, and wallow in penury and destitution. In a dialogue between Ngaruro, Muriuki and Matigari, the latter recapitulates the cause of the conflict between him and the colonial master, Settler Williams, in these words:

> 'You see, I built the house with my own hands. But Settler Williams slept in it and I would sleep outside on the veranda. I tended the estates that spread around the house for miles. But it was Settler Williams who took home the harvest. I was left to pick up anything he might have left behind. I worked all the machines and in all the industries, but it was Settler Williams who would take the profits to the bank and I would end up with a cent he flung my way [….]' (*Matigari* 21)

The above passage shows the exploitative propensity of Settler

Williams and the repetitive use of the first person pronoun 'I' shows that the protagonist is angry with the colonialist's attitude. This passage also shows harmful and nauseating effect of colonialism on Africans. It shows that during this era, Africans suffered from oppression, exploitation, and racial prejudice in the hands of their white colonial masters. Commenting about this period in African history, Frantz Fanon in the *Wretched of the Earth* (1978) writes:

> The originality of the colonial context is that economic reality, inequality, and the immense difference of ways of life never come to mask the human realities. When you examine at close quarters the colonial context, it is evident that what parcels out the world is to begin with the fact of belonging to or not belonging to a given race, a given species. In the colonies, the economic substructure is also a superstructure. The cause of the consequence; you are rich because you are white; you are white because you are rich. (30-31)

Because of the viciousness of Settler Williams, Matigari decides to revolt against him. Through the use of memory, Matigari narrates the events that led him to revolt against Settler Williams. He says that he 'woke up from the deep sleep of many years' and told the colonial master that 'the sound of the trumpet and the sound of the horn of justice' must be heard and given prominence (*Matigari* 22). In metaphorical language, the protagonist reminds the colonialist that: 'The tailor demands his clothes, the tiller his land, the worker the produce of his sweat. The builder wants his house back. Get out of my house. You have hands of your own, you cruel and greedy one. Go build your own! Who deceived you into thinking that the builder has no eyes, no head, and no tongue?' (21-2). This desire to be independent justifies the protagonist's rebellion against the colonialist, Settler Williams. This is because it is only through independence that he hopes to have full control over his own resources and model his society the way he thinks fit for him.

Following the defeat of Settler Williams, which epitomizes the end of the colonial era, the omniscient narrator comments: 'He (Matigari) hoped that the last of the colonial problems had disappeared with the descent of Settler Williams into hell' (3). This shows that the protagonist is visualizing the post-independence period with a lot of optimism. Furthermore, this optimism is accentuated as the protagonist, after the war, goes under a '*mugumo*' fig tree in the forest and buries all the weapons he had used to fight the colonialist. The narrator says:

He rose, turned one more time, looked at the spot where he had buried the weapons murmuring to himself, 'It's good that I have laid down my arms.' He tore a strip of bark from a tree and girded himself with it, once again murmuring, 'Instead, I have now girded myself with the belt of peace. I shall go back to my house and rebuild my home.' He crossed the river and came out of the forest. (5)

The idea of coming out of the forest, as seen in the quotation above, is emblematic of the end of the colonial struggle. This explains why at the beginning of the novel, the omniscient narrator asserts that, 'with the descent of Settler Williams into hell' (1), the last of the colonial problems has been crushed. By burying his weapons, and girding himself with the belt of peace, Matigari shows that he foreshadows a new society where peace and justice will reign, with dialogue being the only way to solve problems in society and not arms as was the case under colonial rule. This depicts the high hopes and expectations Matigari believes will come true in the post-independence era.

The hope for an ideal post-independence society is also seen in Matigari's attitude and behaviour. He makes an effort to search for his family when he comes back to his country. They had been scattered as a result of his struggle with Settler Williams. The narrator says: 'He had made up his mind. He will first go in search of his people; at least first find out where they lived, what they ate and drank and what they wore' (6). This quotation shows that the protagonist is a man of conscience who is not only concerned with himself but his entire society. In other words, the protagonist shows that he has a socialist and communal vision in which it is the society as a whole, that counts and not the individual.

In addition, when Matigari walks along the road, he becomes very elated to realise that Africans as well as Europeans and Asians own cars. This strongly rekindles the hopes and expectations which he envisaged for post-independence society. He believes that this will be the first step in the development of African countries. He hopes that, in the future, they might start producing their own:

> His thoughts soon drifted from the news to the cars, which drove past him. Some had only Europeans in them, others Asians, and others Africans.... How things and times changed! Who could ever have believed that one day Africans would be driving their own cars? Now all that remained for them to do was to manufacture their own cars, trains, aeroplanes and ships. (8)

All the hopes and aspirations that Matigari harboured when he lives the mountain, after the defeat of Settler Williams become evanescent and ephemeral when he comes in contact with the political and social realities of the post-colonial society. He discovers that all the ills of the colonial society that he had been fighting against, are being replicated, perpetuated and orchestrated by the post-independent leaders. These ills in this society lead to political and social injustice against the post-independence masses in the novel.

Matigari witnesses, at the political level, the regime of His Excellency Ole Excellence supporting the activities of Britain and America even though they are unprofitable to the citizens. This is political injustice because the fundamental role of the state is to take care of its citizens and defend their interest. But His Excellency Ole Excellence is prepared to go to any length to defend the interests of these foreign countries even to the detriment of his citizens. In a decree, which is read over the country's radio Voice of Truth, His Excellency Ole Excellence bans a planned demonstration by university students outside the British and American Embassies in protest against Western military and economic aid to the Apartheid regime in South Africa (*Matigari* 7). The obvious reason for this ban is that these countries sustain the regime of His Excellency Ole Excellence. So, allowing the students to go on a rampage against them, for whatever reason, is tantamount to biting the hand that feeds the regime.

In his decree, His Excellency Ole Excellence clearly says that 'A friend in need is a friend indeed' (ibid.: 7). From this, it can be inferred that since these nations do support his regime, he in turn is bound to protect their interests even if it means doing so at the expense of the citizens. This is not only injustice committed against the post-colonial downtrodden masses, but also an aspect of the neo-colonial agenda which is vehemently criticized by Kwame Nkrumah, in *Africa Must Unite*. In this book, which could be described as manifesto against neo-colonialism, Nkrumah argues that:

> The form taken by neo-colonialism in Africa [...] has some of these features. It acts covertly, manoeuvring men and governments, free of the stigma attached to political rule. It creates client states, independent in name but in point of fact pawns of the very colonial power which is supposed to have given them independence. This is one of the 'diverse forms of dependent countries which, politically, are formally

independent, but in fact, are enmeshed in the net of financial and
diplomatic dependence' [....] The independence of those states is in
name only, for their liberty of action is gone. (1963: 174)

Another glaring case of excruciating injustice is seen when
Matigari realizes that the street children are forced to pay a fee to
the guards before they can be granted entrance to the garbage yard.
He is traumatized by this scene and asks the following rhetorical
questions: 'So these five were busy dividing among themselves the
money they had taken from the children? So a handful of people
still profited from the suffering of the majority, the sorrow of the
many being the joy of the few?' (*Matigari* 12). These questions
portray the degree of injustice reigning in the society.

Injustice, in *Matigari*, is particularly manifested in the economic
domain and leads to the portrayal of bourgeois capitalism in
the novel. The neo-colonialists own and control all financial
institutions in the country including industries, companies
and banks. When Africans do take part in the running of these
institutions, they do so as mere subordinates. A case in point is
the Anglo-American Leather and Plastic Works Company where
Robert Williams (the son of the colonialist) is the director and
John Boy Junior (an African) is his assistant. Moreover, foreigners
also own all shopping centres, co-operatives and financial firms
in the country, as the names of these companies make clear, for
example Barclays Bank, American Life Insurance, and British-
American Tobacco. The above institutions are visible sign-posts
of exploitation, neo-colonialism, capitalism and socio-economic
injustice in this society. They show that the economy of this post-
colonial state is in the hands of the neocolonial masters who
are in turn under multinational companies and co-operations.
Kwame Nkrumah argues that the post-independent African state
must improve her economy less her political independence will
be useless. He writes:

> Under colonial rule, a country has very restricted economic links with
> other countries. Its natural resources are developed only in so far as
> they serve the interests of the colonial powers. However, once political
> independence has been achieved, the country's full potentialities can,
> and must, be explored. The domestic economy must be planned
> to promote the interests of its own nationals; and new and wider
> economic links must be created with other countries. Otherwise, the
> newly independent country may fall victim to the highly dangerous

forces of economic imperialism, and find that it has merely substituted one kind of colonialism for another. (108)

Nkrumah's argument, which he put together in the 1960s, could be said to have a prophetic undertone. One realizes in Africa today, as also reflected in the novel *Matigari*, that the economies of most African countries are being controlled from the West through financial institutions such as the World Bank, Bretton Woods and the International Monetary Fund. The citizens in the novel are living in misery because His Excellency Ole Excellence's government is not working for their benefit but for the neocolonialists.

Apart from financial institutions, the neo-colonialists unjustly control the most fertile lands and plantations in this country. As Ngũgĩ wa Thiong'o asserts in *Writers in Politics*: '[…] the wealth of our land has been gripped by a tiny group' (1998: 25). The native Africans, who work in these plantations, are grossly exploited by the neo-colonialists for a very meagre remuneration. They work for long hours on very meagre wages. When Guthera suggests to Matigari that he should go to the plantations and search for his family, Matigari, astounded and depressed, poses this question: *'So they still slave in the plantations?'* (*Matigari* 29). This question is most significant because Matigari had been a plantation worker in colonial days, so he is very conscious of the exploitative propensity of the owners who are the bourgeoisie. The workers, proletarians, labour under deplorable and inhuman conditions. Moreover, in the search for his family, Matigari and Guthera come across a large plantation 'Extending far into the horizon, the tea-bushes were so trimmed that they now looked like a huge bed of green' (41). The conversation between them shows that this land is owned and controlled by either an individual or by foreign investors. The dialogue goes thus:

> 'So fertile this land!' Guthera said.
> 'Does all this land belong to one person?'
> 'Yes… or to foreign companies'. (41)

This dialogue encapsulates the exploitative, capitalistic and unjust tendencies that have gripped the entire country. Matigari even goes ahead to comment that 'This plantation is so big that the owner can cover it only on horseback' (42). This is a satire on the unjust, greedy and insatiable nature of the post-independent neo-colonialists and their agents and stooges.

The forces of law and order are the preserve of the ruling oligarchy in the novel. They are at the beck and call of the neo-colonial political elite who use them to unjustly subjugate the masses with impunity – so that they can continue to wield power. This makes the military so powerful that nobody can bring the forces of law and order to order even when they go wrong. A case in point is the brutal treatment of Guthera by the police because she refuses to satisfy their concupiscence or sexual lust. This act of brutality and bestiality is carried out under the watchful eyes of a crowd but because of fear, they cannot intervene to rescue her (30-31). When Matigari, showing his legendary courage, rebukes the crowd for not stepping in to rescue Guthera, the policemen shouts at him that Guthera flouted the law of the state. Matigari questions the law as follows: 'what kind of law is this which allows policemen to harass defenceless women?' (31). This rhetorical question shows the impartiality of the laws of this society where the police, who are agents of the regime, are allowed to maltreat innocent citizens.

The workers of the Anglo-American Leather and Plastic Works Company are at loggerheads with their employers. This is because they accuse the directors, who are also the owners of this company, of exploitation and partiality. The conflict here is between capital and labour. The former being owned by the company directors while the latter is owned by the workers who argue that they do not receive enough payment or other advantages and remunerations for their labour. This is why Ngaruro, the leader of the workers, says: 'We are only asking for adequate remuneration for our labour. The labour of our hands is all we own . It is our only property .We sell this labour in the labour market' (109). He further summarizes their grievances and plight in this proverb: 'He who sows must be the one who reaps! We refuse to be the pot that cooks but never eats the food' (60).

Furthermore, injustice is found in the conflict between Matigari and John Boy Jr. over the house and estate Robert Williams had sold to the latter. When Matigari insists that the property belongs to him, they alert the forces of law and order and ask for his arrest without any explanation. This action, which is another travesty of justice, shows that the masses have no right to complain when their property is confiscated, especially when barons and cronies of the regime are responsible. More so, Matigari is taken to a cell where he is incarcerated alongside ten other citizens for no crime committed.

The prisoners are forced to live under deplorable conditions; they have no access to food and water. In fact, they are deprived of the basic necessities of life. Out of the ten inmates, eight have been arrested for no reason. One of them 'had been arrested for vagrancy' (54). This arrest shows that there is no freedom of movement in this country. In a very angry and furious tone, the man asks: 'Have I turned down any job? Just imagine being arrested for vagrancy in your own country' (4).

When Matigari escapes from the cell the first time, he undertakes a mission to look for truth and justice in his society. He finds it difficult to understand why what is rightfully due him cannot be given to him. Consequently, he sees his arrest and subsequent detention as unjust. This shows his determination to transform his society from its present state of injustice into one of moral rectitude and impartiality. This justifies why he goes around the country asking the masses where he can find truth and justice. The intention is to prick the consciences of the masses and also to make them realize that there is something wrong with their society that needs to be addressed. His expectations, however, become mere illusions as nobody is prepared to give him an authentic answer. Matigari's conversation with the old woman in the wilderness unveils that the regime has trampled on the masses to the extent that nobody has the temerity to say anything against the regime. The old woman comments:

> 'My dear wanderer, you cannot find answers to your questions where nobody lives. Truth and justice are to be found in people's actions.... But even among the people, you still have a problem of finding the answers to your questions. And do you know why? Let me whisper this in your ear. Come closer. It is fear. There is too much fear in this country....' (87)

Matigari's search for truth and justice earns him another arrest by the regime. This second arrest sends him to a mental hospital. The regime sees him as somebody who is mentally deranged for going round the country in search of truth and justice. It is in this hospital that Matigari realizes that mere words cannot bring change since the custodians of the neo-colonial regime are determined to maintain the existing status quo. In this regard, change demands action on his part and on that of others who desire it. This realization comes to him while in the mental hospital. The omniscient narrator says:

It dawned on him [Matigari] that one cannot defeat the enemy by arms alone. But one could not also defeat the enemy by words alone. One had to have the right words; but these words had to be strengthened by the force of arms. In the pursuit of truth and justice, one had to be armed with armed words. (131)

The novel ends with a popular uprising staged by the down-trodden masses. The aim is to dethrone the neo-colonial hegemony in the society and transform it to a haven of freedom, peace and justice. Though the revolution is still in progress, the revolutionaries are very confident and optimistic about the inevitable dethronement of the regime of His Excellency Ole Excellence. Such confidence and optimism are discernable in the song that is chanted in the background as the revolution is on its way:

Victory shall be ours!
Victory shall be ours!
Victory shall be ours!
Victory shall be ours! (175)

The repetition reinforces optimism in the minds of the rioters as they foresee a new dispensation.

In conclusion, this article set out to analyse Ngũgĩ wa Thiong'o's *Matigari* from the perspective of logical positivism, to prove that the novel is a socio-political discourse on the miscarriage of social justice in post-colonial societies in general and Africa in particular. The article has affirmed that for peace and serenity to reign in post-colonial states, there must be a conscious effort by the ruling elite to draft policies that will guarantee social justice and equality for all its citizens without any exception. If such policies are absent, the post-colonial state will continuously be in the state of political cataclysm and recurrent social revolution. This is because the victims of social injustice, which in this case are the oppressed masses, will not fold their arms and watch while their rights are being trampled upon. For as the omniscient narrator in the novel says: 'Justice for the oppressed comes from a sharpened spear' (131).

WORKS CITED

Achebe, Chinua. *The Trouble with Nigeria*. Enugu: Fourth Dimension Publishers, 1983.
Ayer, J. A. *Language, Truth and Logic*. London: Cambridge Studies, 1935.
Aristotle. *The Politics*. Trans. T.A. Sinclair. Harmondsworth: Penguin, 1962.

Fanon, Frantz. *The Wretched of the Earth*. London: Penguin Books, 1978.

Gakwandi, Arthur Shatto. *The Novel and Contemporary Experience in Africa*. London: Heinemann, 1977.

Killam, D.G. *African Writers on African Writing*. London. Heinemann:, 1979.

Kenyatta, Jomo. *Facing Mount Kenya*. London: Heinemann, 1979.

Laurenson and Swingewood. *The Sociology of Literature*. London: Granada Publishing Ltd, 1971.

Ngũgĩ wa Thiong'o. *A Grain of Wheat*. London: Heinemann, 1964.

——. *Homecoming*. London: Heinemann, 1972.

——. *Petals of Blood*. London: Heinemann, 1977.

——. *Devil on the Cross*. London: Heinemann, 1982.

——. *Matigari*. Trans. Wangui wa Goro. Oxford: Heinemann, 1989.

——. *Writers in Politics* [1981]. 2nd Ed. Oxford: James Currey, 1997.

Nkrumah, Kwame. *Africa Must Unite*. London: Panaf, 1963.

Plato. *The Republic*. Trans. I.A Richards. London: Cambridge University Press, 1972.

Smith, Angela. *East African Writing in English*. London: Macmillan Publishers, 1989.

Soyinka, Wole. 'The Writer in a Modern African State'. *The Writer in Modern Africa*, ed. Per Wasberg. New York: Africana, 1969, 14-21.

Williams, Howard et al. (ed.) . *A Reader in International Relations and Political Theory* . Buckingham: Open University Press, 1993.

'Manhood' in Isidore Okpewho's The Last Duty

Authenticity or Accountability?

DEBORAH L. KLEIN

Isidore Okpewho's 1976 novel The Last Duty takes place in a country called Zonda, in the town of Urukpe, a border zone between the Igabo peoples and the Simba peoples. The two ethnic groups formerly lived at peace, to the point of cohabiting the town and even intermarrying. However, civil war has now driven out the Simbians, and the town is occupied by federal troops. Military commander for the past two years, Brigade Major Ali S. Idris takes his duties seriously and seeks not only to safeguard the town from external attack but also to establish, as much as possible, a just and harmonious community within his jurisdiction. He feels 'equally concerned about the safety of civilian lives and the protection of the civil rights of everybody here, no matter what tribe he belongs to' (4). This noble sentiment echoes the ethical stance of the author and contributes to our understanding of the book's title. However, few of the other characters in the story share or even understand Ali's goals. Ali himself fails through short-sightedness. But in understanding his failure, he ultimately succeeds.

I agree on most counts with those who label this a 'tragic' novel. The two characters who most desire justice and a non-tribalistic society seemed fated to fail even before the first page. Their ineffectiveness does not forecast a promising future for Nigeria, as the problems of the present-day nation bear out. That Zonda represents Nigeria and Urukpe a mid-Western town (probably Asaba) during the Nigerian Civil War or Biafran War of Succession, no one disputes. However, too many readers treat the book as merely a sad commentary on the vicissitudes of one particular war and the disappointing internal corruption on both sides. Few question why Okpewho – or any author – bothers to revisit the war or feels moved to point the finger so long after the apparent end of the conflict. The author's own comments on the novel, however, continue to ring as true today as they did decades ago. Okpewho describes the book as 'essentially . . . the tragedy of any civil war: lofty political speeches, declarations, etc., take little notice of the lives of the small people involved in the war, yet have far-reaching effects on their fortunes' (14). If, for 'civil war,' we substitute 'socially unjust situation,' and if we then look carefully at the uses and abuses of power in this story, we find that the tragedy continues far beyond the closing lines of the book, though not utterly without hope of remediation.

Before analysing more closely the term 'duty,' so important within the novel, we need to both summarize the story and to examine two other terms which recur on almost every page: the words 'man' and 'manhood.' To understand what Okpewho means by duty, we must grasp his definition of manhood. In this novel that task means shifting through the perspectives of eight very different characters, some of whose conceptions overlap, none of whom succeed in accomplishing their 'manly' goals.

Many have remarked Okpewho's narrative innovation in this novel, some likening it to William Faulkner's method in *When I Lay Dying*. We have not only eight characters and eight points of view, but we have eight narrative voices. As J. N. Ogu and Catherine O. Acholonu point out, no voice sees itself as a narrator. Rather, each character speaks only to him- or herself, sometimes with self-deception, but never with the intent of communicating to an outsider. Acholonu labels the readers eavesdroppers, even spies (1990: 69). Ogu calls the novel 'an attempt to recreate the whole drama of the civil war in the mouth of the major actors' (1990: 172). To carry this metaphor further, we can view the narrative method as a series of dramatic soliloquies, delivered without the security of a bounded stage, artificial lighting, and a set time limit. Up till now, the tragedy remains unresolved, unending.

Our opening (and concluding) character/speaker is Major Ali. But unlike the Ali of the beginning, Ali at the end possesses vital self-awareness. When the novel starts, Ali has just finished a daytime survey of Urukpe after a night of rebel shelling. The crowd cheers him enthusiastically, and he inwardly congratulates himself. He believes himself successful in both repelling the rebels and reassuring the civilians. 'I have . . . tried to maintain an atmosphere of calm, understanding, and mutual respect – for how should I know what the people are feeling?' (4). Ali's sentiments are immediately undercut, however, by the next speaker, Chief Toje Onovwakpo, a scheming, self-serving, swollen-headed opportunist. Not only does Toje embody his own praise-singer, but he also justifies his immoral actions and intentions. First he boasts, 'I am a big man, and there is no question about it even if I have to say so over and over. . . . if any army commander here knows what's good for him and for his army, he had better get well attached to me' (5). He goes on to rationalize his underhanded removal of his major business rival three years ago: 'I have not hesitated to recommend a citizen here for detention on charges of collaboration with the rebels, and then suborned another citizen to draw up the details of the indictment. For I felt that Mukoro Oshevire stood in my way' (5). Furthermore, since Toje currently struggles with sexual impotency, 'I have not hesitated to seek carnal pleasure with his forlorn wife now that I feel my manhood flawed, my potency questioned. For it seems only in the nature of things that everything possible should be done in the interests of my manhood' (5). After all, 'what town is there that can survive if it becomes known that one of its most pre-eminent citizens has no claims to manhood?' (5).

In just a few paragraphs, Toje reiterates the words 'man' and 'manhood,' leaving no ambiguity as to his meaning. He is not just a man, he is a 'big man'.. He has power, he has prestige, he has privilege. He considers himself no mere citizen of Urukpe but a leader. He even sees the other members of the Council of Elders, including 'our big chief,' the *Otota*, as actually his inferiors. Furthermore, Toje conflates civic and political power with sexual prowess and believes that his impotence not only robs him of his rightful personal manhood but endangers the prestige of the entire community. For Toje, man and manhood equal power, in every conceivable sense, and he only feels responsible for Urukpe in his belief that any diminution of himself will naturally cause suffering and shame for all.

Our next voice is Odibo, Toje's one-handed nephew. Odibo has two arms, but one ends in a stump, and 'Several times [Toje] has told me openly that my crippled hand has affected my brain, and that my body is useless. Well, I suppose he is right. . . . But I only wish he would stop making me feel so unhappy. After all, it isn't my fault that I came into the world crippled in one arm' (8). Odibo, who serves as Toje's messenger boy to Oshevire's 'forlorn wife', shares Toje's definition of manhood. A man has a whole, flawless body, and with such physical abilities he also exercises power. Strong body equals strong mind equals strong influence. In Odibo's first meditation, seeing himself as lacking in all these areas, he does not use the word 'man' at all.

We next meet Aku, the lonely wife, and her four-year-old son Oghenovo. Aku's definition of manhood overlaps that of Toje and Odibo but goes further. She wonders if she should have left Urukpe when most of her tribesmen fled, for though married to a 'son of the soil', she is a Simba woman, now hated and suspect in her husband's absence. She never anticipated his detention. She 'was sticking with my man because I couldn't conceive of any kind of existence other than with him. . . . it was enough that my man was around, and . . . it was all right for me so long as he was by my side' (11). Now that he has been taken away, 'hostile eyes assail me from all sides' and if not 'for the goodness of the federal army commander here, . . . where would I be today?' (11) No one buys from her market stall any more, few want to sell to her. And now she senses a new threat: 'For several months now Toje has shown us kindness. He has continued to buy clothes, food and other necessities for us, and to give me money from time to time' (12).

Aku does not believe that the old chief acts out of dispassionate kindness. 'I am not a child, and I cannot deceive myself. I know what Toje wants of me. . . . My husband is the first and only man ever to have known my body . . . I can tell what's at the back of a man's mind as he scans a woman's body with his eyes. I can read Toje's eyes, and I can feel the message of his breath as he stands close to me' (12). She determines to remain faithful to her husband, and she tells Oghenovo that all the gifts delivered by Odibo come from 'his father who is away on a journey' (13), yet she does accept the gifts. No alternative occurs to her. Aku, like Toje and Odibo, equates manhood with sexual relations, even though she also sees manhood in terms of character. A true man provides companionship and protection. A man loves and provides for his family.

Little Oghenovo sees few men in his life. The boy believes what his mother says of his father. But he does not even remember Oshevire, Odibo comes and goes, but mostly the men he sees are soldiers. He keeps repeating, as his mother has told him, 'my father is a good man,' but he has no concept of goodness, except that a good man is not a thief. From scraps of wood, he fashions little guns, thinking that a real man has strength and power, like the soldiers he watches. A real man fires a very loud weapon. All of his young life he has lived in the shadow of war, and so for this child fighting defines manhood. He will beat, even shoot (139), his friend Onome for falsely accusing his father, and he will use his little gun to defend his mother from people who make her cry. Manhood equals not just power, but violent power.

Although ever-present in the minds of Aku, Toje, and Oghenovo, and increasingly of concern to Ali, Mukoro Oshevire spends most of the novel in detention at Iddu, one hundred miles away from Urukpe, and we see only glimpses of him. When the federal government, however, decides to hold a tribunal at Iddu, Toje fears that despite his best-laid plans, Oshevire just might obtain his freedom. This possibility means that Toje must rush his seduction of Aku, for her husband cannot return to Urukpe to find her faithful and unsoiled. A newspaper commentary on the tribunal unflinchingly condemns men like Toje:

> It seems clear that certain individuals are using the opportunity presented by the tribunal to settle old scores and to practise new vices which are in no way related to this struggle which the government has been forced to engage in for the unity of our country. . . . No useful purpose can be served by keeping in detention citizens of this country, whatever their tribes of origin, who are merely the victims of vindictive and unpatriotic informers . . . (30)

Instead of taking this denunciation to heart, Toje further justifies himself, accusing the newspaper writer of conniving '[a]gainst the wishes of honourable men like me' (31).

After all, when he first laid his charges against Oshevire to the previous military commander, Major Bello 'rightly reckoned that a man of my stature would not stand up to make a frivolous charge against another citizen' (31). By his position as a big man in the village, all of Toje's actions and intentions are, of course, honourable. Honour, in Toje's world, has nothing to do with morality. It totally relates to pride of place. Honour even includes doing exactly as the papers have charged: 'All that concerns me is that Mukoro Oshevire stays in detention. Long enough . . . [that] I can in safer circumstances establish a commercial lead in the rubber business too comfortable to be threatened by him.' And of course '[l]ong enough for me to be able to use his wife to prove that I still possess that power which I am sure lies within me' (32).

At long last, Okpewho introduces us to Oshevire himself. The innocent detainee defines manhood in a way that Toje, Odibo, Oghenovo, perhaps even Aku cannot understand, and he seems to speak Okpewho's own position – at least initially. 'I don't know what I'm doing here,' he begins. 'But I don't care. The important thing is to be able to stand up to the situation and bear it all like a man' (32). In Oshevire's mind, manhood has to do with truth and honesty and justice. Even if a man dies unjustly, his 'honesty towers tall and superior above everything, like a wild palm, tough and upright' (33). He laughs at the charges against him: collaborating with the Simbian rebels. 'If saving a life means collaborating with the rebels, then that indeed I did. If pointing the way of safety to a little boy . . . fleeing in helpless frenzy ahead of a wild mob . . . I say, if showing the way of safety to a fellow human being means collaborating with the rebels, then of course I am guilty of that. And I am proud to be guilty' (33). Obviously, although he never uses the term, Oshevire considers himself a truly honourable man.

Not only does Oshevire's sense of honour require that he save the life of a boy, any boy, regardless of ethnicity, it also demands that he face his accusers stoically: 'I will go down fighting. Stand up and take it all like a man, I have said to myself.' Echoing the famous declaration of Martin Luther, he says, 'By that resolve I stand' (35). Furthermore, he examines his conscience of all prior actions, and much like Job of the Bible, he exonerates himself. He has never 'sought after another man's wife', he has never – as we know Toje has done – adulterated his latex, he has striven consistently for '[f]air play, honesty, integrity – they have guided my life' (35). And so he faces judges he considers both important and intelligent without fear. 'Stand up to it all like a man. Nothing will move me from that resolve' (36). When another, younger detainee causes a disruption, Oshevire exchanges smiles with a fellow he considers his equal. '[W]e have just looked at each other . . . as a way of seeking reassurance from each other that we will live up to our manhood, whatever happens. . . . God sees through to my conscience. Need I then feel or act otherwise than in accordance with the dictates of a clear conscience and just manhood?' (42). Yes, in a sense, manhood still has to do with power, but it has more to do with the use of strength to defend the helpless and to stand up against injustice. A man does not fear even a mob.

Two other characters make brief appearances in the novel, and their observations round out the conception of manhood in the community of Urukpe. The first of these, Eustace Palmer in his 2008 article on Okpewho calls a 'sadistic soldier' (44). While Okumagba certainly does not come across sympathetically, calling him a sadist may constitute overstatement. To return to the metaphor of novel-as-drama, Okumagba functions much like the chorus of a classical Greek play. Ali seeks out as Aku's protector some soldier from his own command 'who comes from this town' (56). When Ali questions the soldier, at first Okumagba evinces pride, but when asked about Oshevire and his wife, he voices the suspicions and prejudices of the community. How does he know that Oshevire is indeed guilty of collaborating with the enemy? 'Everybody in this town knows that, sir' (57). Likewise, of Aku, he agrees that some may wish her harm, but after all, she deserves it: 'Maybe they will do something, maybe they won't. I can't say, sir. But she is a rebel' (58). He represents the position of the common man of Urukpe. Despite this attitude, Ali assigns Okumagba the duty of officially protecting Aku, from a distance.

Okumagba of course does not defy his commander, but he highly resents his assignment. 'Only the consequences of such an action deter me from sticking the barrel of my gun through the window and blasting the brains clean out of that woman and her child. For that is what they deserve, like all rebels' (130). He even plots to use the next air raid as a cover to do exactly that, though when the opportunity presents itself, he cares too much about saving his own neck to act on his intentions (199ff). He meanwhile watches 'the cripple Odibo' (132) coming and going and questions Aku's faithfulness to her husband. He will be an obedient though reluctant soldier. 'But the trouble with the Major is,' he thinks, 'he is crazy. He doesn't know anything. Besides, he a stranger from up-country and he doesn't understand our people down here' (132).

We see Okumagba motivated not so much by innate cruelty as by the ethnocentric attitudes of Urukpe. Yes, he fights on the federal side. But he does not and seemingly cannot internalize the slogan, 'To keep Zonda one is a task that must be done.' Emmanuel Obiechina sees this soldier as 'a simple man imbued with the prejudices of the ordinary people of his town' (1993: 269), prejudices that undermine the development of any sense of national identity. Chidi Amuta misreads this aspect of Okpewho's narrative style, accusing the writer of ignoring 'the social and historical setting' and focusing excessively on individualism (1984: 97). On the contrary, an important point by Okpewho is that most of the individuals fail to see the larger national setting in which their personal dramas play out. Their narrow-mindedness, not Okpewho's, creates the tragedy of the novel. As the late Chinua Achebe notes about the period leading up to the Nigerian-Biafran War,

> The social malaise in Nigerian society was political corruption. The structure of the country was such that there was an inbuilt power struggle among the ethnic groups, and of course those who were in power wanted to stay in power. The easiest and simplest way to retain it, even in a limited area, was to appeal to tribal sentiments . . . (2012: 51)

While Toje demonstrates this attitude most overtly, he could not succeed in his corrupt empire-building did not 'little' men like Okumagba share his provincial view.

The final character to whom Okpewho introduces us we meet only once, and in one role, he serves as a brief and welcome interlude of comic relief. At the same time, Emuakpor the herbalist also represents an older, more noble tradition of viewing manhood. To him, Toje is only 'a cock shorn of his comb' (164), a 'mischievous little man' (165), even a 'boy' (166). While he claims to his face that curing Toje of a sexually transmitted disease temporarily made the chief 'a whole man again' (166), he really looks down on his client: 'I have always said that money makes a fool of a wise man. And some of the men we have around here don't strike me as the best example of wisdom. Look at a man like Toje. . . . he is too full of himself to accept any kind of handicap' (169). And so he gives the impotent man a medicine of which the chief ingredient is sheep's dung, a stinking, stinging preparation which he instructs Toje to apply to his afflicted 'manhood' every evening at bedtime and whenever he lies with a woman (174-5). If we accept the oral wisdom of Emuakpor, then we can laugh at Toje and his posturing. A man does not strut and preen and have to remind everyone of his worth. A real man puts his people and their welfare ahead of himself. He also holds to certain moral ethics, like marital faithfulness. The old values do not hold, however, in this modern situation, and attitudes like Toje's have passed from laughable to dangerous. Emuakpor's attempt to humble and reform the 'little man' comes as too little too late.

The novel takes a surprise turn when Odibo rebels against Toje's domination. One evening, after Aku has left the house to meet Toje – as commanded, and he remains in her stead to watch over Oghenovo – as commanded, he thinks seditiously, 'I cannot be fooled any more. I may have too little sense or ability to help myself, but I am certainly not a child and I cannot be fooled' (139).

Then he dares to determine, 'One day I shall be able to stand on my two feet, and I will no longer have to be at anyone's mercy or be made to suffer disgrace in front of a woman. Someday I shall find something to do, and I may yet be my own man' (139). His 'one day' arrives sooner than expected, due to the combined effects of Toje's frustrating groping of Aku, his keeping her out past curfew, and a Simbian air raid. All of these circumstances force Odibo to twice stay the night at Aku's house.

The first time, Aku wakes in the semi-darkness to find Odibo standing by her bed, observing and inhaling the scents of her body. The second time, she allows him to see her completely naked, and when he starts to leave the room, she grabs first his body, then specifically his 'member' (181). Odibo, surprised but more than willing, 'fell upon her lap and knew desire' (181). The next morning, he experiences an epiphany. 'Now I know that I am a man like any other man. I have desires that should be satisfied, impulses that should be realized, and my big strong body is no longer there for nothing . . . Now when Toje calls me a useless man I am simply going to swallow his words without a care' (179-80). He feels that he has gotten his revenge against Toje and that should Toje ever learn of his actions and threaten him, he will reveal Toje's own plotting to the entire town. Meanwhile, he plans to stop playing Toje's 'boy' and find some kind of meaningful employment for himself: 'The war is still here, and many of the old chances of paid labour are now closed. But as I reflected further, a few places came to mind. . . . I knew life was not easy for a man with one arm, but it certainly wasn't hopeless. God was sure to lend a hand at some point' (182-3).

With heartbreaking irony here, Okpewho presents glory and disgrace simultaneously. On the one hand, we rejoice to find Odibo triumphant, Odibo exulting and freed of humiliating servitude. An oppressed man has shaken off his bonds. We have here one of the few overtly happy scenes in the novel. On the other hand, Odibo's victory comes at the cost of Aku's marital virtue, and for that he gives credit and praise to God. As V. U. Ola observes, 'Odibo's hour of victory is Toje's and Aku's hour of failure' (67). Furthermore, as Palmer notes, while Odibo loves the pleasures of Aku's body, he does not seem to love the woman herself. When Toje discovers the couple together in Odibo's room a few days later, Odibo thinks only about proving his superiority over Toje. Aku weeps and begs to go home, but he speaks harshly to her and forces her to stay. In part, he knows that if she leaves and Toje catches her alone, she will probably die, but

> Odibo is not the tender chivalrous lover; he is a traditional man who has just discovered his manhood and power and feels that it is consistent with that manhood to be brusque, sharp, and authoritative with a woman. Taking his cue from Toje, his concept of manhood had included sexual prowess and physical strength, not honor or gentleness. (Palmer 2008: 54-5)

With no surprise then, we learn a few pages later that Toje returns to Odibo's house with a machet, and the two men fight until both collapse on the floor. Aku, forced to witness the vicious combat, finally 'could no longer stand it all – the sight of two groaning and gasping men, and all that pool of blood. So I ran – ran – ' (217). Though many readers assume that either both men have killed each other or that at least Odibo has killed Toje, Okpewho leaves their fates hanging. We know only that Okumagba has brought Aku and her son the barracks, that a crowd outside demands the death of 'the rebel woman', and that Ali has had both men treated by the military doctor and then sent 'to the hospital at Okujere, fifteen miles away' (218).

Two more ironic twists remain to the story. The first concerns Oshevire. Despite Toje's hiring of a false witness against him and Toje's own attempts to directly intervene, the tribunal declares Oshevire an innocent man and sets him free. Okpewho does not give us a definitive time frame, but it appears that the detained man gains his freedom about the same time Aku surrenders to temptation. Oshevire has worried about his family: 'what hope of protection can there be for a woman and child deprived of the presence and security of a man and exposed to the resentment of a whole population?' (156). He tells himself that 'I know what women are, but I also know my woman,' and she would never 'submit her honor' to another man (156). But he has no way to contact her, no way to comfort her, no way to inform her of his impending arrival. During Oshevire's arduous journey home, Toje and Odibo enact their personal civil war, and by the time Oshevire actually reaches Urukpe, he finds his wife and son not in their home but within the federal army barracks. Instead of a joyous family reunion, he meets a woman who throws herself at his feet, weeping hysterically, and a little boy who shrinks away from his gaze (229).

In private, Ali explains the situation as he understands it, and at first it seems that Oshevire will uphold the ideals of compassion and justice he has espoused throughout the book. He determines that he will not remove his family from Urukpe, regardless of others' opinions: 'why should I tremble when small men here, people whom I know only too well, try to threaten the life of my family?' (236). He correctly infers the true culprit in this calamity: 'I don't think I would be far wrong to say that Toje Onovwakpo had a good hand in all that has been happening' (237). Yet when he thinks a bit longer, his pride overrules his principles. He falls back upon an inferior perception of manhood:

> But if she has allowed herself to be put to such unworthy use by two men, whatever the predicament that she found herself in, what else is there but a strong likelihood that right now she is bearing within her bosom the seed of such vile communion? And what man would choose to be alive to face every day the ill-conceived fruit of shame? (238)

Olu accuses Oshevire of hubris here. He never doubts 'the justness of his [own] cause' but he also 'fails to take cognizance of human frailty. He therefore refuses to forgive his wife' (1983: 67-8). Obiechina agrees that Oshevire 'fails to take into account the nature of the temptations to which [Aku] is exposed and the pressures that break her in her loneliness' (270). In the end, concludes Palmer, Oshevire 'shows . . . that he cannot really bear it all 'like a man'.' He loses his nerve' (50). I agree with Palmer's sad assessment that Oshevire's 'male pride, his sense of reputation. . . is affronted, and he thus moves significantly away from his early conception of manhood . . . Oshevire refuses to face up to the truth and lacks the courage to accept the totality of the situation' (51). We have noted earlier how Okpewho values courage as an essential trait of manhood.

The penultimate speaker, Oghenovo, tells how his family left the military compound and returned to their home, where Oshevire poured petrol throughout every room and set the house on fire. The family now walks through the dark night, past the hours of curfew, beyond the borders of Urukpe, and whenever the boy turns to view 'the big fire', his mother forces him to face forward and keep walking. He decides, 'I do not like my father because he will not let me sleep and my mother is crying and my father has set fire to our house.' Taking all of this together, he now concludes, 'my father is not a good man' (241). No, 'I do not like my father and I don't think he is a good man' (242). At this point, someone on border patrol orders the family to stop, and Aku obeys. Oshevire, however, whether out of pride, stubbornness, or self-imposed deafness, keeps walking. As Oghenovo grips his mother's hand, gunshots growl out twice, and something drops to the ground. Aku falls to her knees, weeping, and the boy watches the cat-like eyes of a soldier in the bush. The story ends here, except for a concluding paragraph from Ali.

A chastened Ali, relieved of duty and awaiting his successor, acknowledges that his pride led him to misread people, to misinterpret important clues, and to grossly misjudge character. And in his honesty he recognizes that given the opportunity to relive these last two years, 'I'd make the same mistakes all over!' (243). His situation, even his newly-gained self-insight, provides Okpewho's final ironic touch.

Early in the story, Ali executes a soldier whose situation mirrors and foreshadows the triangle of Aku, Toje, and Odibo. In this case, a private who 'loves' a girl of the town discovers her in flagrante with his sergeant and shoots the lovers dead. Of course Ali must discipline the military infraction of killing one's senior officer, but he also thinks that his handling of the incident will give the townspeople a greater sense of protection and security. Instead, people's fear of the military increases. Despite Ali's early acknowledgment that he does not really understand the mindset of Urukpe, we do not see him going to anyone for advice – except Toje, the one person of all the townsfolk he should least believe. After the execution, 'as I was being driven home, I sat pondering the unglamorous grandeur of justice and bounden duty' (23).

Even when doubts about Toje creep in, Ali dismisses them. He listens to Toje's arguments against acting on Aku's behalf, wanting to believe that Toje really helps and protects the woman. At the time Ali feels 'torn between duty and deference to a noble heart' (51). Toje's words don't quite ring true, but 'I was sure the Chief was an honourable man' (55). At the same time, 'I could not fight the feeling that I was taking a chance. What if there was something in all this? . . . For how much goodwill could the Chief have felt towards her, if he felt so badly about her husband's role during the rebel occupation . . . ?' Furthermore, it bothers Ali that Toje urgently 'objected to my taking the woman into protective custody, when if he really cared for her welfare he should have been sure that she could count on no better safeguard against the town's thirst for vengeance' (56). To soothe his conflicted conscience, he then orders Okumagba to guard Aku, obviously not understanding the extent of this young man's true feelings either.

When everything comes out in the end, Ali berates himself:

> How could I have known that by giving the woman freedom and protection I was only exposing her to this sort of exploitation and making her the target of a rotten relationship? . . . [H]ow could I have guessed that a man of Chief Toje's calibre, a man I continued to respect in spite of everything, was going to take advantage of the trust . . . ? Perhaps I should have known . . . that such a woman had too little chance of living a normal life whatever assurances and protections I tried to give her. I should have known . . . (219)

Palmer faults Ali as overly 'self-satisfied', 'rather deluded', and 'liable to misunderstand the significance of events and to overestimate his own importance' (56), as having a too 'limited range of vision' (48-9). But considering his age and inexperience, how could he have known? Who did he have to advise him? Perhaps had he known about Emuakpor, he could have gained wisdom from the seer? But how would someone not of Urukpe know of such a man? And even if Ali found him, who would have served as a reliable translator between the two men? Left unguided, operating under his own noble but naïve sense of honor, Ali has, through the very actions intended to prevent the novel's tragedy, only abetted it. Like Oedipus, every step he takes to avert disaster accelerates it. Yet what else could he have done?

In a sense, however, Ali's failure completes his growth into true manhood. The one essential trait he has lacked, he finally gains: humility. No, he did not succeed at protecting all those he so tried to aid. No, he has no power to change the hearts or minds of his commanding officers. But he does now recognize his blindness, his self-deceptions, and unlike Oedipus, he accepts he own weakness. A true man now, he has the power to stand tall even in understanding his lack of power.

Thus we return to Okpewho's own words about the novel. 'Why that title *The Last Duty*? Basically because the story makes the point that a man's ultimate concern, his 'last duty', is to his conscience – his deep human conviction of what he *must* do in accordance with the dictates of his manhood or his sense of justice' (14). As we have seen, most of the characters, even Oshevire, fall short of fulfilling that duty. Their pride, their fear, their desperation, turns them aside from their sense of duty. Ali alone stands firm to the end, acknowledging his failures and shortcomings, and thereby maintaining his sense of honor and duty, an honor Oshevire has lost, a duty which he defaults. Unappreciated by the federal government which he represents, Ali still holds to his integrity.

What, then, for Okpewho, constitutes true manhood? How does he define justice? And how does this message continue to resonate today?

Chinyere Nwahunanya argues that of all the characters only 'Major Ali's sympathetic understanding of Aku's position is isolated for applause' (1987: 55). For him Ali 'stands morally upright in such a trying situation where he could easily have pawned has conscience' (55). Likewise, to Obiechina, Ali 'is imbrued with the vision of the nation as a civic society with obligations to guarantee the security of every person' (1993: 271). Ali fails to some extent less because of personal limitations than because, as Koku Amuzu points out, the concept of war is inherently antithetical to the concept of justice. Amuzu argues that this book gives 'an account of the way in which one individual seizes upon the opportunities the war has created for evil, and by using his social position, influence, and money, turns virtues of innocent individuals into evil tools with which he subverts the moral foundations of his society' (2004: 193). By the end of the book, 'the sense of futility which now burdens us is, in truth, the nihilism of war' (196).

Ola agrees that for Okpewho, the matter of concern is not the specific politics of a particular war but rather 'the human and emotional dimensions of war – broken homes, the fate of widows and widowers, marital infidelity, the sufferings of orphans, even insanity and general moral decadence' (65). Nwahunanya adds that for Okpewho, war opens the door for 'power-profiteering, witch-hunting and the exploitation of the weak by the strong' (54). Within a war situation, Ogu points out, the 'violation of basic human relationships is both the cause and symptom of the more general social corruption brought about by the war. . . . truth goes unbelieved, civilized society becomes impossible and the sanctity of bonds disintegrates' (1990: 174-5). As Ogu rightly concludes (176), a major question of the novel is not whether or not we should consider Oshevire a 'saboteur,' but rather, in such a topsy-turvy setting, how should we define 'saboteur' in the first place?

In other words, while everyone agrees in labeling Toje a villain, Okpewho does not merely show us how villainy thrives in war-time. *The Last Duty* really argues that people like Toje, exploitive managers of power and authority with warped definitions of manhood, create the social settings which engender war and lack of justice. Obiechina argues, and I agree, that for Okpewho 'there cannot be true national stability without justice, and there cannot be justice without a broad enough vision that transcends the narrow limits of each individual's ethnic loyalties' (1993: 271). While many insist that ethnic narrow-mindedness has now given way to sheer corruption in Nigeria and that all the corrupt politicians share in parceling out choice slices of 'the national pie,' regardless of ethnicity, Achebe argues that 'Corruption in Nigeria has grown because it is highly encouraged' (2012: 249). The federal government, he insists, 'has turned a blind eye to waves of ferocious and savage massacres of its citizens – mainly Christian Southerners; mostly Igbos or indigenes of the Middle Belt,' and this attitude has 'doomed' Nigeria to 'endless cycles of inter-ethnic, inter-religious violence' (251). He believes that the original coup 'of January 15, 1966, is something Nigeria has never really recovered from' (65) and that the government which resulted 'has had the effect of destroying the basic mutual trust and confidence among the people . . . and has created the decentralization to the Nigerian people into tribal groups. This action . . . has had the greatest effect on the dismemberment of Nigeria' (261).

Sadly, as we have seen, few of the characters possess the needed 'broad enough vision' (Obiechina 271) to see past their personal desires and the prejudices of their communities. Emuakpor understands the destructive effect of someone like Toje but cannot shame him into better behaviour. Aku chooses to stay with her husband rather than her people, but she lacks the fortitude to ignore her own physical desires. Oghenovo remains too young for us to determine the position he will hold, but if federal soldiers have killed his father, he seems unlikely to embrace the national identity such men represent. Oshevire, like his wife, sees beyond ethnicity to personhood, but his insulted pride will not let him show Aku the same compassion he once showed a hounded boy. Toje, Odibo, and Okumagba embrace the prejudices of their Igabo people, attitudes which include taking pride in their ability to control and even injure others. Only Ali maintains his high vision, even if the federation, it seems, has no role for men like him. Okpewho would discover more Alis, men who see beyond both the limits of their particular ethnicities and the self-blinding delusions of their own hearts and reason.

The book gives us a chilling prophecy. Whether or not Nigeria faces another civil war, the nation seems doomed to fall apart. Injustice and narrow-mindedness prevail, and no one, however well-intentioned can establish equity or unity. Considering current events in the nation, we cannot call such myopia a problem of the distant past. Only if readers heed the warnings of Okpewho and other writers can we hope to see an end to the abuse of power in the name of manhood.

WORKS CITED

Achebe, Chinua. *There Was a Country: A Personal History of Biafra*. New York: Penguin, 2012.

Acholonu, Catherine O. 'Upthrust or Downthrust? Technique in Okpewho's *The Last Duty* and Iyayi's *Violence*.' *Black Culture and Black Consciousness in Literature*. Eds, Ernest Emenyonu, et al. Ibadan: Heinemann, 1990: 69-70.

Amuta, Chidi. 'Ideology and Form in the Contemporary Nigerian Novel.' *Commonwealth Essays and Studies* 7.1 (Autumn 1984): 94-105.

Amuzu, Koku. 'The Nigerian War Novel.' *An Introduction to the African Prose Narrative*. Ed. Lokangaka Losambe. Trenton, NJ: Africa World Press, 2004: 184-98.

Nwahunanya, Chinyere. 'Nigerian Literature and the Search for Socio-Political Alternatives: The Relevance of Nigerian War Fiction.' *Nigeria Magazine* 55.2 (1987): 50-55.

Obiechina, Emmanuel. 'Isidore Okpewho.' *Dictionary of Literary Biography. Vol. 157. Twentieth Century Caribbean and Black African Writers*. 3rd Ser. Eds, Bernth Lindfors and Reinhard Sander. Detroit: Gale, 1993: 262-276.

Ogu, J. N. 'Literature and Truth: The Epistemological Imagination of Okpewho in *The Last Duty*.' *Literature and Black Aesthetics*. Eds, Ernest Emenyonu, et al. Ibadan: Heinemann, 1990: 169-76.

Okpewho, Isidore. *The Last Duty*. Burnt Mill, Harlow: Longman, 1976.

—— 'The Last Duty.' *African Arts* 6.2 (Winter 1973): 14-15, 70-77.

Olu, V. U. 'Identity Crisis in the Tragic Novels of Isidore Okpewho.' *African Literature Today* 13 (1983): 56-68.

Palmer, Eustace. 'Isidore Okpewho: *The Last Duty*.' *Of War and Women, Oppression and Optimism: New Essays on the African Novel*. Trenton, NJ: Africa World Press, 2008: 43-58.

Remembering Kofi Awoonor

13 March 1935–21 September 2013

Kofi Awoonor
In Retrospect

KOFI ANYIDOHO

Rediscovery and Other Poems, Kofi Awoonor's first collection of poems, was published in 1964 by Mbari Press in Ibadan, Nigeria. By a significant coincidence, *The Promise of Hope: New and Selected Poems, 1964–2013,* is being released in 2014 by University of Nebraska Press, the first publication in the African Poetry Book Series. In many ways, the new collection offers a unique opportunity for critical retrospection, a backward glance over a half century of Awoonor's distinguished career as a Guardian of the Sacred Word.

The collection opens with poems that point us in two directions, to a reconciled past and to a future of new challenges and new possibilities. First, to a past where we meet poet and country, young as the new moon and filled with hope and the promise of hope. We see in that past many memorials of struggle, inviting a stroll across a landscape of birds and flowers strewn with graveyards. But we walk arm in arm with the poet, with little fear of mortality. We hold our breath as the poet looks across a new dawn and introduces us to Death holding out his own 'inimitable calling card' only to be ushered into

a homestead
resurrected with laughter and dance
and the festival of the meat

of the young lamb and the red porridge
of the new corn.

Here is a constant return to old familiar themes and subjects and
the need to postpone dying 'until the morning after freedom.' So
we find in 'To Feed Our People' a gentle plea with the pallbearers
and mourners to hold back, just a little bit, while the poet persona
attends to a few outstanding concerns:

> I still have to meet the morning dew
> a poem to write
> a field to hoe
> a lover to touch
> and some consoling to do
> I have to go [to India] and meet the sunset.

Above all, we must join the poet in 'herding the lost lambs home.'
Only then can we pass on to a deserved ancestorhood. The final
lines of this particular poem sum up probably the most important
concern at the core of Awoonor's poetry, from the earliest to the
latest in a long distinguished career: the duty we owe to our
country, our people:

> When the final night falls on us
> as it fell upon our parents,
> we shall retire to our modest home
> earth-sure, secure
> that we have done our duty
> by our people;
> we met the challenge of history
> and were not afraid.

Despite the bold assertion in the last two lines, we find in his
most recent collection, 'Herding the Lost Lambs,'[1] a constant return
of the funeral mood and voice so typical of the early Awoonor. As
the poet himself acknowledges in 'What More Can I Give?'

> I did not know it will return
> this crushing urge to sing
> only sorrow songs;
> the urge to visit again
> the last recesses of pain.

However, it is important to note a fundamental difference between the funereal voice and mood in these last poems and what we find in the early ones. These are not typical songs of sorrow. Rather, they demonstrate a mature reflection on life, a philosophical balance sheet carefully drawn to weigh life's gains and losses, with the final balance showing an impressive credit in favor of hope and the promise of hope. Through the thin mist of doubt, of uncertainty, we can see 'a new beginning' in almost all the recent poems, as in 'Up in the Garden,' where in spite of tears that are still wet, the poet gathers 'the courage of cobras' and surges on relentless, 'each chronicle renewed/ each earth reclaimed/ each hope refurbished.' His final victory, he assures us, 'shall be recorded on a tombstone to be designed by my sons.'

It is indeed, more than mere coincidence, that the first two poems in 'Herding the Lost Lambs' are dedicated to Kekeli, the poet's youngest child, who arrived 'one October day' 'large-eyed, replica of the first/ princess, and now the prince.' The coming of Kekeli signals a victory over age and thoughts of death, a transformation of the long night of shadows into the light of a new day. Kekeli in Ewe means 'light,' hence the title of the first poem in the collection: 'The Light is On.'

From the very beginning of a half-century career in the service of poetry, increasingly and indeed persistently, Awoonor takes us beyond the grave into the land of ancestors. With the earliest poems, especially in 'Song of Sorrow,' the ancestors are called to order and even accused of neglecting homestead and offspring. The poet sends a direct query to Kpeti, Kove, and Nyidevu – all personal ancestral figures – asking why they idle there in Awlime while their offspring suffer and 'eat sand' here in Kodzogbe, surrounded by termite-eaten fence, with strangers walking arrogantly over the homestead. This kind of negative homage is not unlike what we find in many traditional Ewe libation texts, where the ancestors are often reminded of the obligation they owe to the living, that if they expect their offspring to honor them with sacrifices and success in life, then they owe it to themselves that their offspring are blessed with long life, *with good health,* and of course some wealth.

Over the years, however, Awoonor's homage 'to those gone ahead' has taken on much more positive and indeed laudatory attributes. Many poems invoke ancestral figures as a source of countless blessings and renewal of hope. And there are also the many poems dedicated to comrades in struggle who fell too soon, but whose memorials are the best testimony to a life led with profit, a life devoted to the resurrection of the best dreams of society. It is significant that *The Latin American and Caribbean Notebook* (1992) opens with the poem 'In Memoriam,' with its 'single line honor roll':

> For friends gone ahead; Joe de Graft, Ellis Komey, Paa Keyper, Camera Laye, Chris Okigbo, Alex La Guma, Robert Serumaga, and Geombeyi Adali-Mortty, all the Brothers who sang our song, and went home to the ancestors.

The poet's invocation of these comrades fallen in struggle ends with a promise of hope:

> we shall build the new cities
> over your bones,
> that your mortuaries shall become the birthplace,
> that our land and people
> shall rise again
> from the ashes of your articulate sacrifices!

Some of the comrades mentioned here were already listed among a long line of fellow writers celebrated in the earlier longer poem in homage to a leader among Awoonor's generation of activist writers, Ezekiel Mphahlele, in the poem 'For Ezeki,' published in *Until the Morning After*. The poem celebrates Mphahlele's courage in his decision to return home to an apartheid South Africa, even against a storm of protests from friends and comrades. Somehow, the poem manages to convey the long-exiled combatant's conviction that it was time to return home, that even as his own life was drawing to a close, he could feel the inevitable logic of struggle overtaking the arrogance of apartheid. At any rate, beyond apartheid, the call of home is a primal necessity:

> So you went home Zeke
> to seek memories along the goat paths, home
> to those lingering shrubs of childhood
> denuded by exile tears.

The need to return home to the soil that gave us birth is a mandate of nature we cannot deny: 'We say / the snake that dies on the tree / returns home to earth.'

Another homage poem of special significance is 'In Memoriam: Return to Kingston.' Unlike 'For Ezeki,' 'In Memoriam' is dedicated, not to a comrade still alive and staging heroic struggle against oppression, but to a lifelong comrade and brother now 'gone like the furious wind of the hurricane mouth,' Neville Dawes. Those of us who have had the privilege of listening to Awoonor speak again and again with love and deep respect for Neville Dawes understand why the poet had to travel all the way from Africa to Kingston, to be present at Neville's 'furious homegoing,' and why the poet grieves so much over this brother's death, and why, ultimately, his lamentation becomes a celebration. We note that Awoonor's novel *Comes the Voyager at Last* is dedicated, among other 'extended family members of Babylon,' to 'the memory of my brother and comrade Neville Augustus Dawes who revealed to me the miracle of story time, and gave us hope for liberation.'

In many ways, this relatively long poem becomes a series of snapshots of countless times spent together in combat as in revelry, in fields of struggle and in memorial halls of fragile victory, recollections of significant stages of a long journey from

> slums and cold tenements
> on urine-wet floors of tram-ways
> . . . .
> across snowfields
> fired on storm nights of blazing friendless territories of exile
> and exile tears.
> We hear the poet weep anew 'for historical follies I could not shed,' but
> soon, we watch him smile in memory of toasts drank 'to struggle with
> the people' and of
> meals we shared
> at early sunset or sunrise
> in smoke-filled rooms redolent with conspiracy
>   and strategies.

At final countdown, we are not surprised to witness 'the doors of Babylon closed again' this time behind the poet and his comrade and brother, 'with Neville and I on the freedom train, / going home, yes, going home.'

As we step back in time from one collection of poems to the preceding ones, we find a constant return to and variations on old themes, but we also follow the poet on a return voyage away from those narrow shores of childhood into an expanding universe of exciting vistas of new and newer worlds, each with its own agonies, its own fields of sorrow giving way to monuments of struggle and victory and promise, each new world with its own history of endless human possibilities. Once, we listened to the poet as he heard a bird cry again and again in agony over fallen homesteads of his birthplace. Now we follow the poet and eavesdrop on his jubilant songs as he imitates the joyous calls of mating birds on that almost mythical Isla de Juventad, the Cuban Isle of Youth.

The Latin American and Caribbean Notebook occupies a unique place in all of Awoonor's collections of poetry. Written during and out of the poet's sojourn in Brazil and later Cuba as Ghana's ambassador, these poems bring us farthest away from homestead and country only for us to discover that our steps are constantly treading not only new and unfamiliar territory but also replicas of ancestral grounds filled with memories of historical injustices and monuments of struggle. Some of the faces we encounter in the streets of Montevideo, Rio de Janeiro, Kingston, and Havana could have been those kinsmen and women back home long gone into the shadows.

Another early fruit in Awoonor's garden of poetic delights that matures into full bloom in *The Latin American and Caribbean Notebook* is the poet's constant dwelling on images drawn from nature – his constant reference to specific animals, birds, trees, flowers, rivers, and above all, the lagoon and the sea, the land, the soil. If ever we are invited to a festival, it is most certain to be the festival of the new corn, ripened with golden rays of the sun and mellowed with the silvery shine of the moon and stars. Most of our journeys are over the land, not on highways or boulevards, but on bush paths through thorn fields, with occasional stretches of salt flats and flower fields. Sometimes, we journey by sea, by lagoon and river, often in leaky boats. But the boatman and oarsman are unfailing dependable, their gaze on a final destination constant. Even when the boatman happens to be Kutsiami, Death himself, we have no fear of disaster, knowing that we will land safely on a shore bustling with familiar ancestral faces, a welcome festival waiting for our safe return home.

The abundance of images of nature we find in *The Latin American and Caribbean Notebook* may have been reinforced by the fact that Awoonor's childhood love of nature found fulfillment in the wonderful opportunity to pursue his old hobby of hunting, especially in Cuba, that magical island with a landscape that inspires even as it intimidates with relentless hurricane seasons. But we note as well that even from prison, that house by the sea, Awoonor's poetic imagination is on constant lookout for snatches of nature's reassuring presence as he peeps through the tiny window and catches the swift flight of a seagull, or the sun's rays retreating beyond the horizon only to give way to the a rising moon, even if only a half moon. Wherever we look in his poetry, Awoonor's love of nature is constant and provides occasion for some of his loftiest poetic statements. But this deep love of nature is always connected to a deeper love for social justice:

> I know a paradise
> when I come into one
> of an evening over a hill
> on an island
> when mountains crouch like lions
> and rivers are threads
> soaked in the hero's blood
> deep dyed in many tears. ('The Hero's Blood')

And if the poet is never incapacitated by thoughts of Death, it is because he knows for certain that 'where the worm eats / a grain grows' ('Across a New Death'). The promise of hope so briefly, pointedly captured in this recent poem, was already there in an early one ('The Gone Locusts,' in *Rediscovery*), where the poet 'watched the locus / From the east come in clouds; / And then the tops of the trees were no more.' But rather than break into ululation, the poet invokes his

> wish for the return
> Of the sowing season
> In which the farmer
> Will remember his harvest.[2]

In another early poem, 'The Weaver Bird,' one of his most frequently anthologized pieces, Awoonor portrays the weaver bird as an archetypal colonizer, who came and laid his eggs 'on our only tree' and ultimately destroyed the tree, desecrated the scared shrines, and took over the house, indeed 'preaching salvation to us that owned the house.' Again, significantly, the poet spares little time for cursing, for lament. Rather, he insists on inviting the comrades to a demonstration to repair the damage done, lest it becomes a permanent disability: 'We look for new homes every day, / For new altars we strive to re-build / The old shrines defiled by the weaver's excrement.'

Perhaps, it is this unfailing anchorage in hope that seems to have seen the poet through probably his moment of greatest stress, political imprisonment without charge, and for a long time without trial, as recorded in *The House by the Sea* and in a few recent poems. Of all of Awoonor's collections, *The House by the Sea* is perhaps the most challenging to read, to fully digest without a lingering sense of discomfort. Even in part 1, 'Before the Journey,' in poems mostly written in Awoonor's final years of exile, there is a sense of brooding disaster hanging in the air, despite the obvious sense of anticipation as we count the days toward the inevitable return to the native land. There are too many reports of killings, political assassinations, and Death, 'the removal man/ reaper-angel of profaned destinies / locks the door and hides the keys.' Miraculously, the land endures, but there is some sad reckoning to be done, as we seek in vain the passionate pleas, the voluble chants of Pablo Neruda, now lost to a reign of terror,

> when Ugarte with his cohorts
> slit the throat of Salvador Allende
> in the name of American liberty
> and you [Pablo] had to die.
> In America, the poet could not rest easy:
> Between the sun and my head
> a pen of blood rests to write the story
> of Negroes hanged in Jackson
> black boys shot in Memphis
> . . . .
> The guns still patrol the streets
> for Law and Order.

And back home across the Atlantic, much of hope goes up in flames as thunder rumbles through the land: 'Whole in the Nigerian jail / Okigbo in flight to the musical burst / the last dance of our drums.' In the midst of all these heartbreaks, the poet embarks on the homeward journey out of exile, from his own account, a return journey made by sea, by choice. The poem 'Departure and Prospect,' most of it written on the Atlantic voyage of return, is one of the most memorable in the entire collection. It opens with a pledge to country, to self, and to Mother Earth:

Seven years, and I'd like
to care for the dying
clean sores in the iodine mornings
on tropical grasslands and scrapes;
I'd like finally
to start the foundations of my dream house
Smell again the public groin
of my ravish earth.

Against this noble declaration of plans, most of the piems in part 2 of *The House by the Sea* read like a sad reversal of the poet's best intensions and fortunes. The poetic voice itself comes and goes in brief, fragmented statements, sometimes of historical facts long forgotten, sometimes enduring fond memories of loved ones, often of recurring and lurking dangers to self and nation, evil men dressed in camouflage as revolutionaries with sinister designs. Even the final poem that closes this collection, 'The Wayfarer Comes Home – (A poem in five movements),' one of his longest, is generally devoid of the bold declarations of hope we encounter in the most of his other collections. The poem opens on a note of personal and collective tragedy:

Even here in my cell
in the house of Ussher
I hear the guns
They are killing the children of Soweto.

And it closes with little promise of hope, as the poet confesses, 'I will have no trophies to show.' Of course, there are many hopeful moments in *The House by the Sea*, such as in poems like 'On Being Told of Torture,' but such moments are too quickly overshadowed by the brutal reality of life in prison, presided over by fellow citizens who are ready to torture you to death, as they did to Allotey, one who had died earlier in the cell now occupied by the poet, as they almost did to the poet's brother and comrade in struggle, Capt. Kojo Tsikata.

In a prison yard they crushed
the petals of our being
against a long row of ancient walls and
a line of assorted flowers.

This memorable juxtaposition of rare beauty and immeasurable pain is redeemed, a few lines later, by probably the strongest affirmation of hope in *The House by the Sea*, lines so lofty that they provided the title for Awoonor's comprehensive selected poems, *Until the Morning After*: 'So much Freedom means / that we swear we'll postpone dying / until the morning after [freedom].'

Until the Morning After: Collected Poems 1963-1985 (1987) has the distinction of being selected as winner of the Commonwealth Poetry Prize for the Africa Region in 1986. Except for the last nine poems grouped under 'New Poems,' the entire collection features most of the key poems from Awoonor's first four collections, namely, *Rediscovery; Night of My Blood* (1971); *Ride Me, Memory* (1973); and *The House by the Sea* (1978). The nine poems listed here as 'New' seem to belong to a period of meager harvest, most likely the transition between Awoonor's American years and his return home in 1975 to a land trembling under considerable stress and deprivation imposed by a military dictatorship best remembered by many for its nervous reaction to dissent, with the generals and their hangers-on freely looting the national treasury and growing prosperous in an economy marked by a proverbial scarcity of every conceivable 'essential commodity.' Considering the poet's stand on the side of dissent in a time of repression, it is not surprising that most of these poems reveal a mind constantly haunted by premonitions of death. His fears were soon to take concrete form in his arrest and detention without trial in an old slave fort still filled with the constant smell of death:

> Along a hope hill and fields
> when dreams crush like petals
> . . . .
> We move on, carrying I say
> a singular faith in death
> the only companion in this valley. ('Life's Winds')

Against this image of a black world dominated by constant thoughts of death occasionally relieved by an instinctive faith in the eventual, ultimate order of a free and just world, the very last poem in the group and indeed last poem in the collection, 'For Ezeki,' stands as a powerful monument to revolutionary struggle anchored in the firm belief that every soul lost in struggle shall not have died in vain. As we wait 'For the coming excellence of days/ For the lovely resurrection time' it is crucial that we remind the young ones not only of a past made proud and memorable by heroic struggle against oppression, but also especially of a future beyond looming catastrophes of a present life ensnared in death and dying:

> Above all Zeke
> tell them of hope and the promise of hope
> encrusted beneath death
> and death's tears.
> of the excellence
> and the vision
> that no perfect armament can destroy:
> of the human will that shall endure,
> of the coming festival of corn and lamb
> of the freedom day that shall rise
> as the sun tomorrow.

Of Awoonor's *Ride Me, Memory*, we may take note of the following critical observations made in an earlier essay:

> A remarkable change occurs in Awoonor's poetry in his third collection, *Ride Me, Memory*, mainly through a widening of the thematic and stylistic range of his poetry. There is no clean break with earlier preoccupations. The dirge mode and style, for instance, continue in the final section, 'African Memories'.... But *Ride Me, Memory* as a whole, moves away from the lament into other areas of the oral-poetry tradition and into artistic traditions outside Awoonor's immediate ancestral heritage.... The work is a testimony to the commonality of human suffering, struggle, and aspiration, compelling a celebration of various successes, however small. Quite understandably, Awoonor displays deep sympathy for the experiences of the African peoples of the diaspora, incorporating several lines and themes from African-American literature and music into his poetic sketches.[3]

These observations must be seen against the background of the main trends found in Awoonor's earliest collection, *Rediscovery*, and especially in the more comprehensive *Night of My Blood*. The widening of thematic and artistic range noted here must also be seen as a logical outcome of the poet's travels outside his homeland into the wider world of human experience. His initial entry into the United States, following his sojourn in the United Kingdom, coincided, significantly, with the unfolding historical drama of the civil rights movement and with the rising heat of the Cold War as well as the Vietnam War. The impact if these world-changing events on the poet's expanding consciousness and artistic sensibilities is very effectively captured for us in part I of his 2006 collected essays, *The African Predicament* (Accra: Sub-Saharan Publishers). A brief return home during this period, which the poet used to conduct field research into African oral literature, eventually saw the publication of two of his most valuable scholarly works, *Guardians of the Sacred Word: Ewe Poetry* (New York: Nok Publishers, 1974) and *The Breast of the Earth: A Survey of the History, Culture, and Literature of Africa South of the Sahara* (Garden City NY: Anchor Press, 1975). In both works, Awoonor provides a rich scholarly demonstration of the unique Ewe tradition of *halo*, songs of abuse. But even before these two works were published, Awoonor had already drawn on the tradition to write his own satirical songs of abuse, as seen in *Ride Me, Memory*.[4]

Awoonor's literary career provides a significant instance of various ways in which the critical insights of the research scholar and the creative impulses of the poet-novelist offer mutually beneficial influences on each other. Indeed, some of the earliest critical statements about meaningful ways of reading aspects of Awoonor's early poetry and those of some of his contemporaries, especially Mazisi Kunene and Christopher Okigbo, may be found in Awoonor's work as a scholar. The principle of creative continuity between African literature written in colonial heritage languages and the rich heritage of African oral literature is now a well-established fact, but a coherent critical demonstration of this fact was a relatively new and still-contested notion prior to the publication of *The Breast of the Earth*.

Awoonor's early poetry, presented in *Night of My Blood* and *Rediscovery*, attracted a great deal of critical attention and quickly secured for him a place of honor among Africa's leading poets of the twentieth century. Some of that criticism may be found in a very useful bibliography compiled by Kwaku Amoabeng and Carrol Lasker, 'Kofi Awoonor: An Annotated Bibliography' (*Africana Journal* 13 (1982): 173-214). A useful update is provided in a major bio-critical essay published in *Dictionary of Literary Biography*.[5] In the essay, Awoonor's very first collection, *Rediscovery*, is considered 'remarkable for its confident handling of metaphor, thematic consistency, and pure lyricism' (117: 81). And *Night of My Blood* is praised for its firmer grasp of style and technique, its sense of increasing urgency, and especially the deployment of a special technique of 'the collage' in the handling of a wide range of historical and contemporary events and experiences.

Ezekiel Mphahlele in his introduction to the original Doubleday edition of the collection, describes such a style in terms of a musical medley.... At one level, Awoonor pulls together themes, images, lines, and line sequences from several of his earlier poems. At another level, he draws on a baffling range of apparently disparate and fragmentary experiences, historical, mythical, or purely symbolic. All these scattered bits are then passed onto a wide canvas and are held together by a coherent rhythm and movement, the essential unity of which is sometimes registered in certain basic thematic lines repeated in a carefully regulated pattern. The poems in which this technique is best seen are necessarily long, among them 'Night of My Blood,' 'I Heard a Bird Cry,' 'This Earth, My Brother,' and 'Hymn to My Dumb Earth' (117: 84).

A close reading of much of Awoonor's poetry, especially the first three collections, is certain to profit from another dimension to his versatile literary career, his autobiographical work, as seen in some of his essays, but especially in 'Kofi Nyidevu Awoonor,' in *Contemporary Authors Autobiographical Series.*[6]

In the epilogue that closes this commemorative selection, the poet himself declares: 'This is the source of my poetry, the origin of my commitment – the magic of the word in the true poetic sense. Its vitality, its energy, means living and life giving. And that is what the tradition of poetry among my people has always meant.' We only need to turn to his elaborate autobiographical essay, to see how firmly his artistic vision is rooted in the ancestral soil and soul of his heritage, but with the liberty to travel far afield for the exploration of other essential dimensions of our common humanity.

The very last poem in this collection, 'Songs of Sorrow,' is included here for the first time in any Awoonor collection. Although it is perhaps the one poem by which generations of lovers of Awoonor's poetry best remember him, he has never put it in any of the earlier collections, in due recognition of and respect for Henoga Akpalu Vinoko, the best known of Ewe oral poets and the single greatest influence on Awoonor. As explained by the poet himself, 'many of [his] early poems are built around central thematic lines directly translated from Akplalu.' In the particular case of 'Songs of Sorrow,' the entire first segment consists of a translation of lines from two well-known Akpalu songs. The point of 'creative continuity' emerges, especially in the closing segment, where the young poet does honor to the older singer by using his craftsmanship as a model to draw directly on his own family history to elaborate on the ancestral story began in the songs of the older poet, Akpalu.

It is this ancestral story of sorrow and of ultimate victory over sorrow especially in the death and resurrection of Hope that the young Awoonor took up half a century ago and through various creative transformations and adaptations as he traveled around the world, the now statesman and elder Awoonor has brought the old and changing story back home in the voice of the sage and Guardian of the Sacred Word, inviting us to join hands and minds and souls as we Gather the Lost Lambs Home. We welcome our long lost kith and kin back to the ancestral land and to a harvest of powerful images, of sun, of moon, of thunder, of lightning, drums and trumpets, and of course dance, in the company of fellow humans from all corners of Earth, joined by all creatures of the Earth – an amazing Festival of the Word, appropriately captured in a vintage Awonoor prose poem that closes his novel *Comes the Voyager at Last*. In this final entry, we pay homage to Kofi Awoonor not only as a poet with a profound vision and articulation of the world, our world, but also with a gift of words that is at home in poetry, in prose, in critical literary studies, and equally in major essays about our African, our human condition.

NOTES

1   This collection was put together for release in 2003 as a bilingual text, with English and corresponding Ewe pages facing each other. But the publisher/printer made such a mess of the final product that the entire project had to be abandoned, and the copies printed were never released for distribution.
2   This reference to the coming of locusts could have been inspired by the poet's recollection of a major plague of locusts experienced in his birthplace in 1939, an incident still cited today in oral history.
3   Kofi Anyidoho, 'Kofi Awoonor: A Bio-Literary Essay,' in *Twentieth-Century Caribbean and African Writers*. Vol. 117, *Dictionary of Literary Biography*. Ed. Bernth Lindfors and Reinhard Sander. (Detroit: Gale Research Inc., 1992): 77-92.
4   Kofi Anyidoho, 'Kofi Awoonor and the Ewe Tradition of Songs of Abuse (*Halo*),' in *Toward Defining the African Aesthetic*. Ed. Lemuel Johnson et al. (Washington DC: Three Continents Press, 1982): 17-29. Reprinted in Richard K. Priebe, ed., *Ghanian Literatures*. (New York: Greenwood Press, 1988): 87-102.
5   Anyidoho, 'Kofi Awoonor: A Bio-Literary Essay,' 117: 77-92.
6   'Kofi Nyidevu Awoonor,' in *Contemporary Authors Autobiographical Series*. Ed. Joyce Nakamura. (Detroit: Gale Research Inc., 1991) 13: 29-54.

Kofi Awoonor

Poem for a Mentor & Friend

GHIRMAI NEGASH

In the cave of my bedroom, slumbering to sleep
I often listen to poets whose verses force a grin or a weep.
Lesego Rampolokeng and Lemn Sissay stopover
To deplore, in the manner of a knowing griot-warrior,
The Boer's logic of hate and Anglo racism of late
Meles Negusse tells me about Mammet's flight
Into the Red Sea, about her escape from the emperor's morbid gape,
Although playing hide and seek with lovers – who worship her wisdom,
Actually teasing them, biding time
Until wounds wringing in lies, patch up by the salt water's coral gem.
In the background, I hear the Chinese poet Bei Dao murmur startled
'When the Cape of Good Hope has already been arrived'
Why the heck take the vessels to wreck in the Cape of Death?
But today disaster has struck, bringing close the twilight
Kofi Awonoor has left this life, in an unscheduled flight
To join the other life that may be gentler and eternal.
I wept, I will not lie
So many memories come by
One of 2007, when on a beautiful summer's day we congregated in
     our garden
He started singing songs of freedom; whistling and chanting like a
     contented nightingale
Still with a raw anguish that somehow balanced the scale
Whatever you do in word or deed, do all in the name of the wood,
Words I didn't fathom then but wish I could.
Summers later yet another beautiful day, sitting in his home in Accra
Hearing my long story of the container-prison – our present day Naqura
I saw his protruding eyes flamed red,
Like roasting grains of red flax seed
And so, vainly though,
I had to withhold the news about the hiding of Mammet,
The mythical muse of the brave, who vanished in the custodial make

shift cells of iron and steel
Artfully designed by fatalists with a license to kill,
Alas, how hard it seems to believe in the wood and how easy to deceive
and steal.
Were the Nairobi butchers thinking?
If they were thinking, what was the purpose of their doing?
If there was a purpose, what was the logic of the ugliness –
Beyond its deadliness?
The warrior-poet Awonoor is gone forever and for sundry to miss
Somewhere in Ghana the drums are beating to start off the borborbor
dance
Inviting dancers who had learned his death from the wailing women
Who learned from the choking men, who follow the poets' dirges,
Who in their Kente clothed well, empty wonderful rhyme for the
agbadza dance,
to crescendo the farewell.
Ghana will brace itself to send off its beloved son
And let Africa express its grief, respect and veneration
To this land of African pride and the symbol of liberation
The land of Nkrumah and Awonoor, truthful soldiers of freedom,
Whose glory intensifies every time, with the calling of their name.
Ancestors, prepare to welcome one of your bravest sons
Awonoor has taken the flight to join you in the heavens.

Looking Death in the Eye

The Human Condition, Morbidity & Mortality in Kofi Awoonor's Poetry

MAWULI ADJEI

Kofi Awoonor's fascination with the Anlo-Ewe dirge as a poetic form has been established in various critiques of his work. What has invariably been highlighted, is his sometimes liberal borrowing from the Anlo-Ewe poet-cantor Vinoko Akpalu, whose fatalistic commentaries on his personal life resonate loudly in Awoonor's poetry. However, not much attention has been focused on Awoonor's own views regarding the human condition, morbidity and mortality. This article discusses Awoonor's attitude to death in his poetry, particularly as it relates to the poet's acceptance of the inevitability, anticipation and, sometimes, defiance of death. It also highlights Awoonor's evolution as a poet with a distinct voice.

The theme of death features prominently in world poetry, but attitudes to death vary from poet to poet – Sylvia Plath, Emily Dickinson, John Donne, Alfred Lord Tennyson, etc. Death could be mocked and demystified, as in Donne's popular sonnet 'Death Be Not Proud'; seen as terminal, regenerative, inevitable as a normal rite of passage in the life cycle, an eternal reward for the individual's good deeds, or simply 'going home' to join one's ancestors. For Tagore, death is the 'Great Unknowable' where the 'mortal bonds' perish.

Often, in dealing with death, the individual poet either projects his personal views on life and death, or grounds his views in his people's culture and worldview; or conflates both. Awoonor's understanding of death was imbibed at a very tender age, and it has to do with his people's belief in the idea of death as the result of the interplay of cause and effect relationships, both physical and metaphysical; a fact he re-affirms in 'Reminiscences of Earlier Days' (1976).

In his poetry, Awoonor explores death from a multiplicity of perspectives. He treats the theme of death as if he is constantly expecting his own death; he sees death in a Manichean / cathartic sense; as a disruptive natural phenomenon; as an opportunity to link up with 'those gone ahead' in the cyclic trajectory of birth, death and renewal and as an emblem of his accomplishment of, or failure, in life's tasks – divine or self-imposed. There is also a sense of ambivalence, or equivocation, in the way the poet confronts death; he is in constant dread of death, sometimes defiant and unafraid. The latter posture he prophetically underscored in a light-hearted speech hours before his tragic death in the West Gate Mall terrorist attack in Nairobi in September 2013. Addressing a workshop of the StoriMoja Hay Festival, he stated:

> I have written about death also. Particularly at this old age now, where at 79, you must know, unless you are an idiot, that very soon you should be moving on. I have seen friends of mine who are petrified of death. I say; what are you afraid of? You have done everything already; you have fathered your children, your grandchildren are thriving. So begin to pack your things because the man will come.

The sentiments expressed above echo, in particular, Tennyson's 'Crossing the Bar', which the renowned English poet asked to be etched on his tombstone, secure in his heart that death is a passage to a bigger realm where he will be reconciled to his 'Pilot'. Thus, much as Awoonor is reputed to have been influenced by his native Anlo-Ewe poetic tradition, particularly the dirge, he is also a mortal being who sees death in ways similar to other great poets in world literature.

PLACING DEATH AND THE POET IN CONTEXT: TRADITION AND CONTINUITY

The theme of death, in whatever configuration, manifestation, circumstance or expression, that pervades Awoonor's poetry spanning half a century – from *Rediscovery* (1964) to *The Promise of Hope* (2013) – is a function of the poet's origins, personality, upbringing, education, philosophy, politics, among other things. It is, therefore, imperative to place the poet, his people, both ancestral and contemporary, the world at large and the human condition in the contexts in which death is addressed, alluded to, confronted, embraced, anticipated, demystified or treated normally as an inevitable rite of passage. It is also important to clearly define the poetic mediums in which he functions.

To say Awoonor's poetry is enriched significantly by the Anlo-Ewe poetic and song traditions is to over-flog the obvious. Very early in his poetic career, he himself states:

> The Ewe dirge has fascinated me as a complete poetic form. Its use of the elegiac tone, statement, exhortation and prayer combine into a totally effective poetic medium. The expression of philosophical concerns is incidental to the total mood of sorrow [...]. Some of my earliest poetry was an attempt to carry over from the dirge a series of segments or individual lines around which to create longer pieces that still express a close thematic and structural affinity with the original. (Awoonor 1980: 237)

His fascination with his native Anlo-Ewe oral tradition, and the worldview that nurtures it, is discussed in his seminal literary surveys *Guardians of the Sacred Word* (1974) and *The Breast of the Earth* (1975). In the latter, in particular, he explores the content and form of the poetry of the master Anlo-Ewe singers Akpalu, Dunyo and Ekpe. It is from this pool of poets that Awoonor draws his sensibilities and craftsmanship, immersing himself deeply in the worldview of his people.

Why the litany of lamentations, complaints and references to death in Awoonor's poetry – even though, it must be conceded, he has dabbled in and tinkered with other poetic mediums and forms? To begin with, he, like the traditional Anlo-Ewe dirge singers mentioned above, is a deeply introspective artist, a loner plagued by some kind of ennui. As Anyidoho (1995:244) rightly points out:

> Song texts by major Ewe oral poets reveal the poets as loners, frequently celebrated and even envied but marginalized individuals, expressing their opinions beyond the mainstream of their communities though eternally engaged with issues central to communal life. This persistent theme of the poet's ultimate loneliness points to a context of ambiguities and paradoxes in which society celebrates poetry but tends to ignore [...] the poet, a context in which the poet often laments the gift of song as a social handicap but then boasts about the power of song to transpose society's achievements and failures into monuments that may outlast material and social prestige. A close critique of the politics of song in Ewe oral tradition suggests that, at least in certain cases, the dominance of images of loneliness may be an essential artistic, symbolic project that need not reflect actual circumstances of the poet's life and social standing.

It is within the above context that one must locate Awoonor's most celebrated poem 'Songs of Sorrow', which, in part, is a translation of one of Akpalu's songs. The anchor on which Awoonor's poem rests is the loneliness, frustration and anguish of the poet-persona, expressed in being 'on the world's extreme corner', 'not sitting in the row with the eminent' and the fatalistic resolve to 'only go beyond and forget'. These are Akpalu's (translated) words. It is only towards the end of the poem that Awoonor introduces his ancestors Kpeti, Nyidevu and Kove:

> Death has made war upon our house
> ...
> And Kpeti's household is no more
> Only the broken fence stands;
> And those who dared not look into his face
> Have come as men.
> ...
> Let those gone before take note
> They have treated their offspring badly.
> What is the wailing for?
> Someone is dead. Agosu himself
> Alas, a snake has bitten me
> My right arm is broken,
> And the tree on which I lean is fallen
> ...
> And the crow and vulture
> Hover always above our broken fences
> And strangers walk over our portion

In 'Songs of Sorrow,' Awoonor sees death as a destroyer and warrior, an idea drawn from Anlo-Ewe cosmogony. The image of death as warrior is captured in the Anlo-Ewe war song tradition (*atrikpui*). In the Anlo-Ewe worldview, war entails death, and life is equated with war. Awoonor's fidelity to this worldview is captured in the way in which he endorses the concept that the ravages of life are similar to a war situation, thus predisposing man to death. Of the Ewe war poem tradition, Awoonor has this to say in *Tradition and Continuity*, 1976: 'I used the war poem as the outer crust within which to push not only its traditional ingredients, but also aspects of the dirge and lament poems.' It is, therefore, logical to link 'Songs of Sorrow' with one of Awoonor's early poems titled 'At the Gates'. Often, travails in life are assigned to one's 'Se' (Destiny). In 'At the Gates', the poet-persona laments:

I do not know which god sent me
To fall in the fire and fall in the river
These have failed me
...
The death of a man is not far away.

The last line echoes an Akpalu song, an extract of which goes:

Soon the singer will be dead and gone from among you
This branch will break off
The singer's death is not far away.

It is, however, more likely that Awoonor draws on a popular
Anlo-Ewe war song, part of which goes:

The death of a man is not far away
It is a woman's death which is far away
Without moving our feet we shall sleep in the battlefield.

What is more certain though is that the title of Awoonor's poem
('At the Gates') is an adaptation of an Akpalu song:

There is war *at the gate*
Vinoko says there is war at our gate
There is war in the very heavens
Akpalu would not plunge into it.

Two early poems in which Awoonor hints at his own death, and
puts forth his views concerning death, are 'In My Sick Bed' and
'That Flesh is Heir To'. They are used to mock Judeo-Christian
doctrines about death – doctrines that encourage Africans to suffer
on earth and await joy and bliss in a hypothetical heaven. In the
former, he poses the question:

Who says there is a resting place elsewhere?
It is here with us
Here with us in the sound of the fall of dust on coffin
And the priestly prayers of the communicants
Not beyond, not beyond O Lord (*Until the Morning After*, p.8)

The sarcastic inflections of the poet-persona's voice resonate
even louder in 'That Flesh is Heir To'. Christ's death on Calvary
and the idea of resurrection are subtly debunked, if only to

project an alter(-native-) or counter-view regarding mortality. Thus, when Awoonor says, 'The mortal coils of flesh peel off / and resurrection awaits us / Large at the front of Calvary', he is merely engaged in a parody of the idea of resurrection as preached in Christendom.

The first hint of the journey motif in Awoonor's poetry – death as a journey, or passage, by boat or ferry – is revealed in 'The Journey Beyond':

> Kutsiami the benevolent boatman
> when I come to the river shore
> I do not have tied in my cloth
> the price of your stewardship. (*Until the Morning After*, p.28)

It is interesting to note that the same ideas and imagery are captured in Tagore's 'Song of Death' where he, too, talks of 'boat' and 'Helmsman'.

'I Heard a Bird Cry' (with echoes of Dickinson's 'I heard a Fly buzz – when I died –,' a poem in which Dickinson investigates the physical process of dying), is a long poem composed as a collage incorporating many diverse issues, but moving back and forth in its references to the human condition and death. There are frequent uses of the addressive/rhetorical 'my people', 'listen', together with philosophical questions and transliterated Ewe proverbs; these are not only literary devices borrowed liberally from the oral tradition, but also tied to the themes of death, loneliness, rejection, frustration and alienation.

Many other poems in Awoonor's early poetic career follow in the oral-formulaic poetic vein; the poet-persona acting as a surrogate voice, or an adaptor of the traditional dirge, whose core themes are built around death. Some critics have raised questions about Awoonor's closeness to the established Anlo-Ewe singers, with Zagbede-Thomas (1985) terming the practice 'plagiarism'. However, in 'Tradition and Continuity in African Literature' (1976), Awoonor explains how, even within the Anlo-Ewe oral tradition, the traditional artist borrowing from the culture can adapt to this culture and still maintain a personal identity. In his words, the artist is both a 'technician' and a 'visionary' and the forms and motifs he adopts 'already exist in an assimilated time and world construct, so he serves only as the instrument of transforming those into an artistic whole, based on his own imaginative and cognitive world', and ultimately, 'in the dynamic impulse of the medium which will bear his stamp'. Awoonor's views, it must be emphasized, are not different from Eliot's 'Tradition and the Individual Talent' (1974), Nketia's 'The Artist in Contemporary Africa: The Challenge of Tradition' (1964) or Irele's 'Tradition and the Yoruba Writer' (1981).

Awoonor's heavy reliance on traditional artists and motifs for his lamentations in his early career serves as our point of departure into the domain of the poet's 'coming of age', as it were, to a corpus of poetry that deals with death, bearing Awoonor's personal 'stamp', but still grounded in the oral tradition, to some extent.

COMING OF AGE

Awoonor's 'coming of age' does not necessarily consist in his casting away a large chunk of his traditional baggage but rather the flowering of his art in terms of its finesse and sophistication. By this time, he has shed much of the (in his own words) 'crudity' of his early poetry. There is a diversity of his interests and a cosmopolitan outlook in the propagation of those interests, though firmly rooted in his Africanness.

Unlike his progenitors the Anlo-Ewe dirge singers, the overly pessimistic tenor of Awoonor's poetry derives from many circumstances, most of all, what he would later in a collection of essays call 'the African predicament.' Awoonor happened to be part of the first generation of intellectual heirs of the post-independence dream in Ghana, and Africa in general; a dream that appeared to be dying at birth before their very eyes. As one of the young energetic, if idealistic, scholars recruited by Kwame Nkrumah to help steer the independence ship to the promised land, Awoonor was disillusioned by the tragic turn of events; the betrayal of the Pan-African independence dream. Then there was the ever-present hand of the former colonial masters re-inventing themselves in all kinds of guises and disguises, a fact the poet bemoans in his allegorical novel *This Earth, My Brother* (1972). According to Early (1988: 52):

> Three of the last poems in *Night of My Blood* show [...] a renewed and increased strength in Awoonor's ability as a poet. 'Lament of the Silent Sister' is an elegy for Christopher Okigbo, the Nigerian poet who was killed in 1967 while fighting on the side of the Biafran forces. 'This Earth, My Brother' and 'Hymn to the Dumb Earth' are also concerned

with the recent violence and despair in West African nations. The last poem, especially, resembles Awoonor's novel, *This Earth, My Brother*, in technique as well as in its pessimistic interpretation of the current West African scene.

Thus, Awoonor's development as a dirge 'singer' in his own right is a reflection of his Christian upbringing, Western education and cosmopolitan consciousness and the burden he carries as an artist – historian, teacher, spokesman, cultural icon, visionary and an embodiment of the people's aspirations.

By the time *The House by the Sea* was published, the scope of the poet's lamentation had enlarged, moving beyond the Ewe enclave and Ghana into the larger spheres of the African diaspora and the world at large – wherever he smells death, or death is enacted in whatever form. The tones of lament are ever present but they are devoid of the copious intermingling of traditional Ewe dirge songs, yet there are still elements that expose, even in their limited form, an Anlo-Ewe dirge paternity. For example, the profusion of philosophical thought which is part and parcel of the Anlo-Ewe dirge is very pronounced in these poems. The affinities between Akpalu and Awoonor are the latter's attempt to explore in these poems his own wretchedness, and the precarious living conditions of other people worldwide.

The poems in *The House by the Sea* were engendered by the poet's incarceration in the Ussher Fort Prison in Accra in the mid-1970s by General Acheampong's military junta on charges of breach of national security. At this stage, the poet professes a new outlook on death. To 'go beyond', Akpalu-style, and win respite from the woes and travails of this world is no longer an attraction for him as is evident in 'Homecoming' because 'death wipes out the red blushes of the rose / the curvature of thistle's neck / the rings on the desert tree.' He, therefore, concludes with the rejection of death as 'counter-productive, terminal and deadly', and choosing only 'the hills' and 'the sea nearby' as refuge. Note that, the sea is used as a symbol of both passage and purification, while the refrain 'the house of Ussher' is used as a symbol of death; reminding one of the gory and grotesque spectacles as well as the hypochondriac sentiments in Edgar Alan Poe's 'The Fall of the House of Usher' (1840).

'On Being Told of Torture' and 'The Second Circle' are also reflections on death. In the former, the poet proclaims that 'for each hair on man', there is 'a ledger in which the account will be written' and that man's sojourn in this world is not measured mechanically by the 'hourglass' but 'by the rivulets of bloodshed'. Towards the end of the poem, the poet simply takes death philosophically, as a necessary rite of passage, 'for as all die, so shall we'.

The reflection on death continues in 'Revolution'. In this poem, there is a strong influence of the walls and iron bars of prison on the poet. Restrained from movement and denied the warmth of human communion, he resolves that, in such a state of misery, 'it is better to die / than lie awake' and 'death by any means' is death. The poet welcomes death if only because it is hoped it would bring rebirth, for out of the ashes of decay would spring new life which must be seen in the 'blossoming of fruit trees', the 'overabundance of rice', the 'overweight of plantain', the 'eternal season of fish', the 'building of roads, schools, hospitals, and all other necessities of life'.

His arena of mourning is ever widening, as we find in 'Going Somehow' where 'time has draped herself in mourning / wandering since last night over the hills singing a dirge swallowing Afghans...' The arena stretches from Afghanistan to Pennsylvania and 'the burning of the Jews', to 'the buzzards of Sharpeville.' There are requiems for Pablo Neruda, Ho Chi Minh, Mao, Salvadore Allende and Okigbo 'in flight to the musical bust / the last dance of our drums'. In other poems, especially 'After the Exile and the Feasts' and 'Departure and Prospects', this cosmopolitan attitude to death is evident. However, the proof that, even at this stage, Awoonor does not abandon fully his reliance on the traditional Anlo-Ewe dirge motif is reinforced by the use of some of the 'old' and familiar images of the 'Songs of Sorrow' era. For example, the 'ferry image' – death as a journey by water – is carried further in 'Sea Time' where the poet, feeling intense loneliness, resolves to 'row' his canoe alone because he needs 'no braves on the ferry' to the underworld. The same idea is expressed in 'The Will to Die', a kind of swansong:

So our silence will sing with the daylight gong
A dirge at birth time that in love
We rise to the ferryport long deserted in dream.
We place our headloads on the platform
To await our friend and ferryman. (*Until the Morning After*, p.183)

TWILIGHT YEARS: HERDING HOME THE LOST LAMBS

By the time Awoonor put together *The Latin American and Caribbean Notebook* (1991), he was already talking about 'A Death Foretold', acknowledging the onset of age and the pain and sorrow it brings:

> Sometimes, the pain and the sorrow return
> particularly at night.
> I will grieve again and again tomorrow
> For the memory of a death foretold
> I grieve again tomorrow
> cull a flower across the yard
> listen to the birds in the tree.
>
> I grieve again tomorrow
> for a pain that grows on
> a pain a friend of my solitude
> in a bed long emptied by choice;
> I grieve again this grievance
> immemorial for this pain
> this load under which I wreath and grieve

With age comes the body's infirmity, with a curb on diurnal activities such as taking his early morning or evening 'obligatory walk'. Now all he could do is use the hour

> to recall the lanes, the trees
> the birds, the occasional snarling dog
> the brown sheep in a penned field
> the dwarf mango tree heavy with fruit
> palms tall and erect
> the sentry-pines swaying
> in a distant field. (*The Promise of Hope*, p.70)

These are sober reminders of his slow march to his grave, a fact he accepts without questioning his 'Se' (Destiny).

It is in *The Promise of Hope* (featuring selections from the unpublished *Herding the Lost Lambs*) that the poet finally comes home to roost. At three-score and ten, and still counting, his preoccupation with death is handled with an air of solemnity and the calculated resignation of the sagacious old man who knows he would soon be plucked away by death. This fact of life he captures in a poem whose title speaks for itself – 'Counting the Years':

As usual, as in the earlier dreams
I come to the whistling shores
the voice of the high domed crab stilled
but a chorus remains of the water creatures
of earlier times, of the birth time
and the dying time, the pity,
when we resurrect the travelers
the anchorman on our singular boat
that will take us home. (*The Promise of Hope*, p.18)

Whereas 'our singular boat' is a euphemism for coffin, 'home' is the grave, the underworld or eternity; it is 'home' because not only is it the final destination of all mortal beings but also where 'those gone ahead' reside, waiting to receive him.

Thus, getting on in years, keenly aware and quite naturally accommodating of the fact of his mortality, Awoonor's attitudes to death are self-centred. In many of the death-related poems at this stage, like the one above, he is concerned not necessarily about the inevitability of death but his duty by his people; tasks to accomplish before exhaling his last breath. There is also a constant reference to his ancestors and the master dirge singers before him. It is a veiled announcement, as it were, that he would soon join them. The poems are sometimes funerary and lyrical, mimicking the pathos of the typical dirge singer; sometimes nostalgic, recapitulating years gone by and reiterating defining landmarks and events in his life and, most significantly, recalling those gone before him. These are captured in 'Across a New Dawn','To the Ancient Poets', 'Once More', 'On the Gallows Once' and the deeply introspective poem 'What Brought Me Here?' With particular reference to his ancestors, as vividly captured in the appropriately titled 'Those Gone Ahead', the poet sees himself as part of that fraternity and seems to be in constant communion with them in his waking moments and in dream visions. As he recounts:

I dreamt again this recurrent dream
of my father
taller ever than he has ever been
in the dream
I travelled on the seventh night
to awlime, the land of spirits
to visit my people,
those I know and those who knew me

On a mat in a corner
under a shady Gbaflo tree
lay my sister Comfort
a bit leaner, her beautiful
smile, frozen by death
as radiant ever (*The Promise of Hope*, pp.24-7)

It is important to state again that Awoonor echoes the worldview of his people as far as the psychic flights to *awlime* (eternity) are concerned. The Anlo people believe that when an old or sick (often terminally ill) person dreams repeatedly of his dead relatives, then that person is himself at the portals of *awlime*; it means his ancestors are beckoning him into their fold. At that point in time, the images and correlates of death – graves / graveyards as well as specific trees that often adorn cemeteries – loom larger and seem to vibrate with the ominous songs of death. As in Lenrie Peters' 'The Panic of Growing Older', Awoonor concedes that:

there is surely a living time
when the recollection of death
slightly shudders
especially when I remember the
burial ground
where the house now stands
among mimosa and [neem].
The second gnarled
the first tender
as the first day
the second the companion
of death and dying
sinewy, arrogant, persistent

But, even in the twilight of his life, Awoonor has this sense of the under-achievement of his country and people and wishes his life would be extended to address the lingering problems that have plagued his people. He sees death as disruptive of the flow of life's targets and dreams. In 'What More Can I Give?' he recalls a 'lifetime used in service' at times 'at the behest of saints…heroes' and at times at the behest of 'not so good men and women'. This lifetime service, looking back, appears to be unfinished business; therefore:

I have fear that I am not done
That my gnat days will be long

Tedious and melancholy
The premonition that not much
Will come from the vigil and sweat
And the tears and the long hours
And the sacrifice (*The Promise of Hope*, pp.22-4)

However, as if to address the fear and premonition stated above, he offers a window of some limited relief 'To Feed Our People'. It is a poem in which the poet looks back at his entire stewardship in life and declares that life is meaningful and worth celebrating, but only when we do right by our people and accomplish the tasks set for us and those we have set for ourselves:

we must bring in our harvest
father the children
and thatch the barns
we must build the roads
clear the paths to the planting fields
and clean the holy places;
and oh, we must meet the
morning dew wet,
work with the early sun till the vertex
when it will come home with us.

Then after the wash, then only
shall we bring out the drums
recall old glories
and ancient pains
with the dance our dance.

All this done, we are assured that history and posterity will absolve us of dereliction of duty. And

when the final night falls on us
as it fell upon our parents,
we shall retire to our duty
by our people;
we met the challenge of history
and were not afraid. (*The Promise of Hope*, p.1-15)

CONCLUSION

Awoonor's poetry, from *Rediscovery* to *The Promise of Hope,* can be described as one long litany of lamentations dealing with the human condition and the theme of death by a poet grounded in his culture and poetic traditions. It is poetry driven by strong Pan-Africanist sentiments and identification with the suffering masses across the world. Awoonor in his poetry seems to be sending a clear message to his readers that death may be a natural phenomenon of the life cycle, but wherever there is human suffering, wherever there is tyranny or oppression, mankind is perpetually predisposed to death.

WORKS CITED

Anyidoho, Kofi. 'Beyond the Communal Warmth: The Poet as a Loner in Ewe Tradition'. In *Power, Marginality, and Oral Literature in Africa,* ed. Elizabeth Gunner & Graham Furniss. London: Cambridge University Press, 1995, pp.244-59.

Awoonor, Kofi. 1964. *Rediscovery and Other Poems.* Ibadan: Mbari Press.

——. 'Reminiscences of Earlier Days', The Writer in Modern Africa, ed. Per Wastberg (Uppsala: The Scandinavian Institute of African Studies, 1968), pp. 112-18.

——. 1972. *This Earth, My Brother…*London: Heinemann.

——. 1974. *Guardians of the Sacred Word.* New York: NOK Publishers.

——. 1975. *The Breast of the Earth.* New York: Anchor Doubleday.

——. 'Tradition and Continuity in African Literature', *Exile and Tradition: Studies in African and Caribbean Literature,* ed. Rowland Smith (Longman/Dalhousie University Press, 1976), pp. 166-73.

——. 1987. *Until the Morning After.* Accra: Woeli.

——. 1991. *The Latin American and Caribbean Notebook.* Trenton: Africa World Press.

——. 2013. *The Promise of Hope (New and Selected Poems, 1964-2013),* ed. Kofi Anyidoho. Lincoln: University of Nebraska Press.

Early, R. 'The Poetry of Kofi Awoonor,' in *Ghanaian Literatures,* ed. Richard Priebe. Westport: Greenwood Press, 1988, pp.52-67.

Eliot, T.S. 'Tradition and the Individual Talent', *English Critical Texts,* ed. D.J. Enright and Ernst Chikera. Oxford: Oxford University Press, 1974.

Irele, Abiola. 'Tradition and the Yoruba Writer: D.D. Fagunwa, Amos Tutuola and Wole Soyinka', *The African Experience in Literature and Ideology.* London: Heinemann, 1981, pp. 174-197.

Nketia, J.H. 'The Artist in Contemporary Africa: The Challenge of Tradition', *Okyeame* Vol.2, No.1, 1964, pp. 57-62.

Poe, Edgar Alan. 'The Fall of the House of Usher', first published in *Burton's Gentleman's Magazine* (September 1839); reissued in *Tales of the Grotesque and Arabesque* (1840).

Zagbede-Thomas, Adzo and Roger Thomas 'Poetic Plagiarism', *West Africa Magazine* (March 26, 1985), p. 527.

Eulogy for an Artist, a Statesman, a Teacher & Friend

Kofi Awoonor

RICHARD PRIEBE

Few people change and shape our lives. I was fortunate that one of those rare individuals for me was Kofi Nyidevu Awoonor. And the changes started unbeknownst to me years before I met the man. As I came to know him, I came to know a grand affecting and effecting presence, a grand epicurean stoic.

The first time I read a poem by Awoonor was in the summer of 1964 as I was preparing to go off to Nigeria for two years; it was a poem published in the Beier/Moore Penguin anthology in 1963. For me it was much like Nigeria, Ghana and Africa, just an abstraction which I could not get my young head around, so little did I know. But the music stuck in a haunting way. 'The Weaver Bird,' still one of Awoonor's best poems, would appear in an Mbari collection of his early poetry in 1964, *Rediscovery and Other Poems*, and Awoonor (then known as George Awoonor-Williams), would through that booklet become a part of the most important Pan-African arts movement of the twentieth century, the Mbari moment that brought together various artists from across Africa. And the writers in this period lasting roughly from the mid-fifties to the start of the Biafran War in 1967, would meet, not just in Nigeria, but in Sweden and Uganda and elsewhere: most we have lost: Brutus, Mphahlele, Achebe, and now Awoonor. All great African artists.

Two years passed, and Africa became less of an abstraction to me, not just because of my being there, but also because of what writers associated with Mbari were doing to redefine modern Africa for all of us.

KOFI, MY FRIEND, NOW I ADDRESS YOU

Kofi, you canoe upturning hippo, you have gone before us, leaving us behind, orphans grieving in the desert. You knew so well that the great trick in art is in making the ordinary extraordinary, and in your living life so fully you taught by example that the grand trick in life is to make each moment extraordinary, and in so doing, to laugh at that ultimate thief, Death. I hear your laughter as when you once said that when Death comes to our door and we say that we have no seat for him, Death always says, 'Do not worry, I have brought my own'. Kofi, I lack your dirge singing eloquence to sing anything befitting your legacy. I remember the tonality and timbre of your fine voice, that smile of yours that was always on the verge of turning into a laugh. Your love of good food, good drink, good conversation, and, of course, women. Your wit. Your kind generosity. Your ability to constantly surprise all of us around you. Was there not a little of Ananse in you all the time? In each smile, each piece of wit, you could light up a thousand rooms. Kofi, I need your umbrella to escape the desert heat; I need your stool that I may sit.

The artist and man I knew
Allow me some context to show the gifts he had and freely gave. I had the good fortune to be at the University of Texas in Austin from 1970 to 1973. I had not gone to study African literature, but how could I not once there. It was not a moment of discovery for me, but to borrow a word from the title of Kofi's first book, a moment of 'rediscovery'. I had lived in Nigeria for two years and thought I had left Africa in 1966. When Kofi appeared in 1970, my path in life was utterly changed.

I rediscovered him as a fine poet as I reread 'The Weaver Bird' in Ben Lindfors seminar in the fall of 1970. It is a powerful poem about external, and perhaps internal, threats to social and cultural order. I read from it:

> The weaver bird built in our house
> And laid its nest on our only tree
> We did not want to send it away.
> We watched the building of the nest
> And supervised the egg-laying.
> And the weaver returned in the guise of the owner,
> Preaching salvation to us that owned the house.
> They say it came from the west....
> Its sermon is the divination of ourselves....

We look for new homes every day,
For new altars we strive to rebuild
The old shrines defiled by the weaver's excrement.

On the one hand, one can see this as a poem about the West in Africa, but it might also well be read as a poem about the destruction of Africa by its leaders; both readings fit concerning the nature of pollution in a society. And both readings fit the larger sense of the poem, of danger always threatening purity. I needed to know Kofi better to understand the complexity of his poetry, and the land about which he wrote.

As an artist Kofi was above all a great poet, even in writing prose. One can see this most clearly in his finest novel, *This Earth, My Brother*. There in his mastery of the rhythms, the repetitions, the sonorities, the poetics of the dirge, one can also see how ironically prophetic he was about his own life. In the following passage we are in the mind of the protagonist, Amamu:

> The seventh night, deep, deep night of the black black land of gods and deities they will come out. First the drums to-gu to-gu to-gu to to to-gu if they insist then I shall die the death of blood I shall die the death of blood. They will march through every lane drums echoing across no one can tell where they are now, no one can tell. They will pause for entrance into thunderhouses.... If they insist and say it must be by every means, if they insist then I shall die the death of blood. The echo recedes... if they insist if they say it must be by every means then I shall die the death of blood....

Kofi delivered a lecture at the University of Texas in 1971 where I met the man; later his work was a subject of my doctoral dissertation. In 1972-73 he became a mentor, and then a good friend of both me and my late wife, Barbara. His year in Austin was extraordinary for us. And the transformations this verbal magician, this alchemist made in our lives continued well beyond. He was later to be godfather to our son, Adam Kwaku, and came to Richmond to perform an outdooring ceremony and taught me that I was no longer Richard, but Kwaku's father.

Some moments in time
There was absolutely no one who could constantly use the phrase 'you must' or 'we must' in such a winning way... It was never a command in his mouth; always a warm invitation to marvel at the world.

Austin, Texas Fall 1972. '**You must** take me trout fishing,' Kofi said. And we floated together down the Guadeloupe River catching trout and talking about Africa. And I realized he had brought an entire continent into my life. (The moment on the river is frozen in photograph of Kofi on the cover of his 1973 collection of poems, *Ride Me, Memory.*)

Austin 1972. I watched in awe as Kofi and Dennis Brutus played ping-pong, watching not for their skill in the game itself but for the witty repartee that passed between these poets, one Ghanaian, one South African, joined in their Pan-African roots through their connection to the Nigerian Mbari Club for Writers and Artists (both being published Mbari authors).

Austin 1972 and for many years later. The wit in Kofi's novel *This Earth, My Brother*, brings a smile. Consider his writing of his protagonist, Amamu, coming to the traffic circle in Accra that was first named for a man, Nkrumah, and then for the abstraction for which they threw him out of office (independence). Years later, there was his more sardonic laughter after his imprisonment in Ghana, referencing his time in prison as a stay in 'a house by the sea'. (He was imprisoned without trial by the then military government, his having been accused of helping to aid someone who wanted to overthrow the government). He was now overtly political and remained active and committed to change through political action. I hear him laughing at the 'imbecilic' (a word he loved) irony of his own death in Nairobi at the hands of 'those idiots' (a phase he often used in referring to those who sought to destroy Africa).

Seattle, Washington Fall 1992; Annual Meeting of the African Studies Association. The girth of Kofi's humanity encompassed a universe – and he could see the universe in a grain of sand. He surprised an audience of about 1500 varied Africanists telling them all, 'You must read the novel, *A River Runs Through It*.' A book about trout fishing? Even I, a trout fisherman, was surprised. He told the audience that the subject of fishing was incidental detail as the book had lessons for all. For Kofi, it was all about moral imperatives and commitment to right action. Trout, the beautiful clean water fish, wasn't anything to him if not first of all a trope.

1978 Sometime after Kofi was released from prison. '**You must** come to Cape Coast and **we must** fish and drink palm wine...' And on this command I got a Fulbright to teach at Cape Coast University in Ghana in 1980-81 where Kofi was chair of the English Department. It was an economically rough period in Ghana but Kofi taught Barbara, Adam and me to share, live well with little and to laugh through it all. On one of the first days there Kofi took me on a drive past the security gate at the entrance to the university. The guard greeted 'Dr. Awoonor', then nodded to greet me as 'Kwesi broni.' I naively asked Kofi how the guard might have known that I was born on a Sunday. Kofi turned to me with his grand laugh and explained that the expression was like the generic, Mr. Charlie. I was white, and Sunday was the day of my god. Later that fall as it was becoming increasingly difficult just finding daily necessities in Ghana, Kofi sensed my growing depression, and came to my campus cottage early on a Saturday morning before breakfast. 'How is Kwaku's father today?' It was clear that all was not well with us. 'You must come with me as I have some of the best palm wine you will ever have?' I had not eaten, and I complained that it was too early to drink. Not to worry, he laughed – come with me and you will be better because of the palm wine we will drink, the smoked Guineafowl (*pintade sauvage*) we will eat, and the words we will hear. (And as he often did, he found a diversion for Adam and Barbara.) He was right to show that every day is an opportunity – and that day, as on many others, his laugh, and all he did for my family, made the year in Ghana a superb year – and positively life changing for Adam and Barbara as well as myself.

A general thought. Truth to say, Kofi was not a good fisherman and was a lousy shot as a hunter, but there was such a joie de vivre in his approach to both sports. He loved to fish for any edible fish and to hunt for duck and Guineafowl and loved even more to make fine meals with them: fish, Guineafowl and wine were also tropes for what is best in life. And for Kofi, process was all...

Richmond, Virginia Fall 1974. Kofi had given a reading at Virginia Commonwealth University; there followed a reception at my house. A colleague of mine, dazzled by the reading, and the physical presence of Kofi, would not leave the reception, wanting to talk with him long after all others had left. Barbara went to bed, and then I left, leaving Kofi in conversation with the enraptured woman. When I returned a half hour later, I found Kofi alone in my living room sitting like a Buddha in lotus position, appearing to be in deep meditation. Moving nothing else he opened one eye and whispered sotto voce, 'Has **that** woman left?' She had and we broke into laughter.

The Chesapeake Bay Spring 1975. Kofi had agreed to come to Richmond to give readings and lectures at the universities here and to teach poetry to children in the public schools. 'But **we also must go fishing**,' he intoned. I chartered a boat with four or five of my English Department colleagues who knew nothing about fishing. We were a motley crew, and with our hooking some large bluefish (aka 'choppers' given their razor teeth) pandemonium and sheer chaos ensued, lines tangled and all of us were slipping on the deck as fish came in. Kofi, having hooked a very large one, stayed standing like Ahab, excited with his Moby Dick, and ignoring the warnings to watch out for the sharp teeth of this chopper. And so, as he brought it into the boat, he got a severe gash in his right hand. Ignoring the bite, he held the fish up in the air, his own blood dripping down, and addressed the fish: '**You must** bite, but **I must** eat you tonight.' We wanted to go in shore right away and have the hand treated, but laughing he refused, saying we **must** stay until we have enough fish for a big feast. And we did. Later, I realized he had been the McMurphy taking us out on an escape from that lunatic asylum we call the academy.

CLOSING THOUGHTS

Long ago, Kofi introduced me to Wole Soyinka and made a feast for us with jerk chicken and much wine. As the wine took hold, Soyinka and Kofi started to take lines from well known verse and substitute the word 'fart' in interesting ways. A comic competition, an epic battle of words ensued: 'A gentle fart turneth away wrath.' 'Do not fart gentle into that good night/ fart, fart until the dying of the light...' Another time and place, Kofi and I were in a crowded elevator going down in awkward silence with no one talking and everyone just staring up at the passing floor numbers . Kofi spoke up loudly to break the silence, saying that in Ghana in such public silence one says 'Ananse farted.'

Kofi, we thank you for your laughter and more. You lived in the possibility of a fairer world than prose. You enriched my life and all who knew you with your wry sense of humor, your work as an artist, a teacher, a statesman, a friend, through your kindness, and your generosity. Thank you.

Post-Colonial Trauma & the Poetics of Remembering in the Novels of Kofi Awoonor

PRINCE KWAME ADIKA

To talk about Kofi Awoonor is to try to re-member a poet, an essayist, a novelist, a political scientist, a diplomat, and a lot more. In the introduction to his monumental study of African culture and literature, *The Breast of the Earth* (1975), Awoonor describes himself as 'a cultural nationalist, teacher, artist and above all, an African' (xi). All these were hats he wore proudly over a lifetime of vigorous dialogic engagements with post-colonial Africa's tortured history, or what, elsewhere in his works, he refers to as the African predicament. Awoonor saw no contradiction in embracing these multiple labels; rather, he saw each as part of a larger chain of complementary roles that actively helped in his cause to be an eloquent analyser of the ills of the African society. More importantly, his active commitment to these multiple roles were, for him, part of the process of finding cures for those ills so as to make 'the world better for others' ('Notes from Prison', *The African Predicament*. 2006: 410). Throughout a career that spanned more than half a century, he never strayed from that commitment to the disadvantaged, and no wonder, at the very end, in his posthumously published collection *Herding the Lost Lambs* (2013), he could summarize his life's mission in the lines below:

> What brought me here
> is the determination to heal
> the thorn-wounds
> of those with eternal miseries
> and the burden of night-time cries,
> of orphans without meals
> of lepers without fingers
> of holy men without faith...
> ('What Brought Me Here?,' qtd. in *The Promise of Hope* p. 21)

In this paper, my primary aim is to bring Awoonor's prose fiction work into the conversation about his legacy of dealing with post-colonial Africa's history, and the continuing relevance of this aspect of his oeuvre to us in twenty-first century Africa. Specifically, I propose to critically analyse how his two major works of prose fiction, *This Earth, My Brother* ... (1971) and *Comes the Voyager at Last* (1992), tackle the traumatic aftermath of the historical dismemberment occasioned by the African Encounter with the West. The paper will analyse how the two works complement each other by engaging the psychologies of continental African and African Diasporan victims of the colonial Encounter. More importantly, the paper will critically examine how Awoonor uses the two works as strategic sites to resist and reverse the dismembering effects of colonial/colonizing practices on the psyches of Africans while at the same time inaugurating a new, empowering poetics of pan-Africanist re-membering through the specific vehicle of *return to homeland* for the victims of colonial dismemberment.

THE HISTORICAL CONTEXT OF AWOONOR'S WORK

The subject of post-colonial African identities and how these are influenced by the history of relations between Africa and Europe over the past five hundred years is one that has attracted major critical attention from at least three generations of scholars both from within and without Africa. For most of these scholars, discussions of the post-colonial are also discussions about lingering effects of colonialism on contemporary realities because although formal colonialism in Africa and elsewhere was supposed to have ended nearly half a century ago, the after-effects are still with us. In gloomier readings, the post-colonial is also seen as being synonymous with the *neo-colonial* since mechanisms of Western control over Africa have remained intact and in active use as well. In recent updates on that on-going conversation, major scholars like Ngũgĩ (2009) and Armah (2010) have drawn attention to the continuing relevance of the subject. For instance, Ngũgĩ asserts in *Something Torn and New: An African Renaissance* (2009), that 'the central character of colonial practice in general and of Europe's contact with Africa in particular since the beginnings of capitalist modernity and bourgeois ascendancy...[is] an absolute act of social engineering, the continent's dismemberment' (5). Armah's important essay, 'Remembering the Dismembered Continent' also contends that in order to come to terms with contemporary African history and the cultural statements associated with it, one has to understand how the African homeland and its people have been ravaged by 'accidents of history' in the forms of

> ...regimes imposed by invaders, from Europe and Arabia, [who] have attempted to configure African space and time in ways beneficial to themselves, cutting off important portions of our space and time, in the expectation that only a residual portion could be acknowledged as ours; that under the European fragmentation of African space and time formalized in Berlin in 1885, the residual fragment was further subdivided into separate plantation-style colonies, the same truncated units we are now invited to identify with, rebranded as our nation-states; that these divisive units, the colonial states, based on the dismemberment of Africa, serve purposes that invariably degrade African life while enhancing European well-being. (Armah, 2010: 9-10)

In making these strikingly similar claims, both Ngũgĩ and Armah re-emphasize a view of the genesis and the consequences of the post-colonial condition of contemporary African societies that re-echo Ashcroft et al. (1989), who define post-colonial societies as cultures 'affected by the imperial process from the moment of colonization to the present day...the continuity of preoccupations throughout the historical process initiated by European imperial aggression' (2).

Having lived a life that straddled both the epochs of direct European colonialism and its disillusioning after-effects in the post-colonial period, Awoonor was well-placed to be one of the most astute readers of this state of affairs. His earliest creative works, not surprisingly, are dominated by images not only of European imperial aggression but more importantly, its debilitating effects on contemporary African cultures and peoples. For instance, several poems in his first, aptly named, major collection of poems, *Rediscovery* (1964), focus on the twin dynamics of colonial violence and the destruction it wrought on native cultures. For instance, in 'The Cathedral,' he reminds us of the symbolically oppressive 'huge senseless cathedral of doom' which was built by imperial surveyors and builders who, in so doing, destroyed a tree that had 'boughs stretched across a heaven/ brightened by the last fires of a tribe' and used to 'shed incense on infant corn' (quoted in *Until the Morning After*, 7). Similarly, 'The Weaver Bird' describes how a bird 'from the west' comes to defile native homes and altars by depositing its excrement on them, thereby forcing the owners of those native dwellings into exilic existences from which they look for new homes and strive to undo the ruins of their old altars. What we see clearly in these two examples and many others like them is not only different layers of destruction caused by colonialism, but also the traumatic after effects of that destruction. Another relatively early poem, 'We Have Found a New Land' extends that metaphor of cultural alienation into a distinctly post-colonial space where African humanity is diminished because it is measured in driblets of ultimately anti-productive imitation of Western cultural values by newly colonized professionals who 'have abjured the magic of being themselves' (*Until the Morning After*, 7–11). Throughout this poem, it is clear that these new professionals are also victims of acts of colonial power that sought to make them docile practitioners of colonizing *dictats*.

But amidst these scenes of dismemberment and subsequent alienation – cultural and otherwise – one also senses a dogged sense of defiance and a will to re-member the scattered fragments even in Awoonor's earliest work. 'We Have Found a New Land' ends on a note of a humble volte-face on the part of the collective persona to 'pause to relearn the wisdom of our fathers,' thereby emphasizing a return-to-roots ideology or a will to rediscover the lost self. Similarly, 'My God of Songs Was Ill,' attempts to undo the sense of exile from oneself by showcasing a persona who goes back to ancestral shrines to undertake rites of renewal solidly anchored in the worldview that colonialist and imperialist ideologies sought to destroy. It is fair to say that the extended prose fiction works, *This Earth, My Brother...* (1971) and *Comes the Voyager at Last* (1992) elaborate on these processes of naming dismembering practices and also showcasing re-membering visions that we experience from Awoonor's earliest poetry onwards, and it is to them that I now turn for the main part of my discussion.

POST-COLONIAL TRAUMA AND REACTIONS TO IT IN *THIS EARTH, MY BROTHER...*

In many respects, *This Earth, My Brother...* is an extremely skilled portrait of the tragic landscape of the African post-colony. Yet it even goes far beyond that. It is as much an allegorical tale of an Africa in the chaotic aftermath of European colonialism as it is a historical document chronicling the hey-day of European colonialism in Africa when, we are told, all sorts of European adventurers run amok and visited mayhem on the bodies and psyches of natives even as they destroyed cultural and political institutions of these same natives. More to the point, the novel begins in a perverse time context in which:

> Britannia rule[d] the waves, through the strong arms of asthmatic officials, adventurers, drunks, homosexuals, visionaries, and soldiers with booming drill ground voices and flashing moustaches. The men – and their women – who took formal possession of distant lands in the name of the King and died in the name of the King so that the great Empire on which the sun never sets shall live a thousand years, nay, a million years. (39)

The motley crowd of warriors for Empire might have been doing their King and his Empire a favour and might even have believed in the sustainability of their adventures in invading and controlling Others, but for the natives on the receiving end of these crude experiments in colonial arrogance, what these representatives of colonialism created was a cauldron of dispossession and dismemberment. Consequently, the central character of *This Earth, My Brother...*, Amamu, is very much akin to what Mbembe describes as 'a subject emerging...in the act and context of displacement' (2001: 17). He is a twentieth-century victim of the social engineering process that far predates him and, as has already been noted, created the dismemberment of African societies. Born into a cultural and physical landscape marked by centuries of European-led and orchestrated violence for the purposes of social control, his 'outdooring' to the world poignantly reflects the very dismembering practices that were to mark his body and psyche in fundamental ways. His father Jonathan, a pawn in the colonial postal service, fails to partake in the important communal ritual of welcoming his son into the world because he fears his boss from Keta will punish him for dereliction of duties. He would rather risk the severing of important paternal bonds than challenge the dominant imperial order. Later in the novel, this same father, determined to snatch a favourable perch on the colonial ladder, would literally shove his son Amamu even deeper into the tentacles of colonial education and alienation where he would soon become one of the 'veritable first victims of every first volley from the cannons of the [colonial] pedagogues' (37).

Under circumstances where the interests of external forces can so easily sever ties of kinship and prevent fathers from doing their duties by their children, the very choice of name for the new-born who would become the most important symbol of post-colonial alienation in the novel is poignantly telling. Amamu, we are instructively informed, meant 'the man has fallen.' The ominous portents of calamity encoded in Amamu's name mirror the fall of the larger society under pressure from European colonizers. As Chinua Achebe points out, Amamu's story, from its very beginning, also parallels Africa's and by extension, his name provides an emblematic reminder of an African society severed from its own interests by foreign powers (1989: 125). In essence, Amamu's life journey, although it detours through exalted halls of Oxbridge and the Inns of Court, is not remarkably different from that of all the decrepit young men who were recruited into 'the glorious carnage of conquest in the name of Empire' (64) and became victims of that carnage in various ways while losing life-nurturing connections with their own people. In fact, their brokenness, confusion, desolation, and even nervous breakdowns mirror Amamu's own beginnings in a household torn asunder by the exigencies dictated by the interests of Europe. We can also read more direct acts of cultural decapitation in the story of the villagers of Sasieme. Their village, we are told, was razed to the ground by the colonial authorities simply because its people insisted on performing 'public rites of cleansing' in order to enlist the favours of 'their gods and the ancestors of the stool in whose shadows they lived and prospered' (89). In addition, majority of those natives were either arrested and incarcerated, or chased out of village. The colonial authorities, apparently, had vested interests in disconnecting natives from the practices and rituals that sustained them spiritually and culturally, and were therefore determined to use all means, including brute force, to ensure that disconnection. In other words, what all the natives in *This Earth, My Brother...* had in common was that they were victims of an external imperial order of being that sought to pacify them in various ways even as it demanded humiliating docility from its victims. The ultimate goal of all these campaigns was to make sure that these victim-natives were disconnected from indigenous sources of social nourishment and sustenance that they had designed and adapted to the needs of their socio-cultural environments over millenia. In that kind of context painted by the novel, even those few natives who enjoyed some of the superficial material benefits of colonialism were victims in this regard since they inevitably ended up being abused for the interests of Empire.

The argument I have been trying to make so far is that the cumulative disaster that we find in *This Earth, My Brother...* is largely due to the deleterious effects of colonialism on the natives. Pressures to conform to colonial and colonizing orders of being had the direct effect of destroying people's bodies and minds just as these same pressures destroyed social bonds and entire ways of life. Fortunately for us, these acts of dismemberment are not all that *This Earth, My Brother...* is about. Amamu might have been a trailed traveler whose path through life unfolded with a tragic inevitability, but through a lifetime of existentialist ennui created by the specific historical anomaly of European colonialism, he does not totally relinquish that deeper impulse to be, even if against all the odds, 'a torchbearer for the gods and ancestors' (12). His entire life may have unfolded like what he himself describes as 'a blind man's song,' but it also had that redeeming quality of constantly 'searching (for) and demanding' (111) connections back to the site of buried birth-cords and communal joys severed by the alienating power of the Encounter with Europe. We see this amply demonstrated in his constant search for a highly symbolic childhood love; that primal and mythical instinct to connect with beauty and vitality in the midst of ugliness and death created by the sterile order first inaugurated by colonialism. Even more so, we see it in that final, highly symbolic journey that he makes from the infernal dark woods of the post-colonial city to the redemption of first love in the space of first beginnings.

If, as Awoonor strongly suggests by his epigraph to *This Earth, My Brother...*, life in post-colonial Africa is akin to trudging through a modern version of Dante's inferno where 'the straight way [is] lost' because of the savage, harsh and dense darkness that colonialism had inaugurated in Africa, he also clearly advocates a return to values that would help recapture lost ways and consequently inaugurate a more progressive African agenda. This is what Amamu's whole life-quest, in spite of its multiple blundering moments, is. Perhaps the most significant passage in the novel is that final moment before Amamu sets out on the long journey back to homeland and what he imagines as the arms of long-sought love. In a dream-like sequence of words that summarize his ultimate vision of re-membering things that had been cut from him, he tells us:

My woman of the sea, I am leaving for the almond tree where I first met you. I shall be there when you rise to meet me at our appointed hour. I am coming down from these mountains of dung from these hills of shame. I shall walk the steps of ancient war drums, I shall move to the beat of husago, atrikpui and agbadza in the twirl of my folded cloth you will read the sign of my coming… I will believe you will come into the same fields I rode with the ghosts the first memorials of my journey from the womb. For now, believe me, the land is covered with blood, and more blood shall flow in it to redeem the covenant we made in that butterfly field, and under my almond. For you I renounce the salvation of madness and embrace a singular hope, your hope. You will dance again in our time the same step you traced in the earth to the ancient drums, and through them reveal the eternal legend of love. (106)

A long passage, yes. But also a highly significant one. It tells us of the resolution of one man to defy the bloody, dung filled, shameful present and embrace the hope of first principles generated through mutual love. It tells of the desire of its speaker to go back to the strategic and mythic space of first beginnings to redeem the sanity that has now been left in the din of an existence marked by metaphors of scatology. It speaks to a new hope of re-membering and renewing community by reconnecting to things that were severed by the colonial process. Amamu's character at the end assumes a new meaning for us, and his attempts to re-connect with dimensions of himself that had been silenced by the palimpsests of colonialism through going back to the strategic space of homeland and re-enacting a ritual of love – self-love, as it were – do not sound inconsistent with the need for modern Africa to reject whirl-windy sojourns into other peoples' dreamscapes and renew a covenant of love with itself as a prelude to marking a progressive return to the world stage.

POST-COLONIAL TRAUMA AND REACTIONS TO IT IN *COMES THE VOYAGER AT LAST*

Kofi Awoonor's second major work of prose fiction, *Comes the Voyager at Last* (1992) returns to the twin themes of dismemberment and re-membering. It is a work of distinction that can stand on its own, but in many respects, it can also be read as a companion piece to *This Earth, My Brother*…. This is because while the earlier work focuses on continental Africans and their travails under various manifestations of Western colonialism, the latter work projects its lenses at a more global picture of Black humanity. *Comes the Voyager at Last* is certainly concerned with the fate of Africans, but does so in a broader, transatlantic framework that focuses on both continental Africans and African Diasporans and explores their shared experiences as victims of Western colonialism. Indeed, it is another artistic depiction of colonialism and its impact on African humans since chattel slavery, such as African Diasporans went through, is nothing but another manifestation of Western colonialism. But as is the case with the earlier work, *Comes the Voyager at Last* also ends on a note of defiant hope by imagining *remembering visions* that are meant to overturn the effects of colonial dismemberment. More to the point, the latter novel also champions pan-Africanist renewal by through the symbolic means of returning to homeland and embracing values from that space.

The coincidence might be lost on some, but it is worth pointing out that *Comes the Voyager at Last* was published in the same year as the poetry collection *The Latin American and Caribbean Notebook Vol. I,* a work that has the distinction of capturing some of Awoonor's most powerful thoughts on the shared bonds between black Africans across the world that make pan-African solidarity inevitable. For instance, the pieces 'Of Niggerhood' and 'As Long as There Are Tears and Suffering' are just two of many in the collection that strongly remind us of the shared bonds of global blackness in the midst of discrimination, with the latter defiantly declaring:

> ...that surging will to march on
> against odds and odds
> against the prejudicial smirks and sneers
> record again the task fulfilled
> hoist a banner for the waging battle
> march in the ranks of our people,
> our black African people, footstools and heroes,
> lynched, massacred, chained in alien lands
> whipped under almond trees, trifled with, abused
>
> as long as there are tears and suffering
> our work cannot be done
> (*The Latin American and Caribbean Notebook* Vol. I : p.71)

Lines like the above, focused as they are on 'our black African people...lynched, massacred, chained in alien lands...' strongly take us back to the African Diaspora and its sufferings while connecting that reality to the global African experience. But the lines also espouse a vision that is ultimately pan-African because they insist on challenging the gloomy status quo until the tears and suffering are brought to an end. More to the purposes of this essay, this vision of reversing dismemberment and suffering is one that Awoonor would elaborate upon in the larger scope that *Comes the Voyager at Last* afforded him.

On close reading, *Comes the Voyager at Last* reminds us even more elaborately about how heavily invested Awoonor's work is in questions to do with the African world at large and how both its Diaspora and Homeland sections fit into an accordion of collective experiences that make constant cross-Atlantic, pan-Africanist dialogue inevitable. It certainly situates what Joseph McLaren has called 'the trope of return and reconciliation' at its forefront.[1] But even before touching on the need for return and reconciliation,the work reminds us about how that trope is closely connected to the history of forced migrations that African Diasporans were made to endure. Theorists of Diaspora cultures like William Saffran, Robin Cohen and St. Clair Drake have shown us over the years that the process of forced exiling of any people necessarily creates victim Diasporas who carry psychological scars in them, and these scars, in their turns become the toxic bases of cycles of tragedy and developmental stasis unless these victims a means of reconnecting – symbolically or otherwise – to the spaces from which they were forcibly severed in the first place.[2]

In *Comes the Voyager at Last*, the genesis of forced African Diasporization is brought to life by a mythic, para-temporal consciousness which paints horrendous images of what the process of forced migration of Africans involved. Through galling episodes of beatings, maimings, frightful nightmares, and the frequent visitation of 'the naked horror of death,' we get to understand just how inhumane the process of the Slave Trade that created the bulk of the African Diaspora in the Western hemisphere was. This latter work also reminds us that the 'caravan of sorrow' that paved the way for the contemporary African predicament goes back at least five centuries to the very beginnings of Western contacts with Africa. In showcasing African victims of the Slave Trade and their traumatic treks from the various slave markets through the Middle Passage to the ultimately hellish conditions of the Americas, Awoonor reminds us about the gruesome details of what the African American poet

Robert Hayden refers to as the 'voyage through death to life on these shores.'[3] But even as horrible as the journeys of these victims might be, the novel also suggests that African Diasporan life, even in the late twentieth century, is often nothing but a continuation of those journeys into the heart of self-deprecation and hate amidst a hostile environment generated by those who engineered the enslavement of Africans in the first place.

The latter point about the contemporary reenactments of the caravan of sorrow is brought out effectively by the structural arrangement of the novel where the mythical time of the past with its woeful visions of slave caravans is matched by the present horrors of living in the racist South or the concrete jungles of the North in the United States for the descendants of Black slaves as epitomized by the experiences of Sheik Lumumba Mandela, the leading character of the more contemporary subplot. So, while we see one plot tracing the journeys of a group of nameless Africans into trans-Atlantic slavery and hence staging the beginnings of the African Diaspora in the Americas, we also notice the striking parallels with the other, more contemporary plot that follows the wanderings of Mandela through the American South, to the North, and eventually to 'home' in Africa. 'Brainwashed by centuries of slavery and the feeling of inferiority' (81), it was only natural that the African Diasporans described in the novel would seek a better life, or a life in which their value as human beings would not be depreciated in any way. In the particular case of Mandela, we are made to understand that these were searches not always rewarding especially when the wrong destinations were chosen, as in that instance when the he tells us about his attempt to locate home in the North of the US:

> For a moment I was seized by a haunting awareness of home coming. I sensed that my journey had at least for now terminated in this aroma of poverty and bright anonymity, and those on the streets in ridiculous hats and flamboyant garbs were my brothers and sisters from whom I'd never really been estranged. I was the prodigal come home. But I couldn't find the entrance to our house, to my father's house, to the homestead from which I had wandered all my born days. No one could tell me, because I asked no one. I stood in the corner of Lenox, confronted by the promise of the feast of homecoming which turned out to be a piece of lenten supper without wine and celebrations and the fatted cow. *I could not find the entrance to the home I had come to.* (Italics mine, 63)

Mandela could not find the entrance to the home he had sought precisely because it was the wrong home and in metaphorical terms, it did not have what it took to grant him reprieve from the sense of displacement that most Diasporans felt. While the slow and painful attempts to undo those disconnections brought into being by the slave trade and other avatars of European colonialism was necessary, one also senses that the call to connect was not from Lenox but a deeper, more spiritually defined space.

Why is this so? We get part of the answers from re-reading the mythical sections of the work more closely. There we get to understand that Mandela's return and re-connection to his African roots became inevitable at the very moment his ancestors were being exiled and disconnected from their African roots. At the beginning of the mythical narrative of the journeys of the 'caravan of sorrow' from the African interior, we are told of 'an old man grey and weak of body, a wheezing sound emanating from his congested chest' who 'kept repeating something in a strange language' (2). This chant, alternatively called 'a magical word' or 'mystic word,' is the incantatory formula that fills the air of the receding African homeland even as the old man and his fellow voyagers made their way reluctantly on the slave caravans towards houses of bondage in the Americas. Elsewhere, another victim of the same mythical caravan uses the vehicle of song 'as if calling down the visitation of powers and forces that can parley with her (27) while the birds and other elements of nature such as trees, magical squirrels, kingly lizards, moonal eclipses, equinoctal blazes, and manatees served as eerie witnesses to the fateful journey (43-6).

The mythical narrator – as opposed to the more contemporary one – also takes time to explain to us how the very journeys into forced exile also showed that 'Day after day in the lethargy of this calmness, the voyager was coming, *brought along by more than chance*, the ocean, its peopled seas, and the inviolable sun. Soon, soon he would be home' (Italics mine, 129). Even as they made their journeys away from Africa, the forced voyagers of the slave caravans were, to the narrator, paradoxically just beginning the first steps of the voyage back. The confidence with which the mythical narrator speaks his prophesy is founded, as Awoonor later shows, on a very traditional belief about the role of the spoken word in keeping the integrity of the society against all odds. Although the scale and the sheer immensity of the rupture caused by the Slave Trade could daunt the most optimistic person, the African world of

Awoonor's mythopoeia was a world that had mechanisms to recall its own. Against that background, I would argue that even the weak old man's words quoted above, spoken in the moment of the clan's separation through enslavement, were metaphysical invocations of a return edict. The mythical narrator himself would lend credence to this dynamic in the narrative when, at the end of the tale, he points out how, in the African society, there was always 'an army of magicians, jugglers, acrobats and sorcerers in whose hands all things were given birth and death, men who held sky and earth in lingering parley, released with their mouth the hidden essence of things, restoring the unity of ALL by the power of the WORD' (137).

In *Comes the Voyager at Last*, the mystical wordsmiths' work of 'giving the names of the departed to the wind' is one of the major prompts that makes people like Mandela, lost in the suffocating and hostile climate of Diaspora, begin to imagine and even act on their desires to reconnect with an African Homeland and explore kinship dialogues in the process. In other words, my argument here is that Awoonor's mytho-narrative makes a case that the verbal edicts of the departing victims of the slave trade were powerful enough to impel feelings of ancestral connections between Africans and African Diasporans. For Diasporans in particular, this sensitivity starts out at the point of self-conception as Diaspora, but ultimately, it finds expression in the overwhelming desire to reconnect to Homeland, and the journey back also becomes a natural consummation consequence of that impelling desire.

Although Mandela's journey to Africa was short-lived and lasted for only a year, and his visions of what Africa is or should be are often colored by the gaps or 'the received biases that refuse to pass over when one crosses the water',[4] his attempts to connect with Africa as 'the homeland, the spiritual birthplace of all black folk' helps ease 'something deeply disturbing lodged in his soul' (84). In the final ritual of return and reconciliation in *Comes the Voyager at Last*, Mandela is welcomed in a tone that suggests that he has always been expected: 'You have come...returned home to the place I prepared for you. A man, a certain man, my husband, my elder, hunter, the brave one' (121). It is an ending that soothes the wandering voyager, but also fills a gap in the homestead the he returns to after centuries of exile. That final connection is deeply spiritual, and the assurance we get is that both Mandela and his native hosts would be positively transformed because of it.

CONCLUSION

This essay has tried to show that Awoonor was preeminently occupied with contemporary Africa's tragic fate, and he saw a large part of that as related directly to the evil effects of the African Encounter with Europe. He bewailed that fate, but he also actively tried to undo the status quo of dismemberment by championing an ideology of self-love which also meant returning to those parts of the African identity that Europe taught Africans to hate. He represented this process of self-love through the specific metaphor of returning home, and both *This Earth, My Brother...* and *Comes the Voyager at Last* represent artistic depictions of the need to return home and embrace the magic of loving the African self. In the twilight of his eventful career, Awoonor penned the memorable words:

> When the final night falls on us
> as it fell upon our parents,
> we shall retire to our modest home
> earth-sure, secure
> that we have done our duty
> by our people;
> we met the challenge of history
> and were not afraid
> ('To Feed Our People,' *The Promise of Hope*, 13)

His two major offerings of prose fiction play an important role in this process of naming and challenging the African predicament by calling Africans back to themselves. He certainly saw this as an important part of doing his 'duty by our people' and fearlessly meeting the challenge of contemporary African history, and these two prose fiction works must be recognized as part of the canon of texts that call us to remembering visions of contemporary Africa.

NOTES

1 See Joseph McLaren, 'Return and Reconciliation in Kofi Awoonor's *Comes the Voyager at Last*,' *Migrating Words and Worlds*. Eds. E. Anthony Hurley, Renee Larrier, and Joseph McClaren (Trenton, NJ: Africa World Press, 1999), 129-38.

2 See William Saffran, 'Diasporas in Modern Societies: Myths of Homeland and Return,' Diaspora 1.1 (1991), pp. 83-99; Robin Cohen, *Global Diasporas: An Introduction* (Seattle: University of Washington Press, 1997), p. 21-5; St. Clair Drake, 'Diaspora

Studies and Pan-Africanism,' *Global Dimensions of the African Diaspora* (Washington, DC: Howard University Press, 1982), pp. 341-404, for more elaboration.

3 The line from Hayden is taken from his poem entitled 'Middle Passage,' and the edition used for this essay is from *The Norton Anthology of African American Literature* (2nd Edition). Eds. Henry Louis Gates, Jr., and Nellie Y. McKay, NY: W.W. Norton, 2004, p. 1520.

4 See Brent Hayes Edwards, *The Practice of Diaspora: Literature, Translation and the Rise of Black Internationalism*. Cambridge, MA: Harvard UP, 2003, p. 14.

WORKS CITED

Achebe, Chinua. *Hopes and Impediments: Selected Essays*. NY: Doubleday, 1989.

Armah, Ayi Kwei. 'Remembering the Dismembered Continent,' *Remembering the Dismembered Continent: Essays*. Popenguine: Per Ankh, 2010.

Ashcroft, Bill, et al. *The Empire Writes Back: Theory and Practice in Post-Colonial Literatures*. London and NY: Routledge, 1989.

Awoonor, Kofi. *The Promise of Hope: Selected Poems, 1964-2013*. Lincoln: University of Nebraska Press, 2014.

——. *The African Predicament: Collected Essays*. Accra: Sub-Saharan Publishers, 2006.

——. *Comes the Voyager at Last: A Tale of Return to Africa*. Trenton, NJ: Africa World Press, 1992.

——. *The Latin American and Caribbean Notebook, Volume I*. Trenton, NJ: Africa World Press, 1992.

——. *Until the Morning After: Collected Poems 1963-1985*. Accra: Woeli Publishers, 1987.

——. *The Breast of the Earth: A Survey of the History, Culture and Literature of Africa South of the Sahara*. NY: Anchor Press/Doubleday, 1975.

——. *This Earth, My Brother...* [1971] London, Heinemann, 1972.

Mbembe, Achille. *On the Postcolony*. Berkeley and LA: University of California Press, 2001.

Ngũgĩ wa Thiong'o. *Something Torn and New: An African Renaissance*. NY: BasicCivitas Books, 2009.

Song for Nyidevu

For Afetsi, Who Survived to Tell

KOFI ANYIDOHO

They say the Panther died in his Sleep
But not without a Leap.
The Hippo drowned in a Pool of Blood
But with a gentle Smile on his Face.

So you took Death by the Hand
brought him Home
to a Harvest of Ancestral Songs.
You took down his Battle Dress
gave him a Gown of Flames
wrapped in Laughter's Tender Care
You removed the Thunder from his Voice
        the Lightning from his Eyes.

You placed a Rainbow on his Face.

You explained to Death
How and Why he must be Brave
Turn his Back upon the Grave
So the Children in their Sleep
May Dream the Future
Filled with Hope The Promise of Hope.

REVIEWS

EDITED BY JAMES GIBBS

Chima Anyadike and Kehinde A. Ayoola, eds, *Blazing the Path:*
Fifty Years of Things Fall Apart
Ibadan: HEBN Publishers, 2012. Pbk. 329 pp. £24.95, available from African Books
Collective.
ISBN 978 978 081 184 6

To mark the fiftieth anniversary in 2008 of the publication of
Chinua Achebe's first novel, *Things Fall Apart*, conferences,
seminars and commemorative events were held all over the globe,
including the United States, Britain, France, India, and Africa. Such
gatherings were the occasion not only for celebration of Achebe's
groundbreaking achievement as a writer, but also for consideration
of this novel's reception in different times and places, its own
history, and its influence on subsequent reading and writing
of African fiction. This volume, edited by two academics from
Obafemi Awolowo University, Ile-Ife, consists mainly of lectures
and papers given at that university as part of the worldwide
celebration of *Things Fall Apart*'s Golden Jubilee. It also includes
essays previously published elsewhere by the poet Niyi Osundare,
and the distinguished academics Professors Dan Ivezbaye and
Olufemi Taiwo.

Obafemi Awolowo University was the first Nigerian university
to award Chinua Achebe an Honorary Doctorate, and it was on
that occasion, in 1978, that Achebe delivered a lecture entitled
'The Truth of Fiction' (later revised and published as an essay
in *Hopes and Impediments*). In his characteristically thoughtful
and thought-provoking keynote address for the 2008 Conference
Biodun Jeyifo takes Achebe's lecture as his starting point in order
to 'affirm but at the same time problematize the consecration of

Things Fall Apart as a classic of world literature.' (3-4). Why, he asks, has *Things Fall Apart* become *the* single Achebe novel that every critic of African literature is called upon to write about, when in his view both *Arrow of God* and *Anthills of the Savannah* are better novels? And why is it Achebe rather than Senghor, Laye, Oyono, Ngũgĩ, or Aidoo who has come to be *the* representative African writer? Jeyifo suggests that the status of *Things Fall Apart* as a world classic derives from the fact that it speaks to the 'defining phenomenon in the encounter between continents and peoples of the world', i.e., the experience of colonialism, but unlike all other colonial novels is entirely free of racism and ethnocentrism. It is, Jeyifo claims, the first work of fiction that takes the full humanity of both colonizers and colonized for granted, treating both with irony and compassion. But *Things Fall Apart* also embodies and plays upon a conflict between valuing of what is uniquely local and openness to a more cosmopolitan awareness. Quoting Marx and Engels, Jeyifo contrasts 'local and national seclusion and self-sufficiency' with 'intercourse in every direction' and the development of a world literature. In the face of post 9/11 narrow-mindedness *Things Fall Apart* presents a powerful warning of the dangers of a retreat into 'local and national seclusion', but we must also be aware of the loss entailed in the single focus on this one novel to the exclusion of Achebe's other fiction and the works of other African writers.

Whereas Jeyifo locates the classic status of *Things Fall Apart* in its humane representation of the universal experience of colonialism, Dan Izevbaye attaches its standing as a world classic to the fact that 'it continues to be read in new ways that remain relevant to its changing reading publics.' It is a novel full of 'hidden meanings', of anecdotes, and incomplete stories which refer to the community, and indeed communities, as a whole, rather than one central character.

Some of those 'hidden stories' are excavated in a fine and closely attentive reading of the novel by Annie Gagiano in her essay titled 'Achebe's Children: Resonance, Poignance, and Grandeur.' Here she links the various references to Ezinma to show her importance to the novel as a spirited, intelligent, and fully characterized young woman. Along with Nwoye and Ikemefuna, Ezinma reveals the consequences of Okonkwo's 'misrule' of his family, a misrule which links to the politics of misrule by the British in their failure to accept the full humanity of Africans.

Gagiano's study, focusing on the fault-lines in Okonkwo's character and his society, develops an approach common to many of the essays in this collection It is an approach articulated most explicitly in Olufemi Taiwo's 'On Agency and Change: Chinua Achebe and the Philosophy of History', in which Taiwo argues that Achebe rejects the notion that Africans were or are merely victims of the European colonists. Megan Macdonald draws on Althusser to examine the 'cracks' in Igbo society and the significance of Okonkwo's suicide. Ajoke Mimoko Bestman responds to earlier critics who have conflated Okonkwo's attitude to women with Achebe's, and insists that Achebe seeks to expose and condemn the misogyny of Okonkwo, and also shows how the failure to incorporate and appreciate the female aspects of his religion and his community leads to things falling apart.

This concern to affirm the agency of Nigerians in determining their history connects with readings of *Things Fall Apart* in the context of African rather than European literary traditions. James Hodapp seeks to move away from criticism which takes Achebe's own comments on Joyce Cary and Joseph Conrad as the justification for a focus on 'writing back'. Such a focus, he argues, 'confines *Things Fall Apart* to a literary genealogy with the works of Conrad and Cary in a limited conversation concerning the faults of European representations of Africa and the merits of Africans correcting those faults rather than acknowledging the contribution of early African literature' (120). Moreover, the persistent claim in critical surveys and histories that African fiction begins with Achebe involves the erasure of earlier African novelists such as Thomas Mofolo, Sol Plaatje, J.E. Casely-Hayford, Mabel Dove, R. E. Obeng, and Peter Abrahams. Hodapp locates a number of tropes which appear in both Mofolo's *Chaka* and Achebe's first novel, and suggests that Achebe draws on Mofolo. While the claim for influence is not altogether convincing, the point about locating Achebe's work within an African literary tradition is well made, and could have been enlarged to include Francophone and Lusophone African novelists as well as others writing in the vernacular. Ebenezer Adedeji Omoteso's essay on the aesthetics of the African novel demonstrates the possibilities of such an enlargement, with its very interesting comparison between *Things Fall Apart* and *Chiquinho*, a novel published by the Cape Verdean author Baltasar Lopes in 1947. Omoteso also makes wide-ranging reference to Francophone novelists who preceded Achebe, including Camara

Laye, Ousmane Sembene, Mongo Beti and Ferdinand Oyono. One would like to see further comparisons of this kind, perhaps also embracing African-American and Caribbean-African novelists such as Richard Wright, James Baldwin, René Maran and Jacques Roumain.

Alongside the reclamation of Achebe as an African literary tradition, the ever-recurring question of language raises its restive head. It is a question that has been debated over the entire fifty years of the novel's existence: Can the English language fully express African consciousness and experience? Several of the contributors to this volume, including Omoteso, Izevbaye, and Jeyifo, accept Achebe's own response to this question, referring to his successful re-creation of English in an African mode. Kehinde A. Ayoola, Helen Luu, and Chima Anyadike all explore in detail Achebe's success in conducting what he termed a 'conversation' between the English and the Igbo languages, and argue that his use of English does not in itself imply that he writes solely for Western readers. On the other hand, the Preface and Introduction to this volume both lament the fact that an Igbo translation of the novel has not yet been published, and assume that the novel cannot truly speak to the citizens of Nigeria unless it is translated into its indigenous languages. Perhaps the most effective response to these opening statements comes from the well-known poet Niyi Osundare. His autobiographical account of his first encounter as a schoolboy with *Things Fall Apart* is a delightfully enthusiastic reminder of how powerfully that novel spoke to young Nigerians in the early 1960s. Moreover, Osundare declares himself 'one of the beneficiaries of the Achebe experiment. A poet with a deep Yoruba sensibility writing mostly (but not exclusively!) in English, I am constantly seeking ways of expressing the sound, sense, and structure of my indigenous language/culture in English.' Achebe's experiment with language showed him, Osundare goes on to say, 'the protean possibilities of the *language-between*' (309; his italics).

Osundare's tribute encapsulates a whole history of responses to *Things Fall Apart*, beginning with the initial pre-independence recognition of Achebe's success in demonstrating that 'African peoples did not hear of culture for the first time from Europeans,' and appreciation of his powerful dramatization of the colonial encounter from an African point of view. More recently, and in the context of nearly half a century of Nigeria's status as a post-colonial nation, African critics in particular have given greater emphasis to the novel's insistence on the agency of its Igbo characters, and to questions of choices within African societies, cultures, narrative traditions, and languages.

LYN INNES
Emeritus Professor of Postcolonial Literatures, University of Kent, Canterbury.

Nana Ayebia Clarke and James Currey (eds), *Chinua Achebe: Tributes and Reflections*
Banbury: Ayebia, 2014, 340 pp., £20.00
ISBN 978-0-9569307-6-7

Through the palm-oil with which words are eaten, readers of Chinua Achebe's novels have been made aware that 'the world is like a mask dancing. If you want to see it well, you do not stand in one place.' Writers, too, are like masks dancing. They must also be watched from different angles, and, because the quality of their 'performances' can vary over time, it is particularly important to look at them over extended periods. Writers can surprise. For example, in Achebe's case, who would have anticipated that his 'performance' would include such a controversial last book as *There Was a Country* (2012)? And, who, apart perhaps from the ever boisterous element among Nigerian literati, sometimes identified as 'bolekaja critics', would have expected that such a lively 'debate' would be provoked by the obituarists who sought to suggest the enormity of the loss to the world of words represented by his death by referring to Achebe as 'the Father of African Literature'? Furthermore, who would have anticipated the controversy surrounding the funeral – and the attendance list – in Ogidi? For a 'dancer' who was often restrained (remember the debate about his 'unrelieved competence'?) a lot of dust filled the air as he gave his final performances and, amid ceremonies, left the dancing ground.

In March 2013, news of Achebe's death stunned the members of the African Literature Association gathered for their annual conference in Charleston, and in April 2014 *Tributes and Reflections* was launched at the Association's Fortieth Annual Conference – held at the University of Witwatersrand. The volume brings together forty-nine contributions by a roll-call of the greats of African writing, African Literary Criticism, and African publishing.

[See Ayebia.co.uk for contents page.] In the main, the contributors offer measured assessments of Achebe's personal and professional impact, but, as the term 'tribute' implies, some are weighed down by the inhibitions created by the short passage of time since the death. Some of these critics reveal how deeply their heads are bowed by concluding their contributions with RIP, or variations on that.

The volume is edited by two of Achebe's publishing colleagues and Achebe's involvement in the business of getting printed matter into the hands of readers is a significant theme in the collection. The title of James Currey's paper is simply 'Chinua Achebe as Publisher' and it includes recollections of vivid moments when the 'Editorial Adviser' provided leadership to Heinemann's African Writers Series. He managed to do so even while engaged in (controversial) missions on behalf of besieged Biafra. In Currey's words: 'Trenchant notes would reach us by mysterious means through the Biafran network' (33).

While Clarke and Currey went through their address books and solicited many original 'tributes and reflections', they have sensibly found space for material that has been in the public domain for some time. Readers are led into the volume through Lynn Innes's obituary. They then encounter Maya Jaggi's profile from 2000, and Soyinka's *Elegy for a Nation: For Chinua Achebe, at Seventy* (also 2000, but reprinted in 2013). Soyinka's verses stand beside other salutations 'in kind': poems from J P Clark-Bekederemo and Odia Ofeimun, and the first part of Femi Osofisan's dramatization of *A Man of the People*. The flexibility of an editorial policy that welcomes such creative interactions makes for a pleasing variety. It reflects an approach that is broad enough to include Toni Morrison's wonderfully warm tribute from September 2000, and an interview with Helon Habila from 2007.

While happy to share documents from the past, the editors allow themselves the scope to look to the present and to a future in which the social media and 'sampling' will loom ever larger. They reprint Ngozi Adichie's 'Chinua Achebe at 82' (from November 2012) and also include Carol Boyce Davies's 'From Achebe to Adichie', that includes observations about the incorporation of social media postings in *Americanah* (2013) and indicates the public interest in that book following Beyoncé's 'sampling' of a section of Adiche's TED talk in her 'popular self-titled album's eleventh track "Flawless"' (123).

The general tenor of the volume is respectful, sometimes, as suggested above, reverential, but there are contributors who are not awestruck. As anticipated above, it is Achebe's 'last dance', *There Was a Country*, that provides a focus for these contributors, among whom I include Akin Adesokan, Kole Omotoso and Ibrahim Bello-Kano. The last named offers his somewhat shrill essay as 'A Dissenting Opinion'. In addition to these three papers there are those by others, including Biodun Jeyifo, who, while maintaining a demeanour in keeping with the predominant spirit of the volume, allude to work they have published in other contexts, written in a different spirit. Jeyifo refers to his six-part review of *TWAC* that appeared in the Nigerian *Guardian* (during Achebe's lifetime) and writes: 'I can now confess that I wrote that series as much for Achebe himself as for the community of the national literati, hoping that one day I would get a response, no matter how indistinct, from the old master.' He added: ' Alas this will not be' (174).

As Jeyifo implies, different platforms and different times draw forth different kinds of writing. *Tributes and Reflections* is a first anniversary offering that brings together a series of elegant, engaging, informative perspectives on the mask dancing. These stand beside interventions from colleagues and contemporaries who enter the arena and engage creatively with the spinning figure. We now await the passage of 'a decent interval' and expect the arrival of the nuanced judgement of history on a writer who grappled with history and who, in March 2013, quit the dancing ground and joined the ancestors.

JAMES GIBBS
Bristol

———————————

François Guiyoba and Pierre Halen (eds) *L'Impact des missions chrétiennes sur la constitution des champs littéraires locaux en Afrique*, Etudes littéraires africaines (ELA) 35, 2013, 223 pp.
ISSN 0769-4563.

This rich collection of essays is the result of a Franco-Cameroonian collaboration which explains the importance given to Cameroonian literature in the publication. The volume is arranged in three complementary parts: the first part is the main focus of the study, with an article on missionary press and literature, three essays on Cameroon writing and two others covering Egypt and the Belgian Congo (now the DRC). The editors' aim is to add to the publication of a first collection of essays on missionary novels and plays (*Approches du roman et du théâtre missionnaires*, 2006) and advance the academic study of the missionary impact on African literatures, an area in need of scholarly enquiry. In their introduction, they highlight the importance of contributing to a better understanding of the role of missionaries in the writing and development of African literatures in both African and European languages, and to the appreciation of the linguistic, educational and cultural legacy of these pioneers in a post-western world.

The studies offered bring out the difference between the attitudes of missionaries and colonial administrators towards African languages. They remind us that missions played a key role in the writing of African languages, thereby providing a solid foundation for African literature in those languages. While bringing to the fore the literary value of the early works inspired by missionary experiences and the Bible, they also highlight the premium placed on morality. The authors were acutely aware of their social responsibilities. In her article on the '*Rayon d'Egypte*', a Catholic literary magazine whose publication spanned thirty years (1928-58), Elodie Gaden illustrates the key role of the press in those early days. She traces the magazine's humble beginnings, brings to light its religious undertone and its literary value, draws attention to its role in publishing local authors and in presenting Egypt to the French-speaking world while simultaneously showcasing French metropolitan literature and culture. In the article that follows, focusing on literature in the Belgian Congo, Antoine Muikilu Ndaye analyses the relationship between Catholic faith, colonial education and the practice of theatre, which was valued for its 'civilizing role'. He takes an opportunity to mention the educational role of literary translations providing additional texts for school curricula. The three studies on Cameroon by Alphonse Moutombi, Francois Guiyoba et Auguste Owono-Koumba bring to light the unusual vitality of the missionary enterprise in that country, fuelled by the competition between Jamaican, British, German, French and Swiss missions, with a clear account of the missionary activity that included evangelistic and educational publications (Bible translations, school manuals, dictionaries), explorations of the main literary genres and the building of libraries and printing presses. Focusing on René Philombe, Benjamin Matip, Ferdinand Oyono and Mongo Beti, these articles reinforce earlier descriptions of the close relationship between the missionary presentation of Christianity, education and the early literary works by Cameroonian writers. Those four writers' works of the 1950s and 1960s, and the virulence of their satire against Christianity and the colonial system, reveal the impact of the colonial government's pressure on Churches. Mongo Beti's literary career, his strained relationship with the Cameroonian censors and his fight for the independence of African writers, are presented to illustrate the difficulties faced by those writers.

This rich array of studies and viewpoints on colonial history and legacy is followed by *varia* – including an article on the impact of the Cold War on African literature by Virginie Coulon that is illustrated by references to Dadié, Mudimbe, Omotoso and La Guma, and another article on Labou Tansi.

The third part of this issue of ELA is no less fascinating, offering an in-depth reflection on Van Reybrouck's essay *Congo: une histoire*, an unusual book – a cross between travel writing, historical research and creative writing that straddles literature, history and anthropology, and gives a voice to ordinary Congolese. This last study definitely adds to the book's value. The final section of the book, amazingly varied, is made up of fifty book and journal reviews covering the whole of the African continent.

FRANÇOISE UGOCHUKWU
Open University, UK

Astrid Van Weyenberg. *The Politics of Adaptation*
– *Contemporary African Drama and Greek Tragedy*
Amsterdam/New York: Rodopi, 2013, li + 215 pp., €56/ US$76, hbk
ISBN: 978-90-420-3700-7, E-Book: 978-94-012-0957-1

This volume brings together four previously published articles on Anglophone dramatic texts written between 1973 and 2004 by Nigerian and South African playwrights. The plays have in common that they are all modern versions of ancient Greek tragedies that have been adapted to engage with political themes in the countries to which their action has been transferred. Van Weyenberg discusses six plays: *The Island* by Athol Fugard, John Kani and Winston Ntshona, *Tegonni: an African Antigone* by Femi Osofisan, *Bacchae of Euripides: A Communion Rite* by Wole Soyinka, *In the City of Paradise* by Mark Fleishman, *Molora* by Yael Farber and *Women of Owu* by Femi Osofisan.

In a wide-ranging and well researched Introduction (pp. xi-li), Van Weyenberg emphasizes that the starting point for her analysis is African drama rather than the Greek tragedies from which they are derived and insists that she views adaptation as a process where different texts and contexts are related non-hierarchically. She describes her methodology as interdisciplinary and based on literary studies, African studies, theatre studies and postcolonial studies. Her discussion of these disciplines shows that she is familiar with the dominant work in the respective fields. However, she might have benefitted from reading Michael Lambert's *The Classics and South African Identities* which would have given her a clearer context in which to explore the South African texts. This book appeared in 2011, but she seems not to have consulted literature which was published after her research for her articles that antedate the present volume.

The first two chapters deal with 'plays that emphasize Greek tragedy's potential to inspire and dramatize political change' (1). Chapter One examines the two Antigone plays that draw on Sophocles' *Antigone: The Island* and *Tegonni*. Attention is also devoted to whether this cultural transfer affects the status of a figure canonical in Western literature. The second chapter investigates the implications of the transformation of Dionysus into a revolutionary leader in Soyinka's *Bacchae of Euripides: A Communion Rite*. The last two chapters focus on adaptations with themes related to the aftermath of transition. The third chapter explores post-apartheid plays that also incorporate reflection on the Truth and Reconciliation Commission (TRC) set up to give a voice to victims of apartheid and to provide an opportunity for perpetrators to reveal the truth about past crimes. The plays discussed here make use of Aeschylus' *Oresteia*, and also of the tragedies of Sophocles and Euripides that deal with the events following Agamemnon's return from the Trojan war. Chapter 4 continues the theme of mourning which is part of the discussion of the post-apartheid adaptations as well as some of the other adaptations discussed earlier. This theme is central to *Women of Owu* which draws on Euripides' *Trojan Women* as a parallel text dealing with the plight of women in a post-conflict situation.

Van Weyenberg is at her best when she engages in detailed discussion of texts and when she makes use of work immediately informing the plays she is analysing, for instance when she relates Soyinka's theoretical writings (76-90) to the aesthetics of *Bacchae of Euripides: A Communion Rite*. In other cases, however, there could have been a fuller investigation of the material used for the creation of the new plays. I refer specifically to *In the City of Paradise* by Mike Fleishman which drew on Euripides' *Orestes* for the last part of the play. This is mentioned in passing on p. 128, but deserves closer study. In the case of *Molora*, Farber herself indicates that she made use of 'a patchwork of quotations from the original Greek plays' (*Molora*, 16). These include not only different translations of the *Oresteia*, and of Sophocles' *Electra*, but also translations of Euripides' *Electra* and his *Iphigenia in Aulis*, and even Sartre's *Flies*, itself a radical reworking of the myth.

Because of her goal of situating the new texts in the wider context of postcolonial studies, the focus on the plays themselves sometimes gets lost in the mass of theory and footnotes. The writing style suffers as a consequence of the jargon of this discipline, for example. 'Adaptation comprises *both* foreignizing and familiarizing gestures, which may coincide with or work against one another, moving beyond the mere historical and temporal, drawing in such issues as geography, culture and race' (xxix). One could ask whether geography, culture and race are 'issues'. There are further instances of infelicities in the English, and an unfortunate misspelling of the celebrated theatre director Peter Hall's surname as 'Hal', twice on p. 76.

Setting aside these quibbles, *The Politics of Adaptation* offers a valuable contribution to the study of the interaction of modern African playwrights with Greek drama. Yet it would have been advisable to use a more modest subtitle than *Contemporary African Drama and Greek Tragedy*. The author herself acknowledges that this is too large a claim (xiii) for a work that deals only with a few plays from two countries on the continent. It is largely due to the fascinating nature of these plays and the detailed discussion of their larger contexts that this study provides much to interest the reader.

BETINE VAN ZYL SMIT
Department of Classics, University of Nottingham

Taona D. Chiveneko, *The Hangman's Replacement Book 1:*
Sprout of Disruption
Chiveneko Publishing Inc, 2013, 489 pp., $29.00
ISBN-13: 978-1482767681, available as an e-book

Taona D. Chiveneko, the author of this serpentine novel, makes a
fetish of anonymity and only communicates through his lawyer.
To save people like me the trouble of trying to find out about
him, the novel's end pages include an interview with said lawyer,
who claims never to have met his client directly and not to know
what he looks like. He once had an assignation with him in an
abandoned confessional in a landfill, but didn't see his face. In
'About the author' all we learn is that he writes with the feathers
of migrating geese and 'is widely regarded as the most anti-social
African author', to the extent that he can hardly bring himself to
voice his thanks in an acknowledgements section where most of
the names are anagrams.

Nonetheless, Mr Chiveneko, you are all over the book, as
publisher as well as author, and in the idiosyncratic presentation of
what in most novels is formal and uninteresting – the declaration
of rights, for example, where the usual disclaimer informs us that
the author is 'unwilling to make the distinction' between fiction
and reality so people and places may or may not be 'real'. You also
invite readers to 'sign up for news about forthcoming books and the
world of *The Hangman's Replacement*' on a number of online sites,
whereby we understand that this novel is by no means a one-off.
Never mind that it's 466 pages long with 23 pages of appendices,
it's only the first, apparently, of a series of 'between four and seven
books', and the second is due out – oh dear, right now, the end
of 2013. No, whew, I checked online and that's been amended to
February 2014, so I might just get this review finished before the
next instalment.

So let's start by looking at 'the world of *The Hangman's Replacement*', which is one of labyrinthine Machiavellian scheming, bloated
self-interest and sadistic extremism, populated by grotesques,
where free-will and coincidence have been hijacked by a sinister
apparition known only as The Harvester who orchestrates events in
the light of a long-term plan known only to himself. In the novel,
this world is located in a place called Zimbabwe. Into this world
wanders a single good man looking for a job, the job of official
hangman to the country's death row prison, which he ardently

desires because it will provide his family with free health care. And, as we learn on about page 381, this desire is driven by the death of his daughter from burns after he had carried her for three days on foot to the nearest clinic, fending off lions with his bare hands, all unknowing that the death had been set up precisely to impel him to apply for the hangman's job ... The urgency about Abel Muranda's appointment as hangman has to do with a shadowy group known as The Bakers, who methodically construct a plot consisting of a series of Ingredients designed to lead to an outcome beneficial to them. These Ingredients include a specially designed gallows; The Carpenter, whose life is dedicated to creating such gallows with a passion that can only be called sexual; a hanging judge who can be relied on to provide a steady stream of victims; and an exceptional legal mind to sift the evidence against them – of whom there are so many that quite who qualifies is a bit obscure, but lawyers play a big part in the novel, not least the pathological recluse, Luxon Hurudza.

Ah, Luxon Hurudza. But just to finish with the plot before we get to him: behind the need to provide a new appointee to carry out the lapsed death penalty is a terrifying carnivorous flame lily which has developed a taste for human corpses which it is threatening to expose no matter where they have been hidden. This is bad for the Bakers, the movers and shakers, the political geniuses, big shots and self-serving apparatchiks who run the country. Hence the need for a supply of legitimate corpses to deflect the flesh-eating flower. One presumes it's no accident that the flame lily, or *gloriosa*, is the national flower of Zimbabwe, which by this token is not only carnivorous but cannibalistic – the country eating itself, perhaps? It's not clear if The Harvester, creator of this Frankenstinian monster, is good or bad, bent on exposing wrong-doing or simply on adding a layer of horror to an already horrible record of official misdeeds. No doubt that's what we get to find out in volumes 2-7, since this instalment ends only with an anonymous explanatory letter revealing The Harvester's hand in the events so far, earning him the title 'the king of predestination', author of this 'macabre tale' in which the characters 'must navigate an intellectual minefield where every grain of sand is booby trapped' and 'frolic in the intrigue of my improbable account'.

But the plot is only part of the story. Far more interesting is the devious mind at work behind the scenes – that of Taona Chiveneko – and his inimitable style, which relies heavily on puns, puzzles, non-sequiturs, wild exaggeration and extravagant humour. A desirable woman is described as having 'the sort of beauty that deserved to be prosecuted for appearing without notice'; a lawyer has a face so symmetrical that 'an ant walking from one side to the other would experience a serious case of déjà vu'; Luxon Hurudza, who is very possibly an avatar of Chiveneko's, sharing his misanthropy and agoraphobia, is described as a 'ruthless perfectionist' for whom a word was never permissible 'until it had been grotesquely tortured and failed to confess to the existence of a better synonym'.

Given that the dominant mode is satire and the characters are grotesques I had a hunch there was another level of meaning secreted in their names, and I looked them up in the online Shona dictionary. Bingo! Hurudza means 'master farmer'; Abel Muranda's surname means 'serf'; the lawyer's name, Gweta, means – 'lawyer'; of the other characters, Gejo is 'plough', Anala is the Hindu fire god, Changamire is the name of a precolonial dynasty that founded the kingdom of Monomotapa, Murambi is the site of one of the worst of the Rwandan massacres and now a genocide museum, Chidoma is a monster created by a witch from a dead child, Kuripa means 'compensate', as in the expression '*kuripa ngozi*' which refers to the ritual of sacrifice of a young girl in compensation for a family dispute and Gudo is 'baboon'. Baboons, however, are ancestral symbols, and Chidoma is also the name of two sacred hills haunted by Shona spirits which provide a sanctuary where baboons cannot be harmed. The name of the national news organ, *Zuva Redo*, appears to be taken from a popular gospel song, 'Mwari muri zuva redo', 'Jehovah, you are our light', therefore, Our Light.

In other words, Mr Chiveneko, you have written a very tricky book. At different times it looks like a biting social satire, a freewheeling fantasy and a skin-crawling horror story. Dig a little deeper, and it's full of references to indigenous knowledge systems, precolonial history and traditional spiritual beliefs. It's also very funny. But come on, 489 pages and counting? OK, Ngũgĩ's *Wizard of the Crow* is 784, but it too is far, far too long. Maybe we shouldn't think of it as a novel, more as a verbal video game, or a blockbuster with multiple sequels? In which case, you really have dragged The African Novel into the electronic, multimedia age. We expect to hear more soon of this elephantine hybrid, in which 'the Determination Gene is the fuel, the flame lily is the vehicle, the gallows are the destination, Cecil Rhodes is the chauffeur and I (sorry, that's you) am his passenger'.

JANE BRYCE
Professor of African Literature and Cinema, University of the West Indies,
Cave Hill, Barbados

———————————

Daniel O. Fagunwa. *Forest of a Thousand Daemons,*
translated by Wole Soyinka, illustrated by Bruce Onabrakpeya
San Francisco: City Lights Publisher, 2013, 140 pp, $14.95
ISBN 9780872866300

The appearance in 2013 of an American edition of Daniel Olorunfemi Fagunwa's classic novel *Ogboju Ode Ninu Igbo Irunmale* translated by Wole Soyinka came at an appropriate time, a time when Fagunwa's work was being greatly enjoyed and subjected to intense critical analysis. Interest in novels by Fagunwa is indicated by the theatrical adaptations, in English and Yoruba, that have been prepared by distinguished teams. In fact, Femi Osofisan's English version, *Adventures in the Forest of a Thousand Daemons,* has reached far beyond theatre audiences since the production has been filmed.

Two thousand and thirteen was an appropriate year for republication since it marked the fiftieth anniversary of Fagunwa's death. That anniversary prompted an intense three-day conference – at Akure in Fagunwa's home state – that brought together some of those involved in the productions together with Yoruba scholars and students who are passionate about the novelist's work. Organized by the Ondo State Government with the Centre for Black and African Arts and Civilization, the D.O Fagunwa Foundation, and the Fagunwa Study Group, the conference offered a programme of events and papers that provided abundant evidence of local interest, national enthusiasm, pride in the Yoruba language, and engagement with issues of translation. The opening ceremony was chaired by the Orangun of Oke-Ila, Oba Adedokun Abolarin, and the partial list of paper-givers that follows indicates the range of distinguished writers, translators and scholars involved: Dapo Adeniyi, Ayo Bamgbose, Karin Barber, Harry Garuba, Abiola Irele, Akinwunmi Isola, Dan Izevbaye, Biodun Jeyifo, Olu Obafemi, Odia Ofeimun, Molara Ogundipe, Foluke Ogunleye and Niyi Osundare.

Wole Soyinka, who began sharing his enthusiasm for Fagunwa fifty years ago, delivered the key-note address entitled 'Fagunwa's Forest Tapestry: Heroes, Heroics, Morals and Moralists'. Although it has not, I think, been published, it clearly draws together ideas about a continuing interest – that was apparent when 'Agbako' appeared in *Black Orpheus*. Soyinka's enthusiasm for Fagunwa was clearly manifest in 1968 when Thomas Nelson published his translation of Fagunwa's Hunters' Saga *Ogboju Ode Ninu Igbo Irunmale*. According to a press release from City Lights Publishers, who are responsible for the new edition, the Nelson English translation has been out of print for twenty years!

When it first appeared *Thousand Daemons* elicited few notices in the international print media. One of those who put pen to paper was R W Noble who provided a somewhat grudging welcome in the pages of *West Africa* – practically ' a journal of record' at that time. He wrote that 'Fagunwa's action (that he regarded as 'allegorical') had been 'rendered by Soyinka with such effectiveness that the novel often comes alive to sweep us into its dance.' Writing recently in *This Day*, Dapo Adeniyi summed up (his impression of) the initial reaction by saying that the critics 'slammed' Soyinka's version – on the grounds that it contained too much of the translator. Adverse criticism can also be found in the Kano *Journal of Languages and Literatures* (2000) where, E B Ajulo suggests that Soyinka 'achieved in the end only terribly limited success'. Ajulo argued that that has been inevitable – 'due to the translation method he adopted'.

However, Adeniyi, who has himself grappled with the task of translating a Fagunwa novel, has also provided discriminating appreciation of the Nobel laureate's work. He wrote that, in Soyinka's 'translation of *Igbo Olodumare*, (he) particularly enjoyed the following solutions to translation dilemmas: 'The Forest of the Lord of Deities' for 'Igbo Olodumare'; 'the man wedded to food to the gates of death' for 'Akara-ogun, Abolonje ku'; 'minnows of the air' for 'alapandede'; 'python of rage' for 'ojola ibinu'; 'The Forest of Impenetrable Silence' for 'Igbo Idakeroro', (and) 'Tiny Fiend of the Border' for 'Esu-kekere-ode'.

The abstracts of the papers presented at the 2013 'D.O. Fagunwa: Fifty Years On' conference can be found on the Fagunwa Study Group website and they indicate the terms in which Fagunwa and Fagunwa/ Soyinka are now being discussed. The debate is vigorous and does not flinch from the major issues raised by examining both Fagunwa's 'fantasy novels' and the translations of them. Forty-five years after *Thousand Daemons* slipped quietly into the world, the new American edition has arrived in the middle of a lively exchange of views. The edition is all the more welcome for having retained the decisive, evocative illustrations by Bruce Onabrakpeya. They, like Soyinka's exploitation of linguistic resources, provide evidence of creative interaction with Fagunwa's narratives; translation into images.

Useful links include: http://www.thisdaylive.com/articles/soyinka-in-the-forest-of-olodumare/139000/

JAMES GIBBS
Bristol

Caroline Davies. *Creating Postcolonial Literature:*
African Writers & British Publishers
Houndsmill: Palgrave Macmillan, 2013, 255 pp. hb. £50
ISBN 978-0-230-36936-8; ebook ISBNs: 9781137328380 PDF, 9781137246363 EPUB

The business logic of the Oxford University Press during the twentieth century was that the recondite scholarly work of the Clarendon Press in Oxford should be paid for by the immense success of high selling lines. These used to be led by Bibles, prayer books and dictionaries. But with the end of empire after the second world war OUP extended the imperial grasp of the English language with school textbooks for all subjects but above all for the teaching of English. Since the turn of the century it has been books for ELT. Oxford English rules the world.

In this revealing book Caroline Davies shows how OUP developed branches and offices in Africa to sell books from the UK but then, with the establishment of editorial offices in Ibadan, Nairobi, Dar es Salaam and Cape Town, to produce books for perceived local needs. In the late 1970s, with oil money and Universal Primary Education, Nigeria became the most successful branch in the whole world. Repeatedly the instructions from Oxford and its London Business were that branches must make a surplus and remit it to England.

This demand led to great tensions between London and Charles Lewis when Manager of the East African branch in Nairobi in the late 1960s. That branch had published the New Peak English Course for the government Kenyan Ministry of Education and this monopoly gave substantial surplus. Lewis employed the poet Jonathan Kariara to publish East African writers in English, Swahili and other languages and to start the pioneering literary journal *Zuka*. He was instructed by the Delegates (i.e. the top board of dons) via the London business to remit his surplus, but in the period after independence he took issue with them because he believed that the mission of the Press was not to squeeze the former colonies for every neocolonial drop they could get.

A similar squeeze was put on the branch in Cape Town. The Editorial Manager was Leo Marquard who had been Commanding Officer of the SA Army Education Corps, an SA delegate at the establishment of UNESCO and a founder with Alan Paton of the Liberal Party in 1953. By the time of his retirement in 1962 he had built up an influential list of scholarly books by South African academics which were published, not just in Cape Town, but for the world market from London or Oxford. Apartheid was of deep international concern. He had followed his instructions to build up a list of textbooks for African primary schools. He and his friend and author Alan Paton had campaigned against the 1952 Bantu Education Act. However they decided to their distaste that Oxford should publish textbooks with the formal approval of the Department of Bantu Education to meet the needs of African schools in as decent a way as possible. (White pupils got their textbooks free and African parents had to buy the approved textbooks for their children.) Marquard invested in the publication of two eight-year class sets of textbooks for English and Xhosa complete with teacher's books; it was this heavy expense on textbooks, and not his academic books laying apartheid bare, which reduced the modest surplus and led to a slight loss in 1962. By the 1970s Marquard's investment and the removal of practically all new publishing was bringing in a substantial surplus to remit to Oxford. Creative stories, plays and poetry had steadily been published in Xhosa, Sesotho and Zulu but not in English. A report by Robert Sobukwe, founder of the PAC said of one script: 'If the obvious political message of this tale is missed it might get approved.' It was! The most successful author, as Ranka Primorac has recently shown, was the detective writer Stephen Mpashi who was writing a string of successful books in Bemba for the Northern Rhodesia and Nyasaland Literature Bureau.

A crisis came to a head in 1970. In 1963 David Philip had taken over from Leo Marquard and continued the Press's commitment to serious academic publishing on South Africa. New laws had worsened the censorship. The great long term project initiated under Marquard was the three volume *History of South Africa* to be published in Oxford. Controversially, it was decided that as so many banned people were quoted in the third volume, a whole chapter was left with blank white pages to enable the rest of the book to be distributed in South Africa. By this time the textbooks commissioned by Leo Marquard were selling profitably, especially in the Transkei Bantustan. Oxford and London, with the total support of disgraceful management in Cape Town, gave David Philip as editor instructions that he should only publish school textbooks and must no longer publish academic books on South Africa. David Philip did not see textbooks as the sole mission of the Press in South Africa and resigned to set up, with Marie Philip, what became known as an 'oppositional publisher' which would publish 'books that matter' for South Africa; the list was also to include creative work by writers such as Richard Rive and Bessie Head. The Philips did not have, as OUP did, the opportunity of cross-subsidising their list with income from textbooks.

Caroline Davis's book, whose subtitle is *African Writers and British Publishers* compares the Oxford University Press's Three Crowns with the postcolonial burst in paperback output by other publishers like Collins Fontana, Longman and, above all, in Heinemann's ever-expanding African Writers Series. Rex Collings's apprenticeship in publishing before going to OUP was with the renowned paperback imprint of Penguin. Joan 'O! What lovely War!' Littlewood first recommended to Rex Collings that he look at the plays by Wole Soyinka. He argues for, cajoles and then just goes ahead with two Soyinka plays first published by Mbari in Ibadan. With fast and determined moves past doubting colleagues he rushed the initial Three Crowns titles into print in 1962. The Penguin style also had a touch of Pelican with non-fiction titles like *Seven African Writers* by Gerald Moore and *Chief Albert Lutuli of South Africa* by Mary Benson. It was also planned to include writers from India, Pakistan and the rest of what was coming to be called 'The Third World'. Three Crowns quickly became renowned for the cluster of playscripts from Africa with plays by John Pepper Clark, R. Sarif Easmon, Tsegaye Gabre-Medhin, Tewfik Al-Hakim and Lewis Nkosi. Caroline Davies has a whole chapter about the ditherings over the appropriate way for OUP to publish Wole Soyinka, who was on his way to become the first African winner of the Nobel Prize for Literature. OUP in the 1970s did come round to treat Wole Soyinka and Athol Fugard, on whom there is also a whole chapter, as worthy of 'the full Oxford treatment' in the general book trade. Three Crowns was allowed to be kept going chiefly as a public relations exercise to try and disguise OUP's concentration on extracting as much money as possible from the postcolonial education market.

The delegates imposed a curious self-denying ordinance whereby they prevented the London business of the Oxford University Press from publishing new novels by contemporary writers, although they did allow publishing in the far less saleable forms of short stories, plays and poetry. All efforts to get an exception for Three Crowns failed. With the departure of Rex Collings with Wole Soyinka to Methuen and James Currey with Tayeb Salih to Heinemann, Three Crowns was firmly lodged in the control of the negative brigade who would only agree, as with Joe de Graft, to acceptance if the exam board will prescribe. Three Crowns was divided in half and the non-fiction was handed to a manager who successfully blocked publication of all titles. The creative half was fortunately put under the wing of Jon Stallworthy, the OUP poetry and drama editor, who long-term managed to secure Athol Fugard for the OUP. After an amazingly complex set of committee meetings and conflicting reports (positive by delegate Maurice Bowra) Stallworthy got out a hardback of the translation of Senghor's verse on his poetry list and a paperback in Three Crowns. After a short period keeping the South African branch running he sub-contracted the subsidiary rights of Oswald Mtshali *Songs of a Cowhide Drum*. The publisher, Sir John Brown, tried to keep Stallworthy out of one meeting about the future of the series because he was 'too emotionally involved'.

In her assiduous combing of the OUP archive Caroline Davis can find no report by any African reader. In 1972, ten years after Alan Hill appointed Chinua Achebe as editorial adviser of the African Writers Series, Arthur Ravenscroft was appointed editor to Three Crowns – his name gave no clue that he was at least South African. The OUP was in severe financial stress at this time. The dismal brigade at OUP could not even make up their minds to stop Three Crowns. It was repeatedly saved by the argument that it was good for the OUP's image to help disguise that their mission to extract from their branches overseas all they could for the benefit of Oxford dons. Philip Chester, the benign deputy publisher who was in charge of the branches worldwide, did point out to his hostile colleagues that average sales of titles in Three Crowns were three times those of those in OUP's 'prestige series' The World's Classics.

I should declare a personal interest in Caroline Davies' meticulously told and sadly disappointing story. Rex Collings, when he went to Methuen, managed with my experience in South Africa especially with the radical review *The New African,* to get me the chance to take over his manuscript cupboard crammed with accepted African studies scripts and with unknown authors for Three Crowns with names like J.Pepper Clark and Lewis Nkosi. All my own proposals for new scripts were turned down in distant committees. In 1967 I went to work with Chinua Achebe, Keith Sambrook and Alan Hill on the African Writers Series at Heinemann. At OUP there was an obsession with committees to secure supposed OUP standards. At Heinemann you got ten, fifteen, twenty AWS titles out a year and learnt what standards the new market wanted by the sales they made. And above all you listened to what was wanted by your colleagues and advisers in Africa.

JAMES CURREY
Oxford

Wumi Raji. *Contemporary Literature of Africa:*
Tijan M. Sallah & Literary Works of The Gambia
New York: Cambria Press, 2014, 282 pp., $ 109.99, hb
ISBN 9781604978674

This volume on Gambian literature, with the respected contributors represented in it, will be welcomed by many of those interested in African writing. From the outset, it is imbued with promise. However, with so much promise, too much can be expected.

Despite including a succession of prominent contributors, it feels as though Wumi Raji has collected together whoever and whatever he could find on Sallah, and included them to make up a book-length volume. This could be why he felt he had the space in his introduction, 'Kora Notes', to be so self-indulgent. He includes details about why he found himself in The Gambia, how he then 'found' Sallah, and what admirers of Sallah's work said to him. All this, with a variety of other ins and outs and information about the compilation of this, book makes the introduction more like kowtowing than critiquing.

The volume is unbalanced. Its focus is predominantly on Sallah's poetry, and very little attention is given to his short fiction. As a result, we don't get a balanced sense of Sallah's strengths and weaknesses as a writer, or even a helpful sense of what he writes about.

The contributions differ considerably in length and this makes the volume feel more like an anthology of papers on Sallah, than an edited book with chapters. Indeed, I see the separate entries as essays since that is essentially what they are: essays written for a variety of contexts and occasions brought together in this volume.

Given this, it is not surprising that there is some overlap. For example, 'chapters' two and three by Dr Tanure Ojaide and Dr Pierre Gomez respectively both take us through Sallah's collections of poems, and sometimes refer to the same examples. They draw attention to Sallah's growth through his themes and quite often say more or less the same thing. When, as in 'An Unusual Growth', an idiosyncratic point is made it is a weak one. Ojaide seems to suggest that Sallah is unusual in having a career apart from being a poet – and unusual in being a poet without a degree in poetry or literature. In fact, setting aside those poets following academic careers, most poets, and indeed most authors, earn their living in other disciplines. These include IT, medicine, agriculture, the sciences and management.

The first essay is by Stewart Brown and is appropriate at the front of the book because Brown asks if there is any literature emanating from The Gambia at all. This raises the issue of literature as opposed to orature – which most people would acknowledge has a strong presence in The Gambia. Brown's statement is, of course, challenging and initiates the discussion about whether there should be a book on Gambian literature at all, since there is so little literature to speak of!

Among the most stimulating essays are Charles Larson's short piece on 'Sahelian Earth', which is described as 'one of the gems of African poetry', Victoria Arana's 'The Ecopoetics of Tijan M. Sallah', and 'Demola Jolayemi's detailed analysis of a single poem , 'Share'. These are some of the joys and illustrate the kind of approaches expected in a book of this sort.

One of the book's major disappointments is not of Raji's making at all, but the fault of the publisher. If Cambria Press, a fairly new operation, wants to become a 'premier academic publisher' they must invest in copy editing. Many African writers have told me that they suffer from lack of access to good copy editors. Without such people, inconsistencies and incorrect statements slip in to publications and often pass for fact. In this volume, there are, disconcertingly, references to 'Gambia', 'the Gambia' (incorrect) and 'The Gambia' (correct). Serrekunda (which can also be spelt 'Serekunda') is also found here (incorrectly) as 'Sera Kunda'. It can rightly be referred to as The Gambia's 'second city', but it isn't, as this volume has it, the 'second-largest'. In fact, Serrekunda is bigger than Banjul.

The most obvious fault of the book is the almost complete absence of women. No women writers are mentioned and there is no discussion of gender issues. This might give readers the impression that women in The Gambia cannot write creatively, or that there is some kind of taboo or ban on their writing. Had Raji undertaken research on this he would have found some emerging writers and he would also have come across relevant work by scholars such as Rosamond King. King was in The Gambia as a Fulbright scholar during 2007, and her research embraced both the academy and the community. A contribution from her would have provided a strong contemporary piece on gender/women and literature. However, she was not invited to contribute to this book that professes to be on 'Literary Works of The Gambia'.

Raji's claim, at the end of his introduction, that this is the first extended reference book on Gambian literature is misleading. The book is solely about Tijan Sallah, and not about him and Literary Works of The Gambia (unless Raji is claiming that all literary works in The Gambia have been written by Tijan Sallah?!) The only points at which other writers are mentioned (and those who make the most appearances are Lenrie Peters and Ebou Dibba) is in the context of their work and its relationship to Sallah. Sadly, a broad view of Gambian literature is only apparent in Brown's essay, and that decries the existence of Gambian literature.

In this context, I trust that Raji's second aspiration will be fulfilled and that this volume will serve to 'deepen awareness of and stimulate interest in or expand the scope of debates and discussion on the relatively neglected but vital aspect of African postcolonial writing.' Hopefully, within that, there can be further discussion. This is a topic broached by Femi Dunmade in his essay entitled 'Stanley Meets Mutesa: Postcolonial Consciousness and the Continuing Conversation between the West and Africa', where he reflects on the usefulness of the term 'postcolonial literature' in respect of Gambian literature. If it is seen as so new, then should Gambian literature be seen as postcolonial literature at all? Surely 'postcolonial' is a term that should be used for twentieth-century writing, rather than for literature that is evolving in the twenty-first century. (When nations such as The Gambia are choosing to disassociate themselves from their ex-colonial masters). One is prompted to ask what does a category such as 'postcolonial' mean to writers who began their writing careers, albeit in a colonialist's language, in independent Gambia?

KADIJA SESAY
Publisher, *SABLE* LitMag and author of *Irki*

Printed and bound by CPI Group (UK) Ltd, Croydon, CR0 4YY

13/04/2025